'Lots of players misplay their drawing hands, especially beginning players and those who have only learned poker by the seat of their pants. *Hold'em on the Come* is a great addition to poker literature, especially so for these players. Rolf is known for giving accurate and easy-to-understand advice, and he does an excellent job in this book of presenting that advice so that any hold'em player can become better at playing their draws.'

Greg Raymer, *2004 World Series of Poker Champion*

'I have played with Rolf for many, many years, and I can tell you from experience: His play is safer than the Bank of England. So this book is a must read for everybody who takes the game seriously.'

Rob Hollink, *2005 European Poker Tour Grand Final winner and one of the world's most successful online players, both in tournaments and cash games*

'Rolf's game is of very high quality – and his writings reflect the level of his play.'

Isabelle Mercier, *2004 World Poker Tour Ladies Night II winner*

'Rolf Slotboom is one of my favourite poker authors. His deep understanding of the game coupled with his clear concise presentation makes this book by Dew Mason and him a sure-fire winner.'

Barry Tanenbaum, *Card Player columnist and a highly successful middle-limit hold'em player*

'This book is a must read for all serious limit hold'em players. It provides the most comprehensive discussion to date on the play of drawing hands. The added comments by poker pro Rolf Slotboom make the book an invaluable addition to your poker library.'

Jim Brier, *Card Player columnist and co-author of* Middle Limit Holdem

Hold'em on the Come

LIMIT HOLD'EM STRATEGY FOR DRAWING HANDS

by Rolf Slotboom and Dew Mason

First published in 2006 by D & B Publishing, PO Box 18, Hassocks, West Sussex BN6 9WR

Reprinted 2006

British Library Cataloguing-in-Publication Data
A catalogue record for this book is available from the British Library.

ISBN: 1-904468-23-3
ISBN13: 978 1-904468-23-3

All sales enquiries should be directed to:
D & B Publishing, PO Box 18, Hassocks,
West Sussex BN6 9WR, UK

Tel: +44 (0)1273 834680, Fax: +44 (0)1273 831629,
e-mail: info@dandbpublishing.com,
Website: www.dandbpoker.com

Cover design by Horatio Monteverde.
Production by Navigator Guides.
Printed and bound in the US by Versa Press.

Contents

Preface

By Rolf 'Ace' Slotboom

In the spring of 2005 I was approached by someone I had never met: Dew Mason. Dew had sent me a manuscript for a book he was planning to publish. He wanted not just my take on it, but also wondered if maybe I would be interested in collaborating with him on this project. Now, even though I get sent manuscripts rather frequently, they are hardly ever really interesting, truly good, or – probably most important – easily marketable. But Dew's work had all of these characteristics. It was well written and insightful, though not an easy read by any means – but in my view clearly a welcome addition to the current poker literature. So, I gave Dew my word that I would try to do everything in my power to: a) help improve those few small things in the piece that still needed improvement, and b) use my contacts to maybe get his (our) work to print.

But then, before I had even started lobbying, an opportunity presented itself. I was approached by D&B Publishing, publisher of many decent, good and even some excellent poker books. They had seen a couple of ratings and reviews of D&B books that I had done on my site, and asked if I was interested in writing a book for them myself.

Now, with all the things I had recently taken upon myself for websites, magazines and TV, I replied that taking on a project like this would simply be too much for me. Knowing that I either like to do things 100% or not at all, it was clear that I would be unable to take on this task, to come up with a quality work all by myself in the time frame they had in mind. That was the bad news for them. The good news was that right at the moment that they contacted me, all the changes and additions we had done in Dew's work were just ready, and that thus we had an excellent piece of work ready for them – one we had completed just a few moments ago! Now, when I proposed *Hold'em on the Come* to them, I was not actually that certain they would appreciate it as much as we did. But once they had seen the manuscript, they had no doubts whatsoever: they loved it immediately.

Now, I hope of course that you guys will love it too. Both Dew and I have devoted a lot of time to come up with a work that will help you in just one specific area of play, in a manner that no other book before this one has done – or at least, not to the same degree. What you will see is an excellent and insightful analysis on the proper way to play drawing hands after the flop, an area of play where even decent to good players often fail miserably. We will give lots of concrete advice and easy-to-implement strategies that will not just help you play according to the odds, but that more in general will try to make you think on a deeper level than most of your opponents. The presentation of this somewhat new line of thinking is taken care of by Dew, and even though we have collaborated on all chapters it should be clear that the complete text of the book most of all represents *his* views. In addition to that, all chapters on counting outs, including the use of 'table action charts' specifically created for this book – all of this is more than anything his line of reasoning. Having said that, I of course endorse fully everything in this book, and in the very few situations where we actually had some disagreements on the correctness of what we were recommending, the text has been modified so that we now stand in 100% agreement. And of course there are quite a few personal comments and short stories by me, written from the perspective that I am known for: the perspective of someone who doesn't take everything for granted, and who is not afraid to go against common wisdom. I hope you will find these contributions to be both entertaining and helpful.

All in all, both Dew and I are convinced that the strategies we present here will have a serious impact on the play and the results of anyone who is serious about playing good poker, and we think they are especially useful for the average player who is trying to lift his game to a higher level. I would say this: Don't just enjoy this book, or just glance at a few things we have written, but study it in depth. If you do this, I am certain you will find it to be well worth the time and the effort.

Questions or comments regarding this book can be addressed directly to Rolf through the 'Ask Ace' section on his site, www.rolfslotboom.com.

By Dew Mason

Whereas Rolf is well-known by most all serious poker players for his accurate and articulate decision-making, Dew Mason isn't quite yet a household name. I'm a middle-limit hold'em player who makes his living by knowing and playing the odds. Drawing hands are my forte. But the fact is, there is no excuse for *anyone* playing middle-limit or higher not knowing how to make educated decisions with these hands. That's how the idea for this book evolved.

This is not a book for beginners. Not that the subject matter is too advanced, nor that the presentation is too difficult, but that the topics presented will be appreciated more if you've first read a couple of other books on poker strategy, and played a couple of thousand live hands, with real money on the table. You should have a feel for the game before reading this book. And I assume that you have a basic knowledge of poker theory and terminology, although I'll give you an overview of some common poker terms. We're here to plug some holes in your game, by rebuilding your foundation. You will be surprised by some of the things you learn. Let me say it again for emphasis:

You will be surprised.

Nor is this a book for the casual reader. It may, indeed, be more intense than some of you prefer. Never has so much been written about drawing hands. Instead of dealing with generalities and unproven rules, you will be shown *exactly* how to play each type of hand, with plenty of charts and examples for study.

This is not a reference book, either. You'll need to read the book from beginning to end. It's a journey; the chapters build to a climax as they do in a novel, and by the time we pull it all together at the end of the book, I absolutely *guarantee* you will have learned more about proper poker play, regardless of your level of play. This book presents a foundation of good, solid decision-making in a way that helps you *understand* the choices you are making... rather than just teaching you to memorise and follow rules.

Poker was never meant to be a dry, unimaginative game. It was meant to be a game about people, not about cards. And it certainly is a much more enjoyable game when you reach the point where you are playing your opponents more than your cards. But this is, after all, limit poker, where odds rule the day. Only by fully comprehending the odds and the correct play in each situation can you really *know* when it is profitable to deviate from mainstream play.

The presentation of ideas in this book is rather original. This usually means one of two things: Either you will love the book, or you will hate it. If you are looking for a study guide to reinforce ideas about playing hold'em that you have already learned, by rehashing the same old topics, then you'll be disappointed! If you are looking for a way to truly *understand* the rules you should be playing by, teaching you to think but freeing up precious decision-making time for you to study your opponents, to really *play poker,* then this is the book for you.

Unfortunately, to take your game to the next level, you *will* have to deal with a few numbers and a little memorisation. It's unavoidable. I'll try to make it as painless as possible.

Writing an original book also means it will be open to closer scrutiny and criticism. I think this is very good for the game in general, stimulating conversation with ideas that haven't yet been put in print.

I had fun working with Rolf on this book, and as always, putting the ideas on paper means making a serious commitment to accuracy. I learned a few things doing the research for this book, and I hope we can pass on our winning ideas to you.

Chapter One

Introduction

This book is about only one thing: Playing drawing hands, in limit hold'em, after the flop.

That's a pretty narrow focus for a book, I know. But it's my experience that this is the second biggest hole in most hold'em players' repertoires (the most common error is playing too many hands, something that can easily be corrected with a little discipline).

Most players think of 'drawing hands' as four-card straights or flushes, where a lucky fifth card turns a losing hand into a probable winner. That's a classic example of a drawing hand, I'll concede, but it's not the whole story. A more accurate picture is, *any* hand that is losing after the flop is a drawing hand. Either you're winning or you're chasing. That's all there is to it. Two types of hands: winners and wannabes.

A drawing hand after the flop has only two chances to win

1) You can get lucky and hit a winning card on the turn or river.

2) You can bluff the better hand(s) out of the pot.

TIP: Either you're winning the hand or you're chasing. That's all there is to it.

We're going to talk mostly about option number one. Mostly we'll be discussing *whether* to play. If you learn nothing else from this book, I want you to learn how to answer the one most important question: *Do I belong in the pot or not?*

This fundamental question, really, may be the hardest question of all to answer in hold'em. Perhaps it sounds like a boring topic—you may prefer to talk about check-raises and semi-bluffs—but I guarantee that proper understanding of the fundamental odds of drawing hands will greatly increase your winnings.

Does this sound simple? It's not. For most of us, there's a lot more to learn than we realise.

What I'm going to do is give you a simple but effective method for estimating the final pot size, along with a basic understanding of counting outs and implied pot odds for various types of hands.

Everyone has heard of pot odds, and everyone pays homage to its importance. Many players can spout words of wisdom about implied odds, drawing odds, reverse odds, and who knows what else. But how many of your opponents really do keep track of how much money is in the pot? How many players run the figures in their head as the hand is being played, counting their outs and calculating their winning chances, and then figuring out whether the pot is laying sufficient odds to continue?

I'll tell you up front: Not very many! I sure don't, unless I absolutely have to. And if *anyone* should, I guess that someone would be me. After all, I'm a mathematician. I love numbers, and I'll go out on a limb by saying I'm pretty good at numbers. I've no excuse for playing lazy; I should be using my abilities to my advantage. But not in the middle of the hand, thank you very much! I want to be studying my opponents, playing the *game*. And most times, I can. Most times, the rules of thumb in this book will help me determine if my hand is profitable enough to play without needing to have a precise pot count.

It's true that, for certain types of hands, you *will* need to keep a tally in your head of the bets as they go into the pot. Then you'll need to guess how much *more* will go into the pot. It's an absolute, if unfortunate, necessity if you really want to improve your game. But I'm going to make it so simple for you, that it'll become second nature after only one or two playing sessions.

TIP: If you learn nothing else from this book, I want you to learn the answer to one fundamental question: Do I belong in this pot or not?

This is where it all starts: Do I or Don't I? Do I belong on this pot or not? Hold'em or fold'em? Do I cross my fingers and push my money onto the felt, or wait for a better opportunity?

Similar circumstances occur over and over, when you are on a draw, and understanding the correct play of these circumstances will go a long way towards making you a fundamentally correct player. Here are some common themes:

Common Themes

- Playing flush draws
- Playing straight draws
- Playing two overcards
- Playing a medium or bottom pair to improve to two pair or three-of-a-kind
- Playing a small pair against overcards

After reviewing how to count outs, we'll delve into these common scenarios and study each one in detail. I want you to know exactly what you are doing, when you choose, for example, to call or raise with A-K against four opponents and a flop of 8-J-Q.

I'm going to teach you how to estimate very quickly whether the odds warrant continuing when you are on a draw. It's all about one thing: *Return on Investment*. It's the size of the pot at the end of the hand that matters. The only pot odds that really matter on the flop and turn are implied odds, and unfortunately, calculating implied odds is a fuzzy concept at best.

Nobody knows what's going to happen next in the hand. Nobody knows who's bluffing, who's slowplaying, who's chasing. But that's where the good investments are made: Implied odds. You want to know how much money you're going to get out of that pot, on average, for the money you put in.

But, folks, *please* don't think I'm here to tell you that there is a single, best way to play each hand. You cannot play poker like it's a game of blackjack. It's not. It's a game of *people*.

The most important knowledge you will get from this book is a basic foundation of which hands are mathematically correct to play. You will, however, often deviate from this 'basic foundation', because playing like a machine will never work in a game of good players, where feelings, impressions, moods, fear, greed, and many other human emotions and rationalisations dictate play. Poker will always be a game of people, even when playing limit poker. Deception will always be important. There is a time for bluffing and a time for picking off bluffs. A time for playing strongly, and a time for timidly calling along. A time for everything under the sun. I want you to mix up your play, but I want you to do it with understanding. I'll show you how.

Some Definitions Before We Begin

What, you've never seen a glossary in the front of a book before? I'd just as soon you read this section up front, so you don't get confused later. It'll just take a minute. Here are a few phrases that I'll be assuming you are familiar with:

Boat or Full Boat: A full house. Don't ask me how this phrase came into vogue. Maybe poker players, in general, wish they could live on a boat instead of in a house? Or maybe a boat is just easier to fill.

Dead Money: Money that has been put into the pot by a player who has subsequently folded. For example, money paid by the blinds before folding. Don't worry; it spends just as good as 'live' money.

Dog: A favourite to lose. It comes from the word 'underdog', I believe. For example, if you are likely to lose a hand two times out of three, your hand is said to be a 2:1 dog.

Double Belly-Buster: Nothing to do with the Heineken in your hand. It means drawing to two inside straights simultaneously, so that you have eight outs, with a hand like 10-8-7-6-4; any five or nine makes a straight.

Drawing Dead: This means no matter what you draw, you're dead. You're so far behind somebody's hand that there's no way to catch up.

Drawing Hand: This usually means a straight or flush draw, but for the purposes of this book, it will mean any hand that is currently not best. You are 'drawing' to make a better hand, and probably headed for disappointment.

Fill Up: To improve to a full house. I mean, a boat. It's what every two pair or three-of-a-kind dreams of, because the straight and flush wannabes are then drawing dead.

Free Card: If everyone checks on the flop or on the turn, each player can be said to be receiving a 'free card' on the next street. This phrase is usually reserved for drawing hands; a player on a draw is given a free chance to catch up. Often, it is said that a player with position can 'buy a free card' on the turn by betting or raising on the flop, where the bets are cheap, so that everyone checks the turn, afraid to bet into him. He then checks as well, taking the free card. Such a card isn't exactly 'free', but hopefully you get the point.

Heads-Up: Playing one-on-one against one other player. In tight games, most hands boil down to a heads-up contest by the turn or river. Not the kind of game you want for drawing hands.

Implied Odds: Pot odds that you calculate on the flop or turn, by taking into consideration anticipated future bets through the river. Winners are good at anticipating how big the pot will *get,* not how big it is right now.

Inside or Gutshot Straight Draw: A straight draw that can be filled by only one rank. For example, 9-8-7-5 is a gutshot straight, since only a six will complete the straight. This comes from the idea that the card you need (the six) is 'inside' the sequence (not at the beginning or end), in contrast to a draw like 8-7-6-5 where there are *two* cards (any four and any nine) that will complete the straight. However, in this book we will generalise the concept of an inside straight to mean, really, a one-way straight, where only one card will help. If you hold A-K-Q-J, it's not technically an inside straight, but we'll call it such and treat it as such, because only one card (a ten) can fill it.

Low Pair: This is not a common poker term, but it's a phrase I'll use a lot in this book to mean 'middle/bottom pair'. By this, I mean one of the cards in your hand is paired on the board, but it's not top pair. Don't confuse 'low pair' with 'small pair'; the latter usually means you hold a little pair in your hand. Since middle pair and bottom pair often play similarly, I'll use the term 'low pair' for convenience.

Modified Outs: Most times, simply counting outs doesn't give an entirely accurate picture of which cards remaining in the deck will win for you, and which will lose. So, after counting outs, you will be learning in this book how to *modify* that count to come up with a more reasonable measure of your chances of winning.

Nut or the Nuts: The best possible hand, given the cards currently on the table. So named, perhaps, because in poker, if you got 'em, you don't need 'em. But having the nuts doesn't necessarily mean you will always win, unless all five community cards have been dealt. For example, you may make the nut straight on the turn, and lose to a flush on the river.

On the Come: This simply means you are on a drawing hand. You're beat right now, but hoping to improve on a later street. You can call it 'chasing', if you like, but 'on the come' just doesn't sound quite so derogatory. My first printing of this book, titled *How to Chase in Hold'em,* was a miserable flop.

Outs or Out-Count: An 'out' is a card that could come on the turn or on the river that will hopefully turn your drawing hand into a winner. The 'out-count' is a tally of all such outs. For example, a flush draw could be said to have nine outs, and the out count would be nine.

Open-Ended Straight Draw: Any connected straight draw, so that there are two ranks that will help you. For example, if you hold 7-6-5-4, then any three or eight will make a straight.

Overcard: This term may be confusing, because it is used two different ways. If you hold a card in your hand that is higher than any card on the table, it is called an overcard. If, however, you have a pair, either in your hand or by pairing one of your cards on the table, then any other card on the table that is higher than your pair is also said to be an overcard.

Overpair: If you hold a pair in your hand that is higher than all of the cards on the table, then you hold an overpair.

Position: This term usually refers to how close you sit to the button. Because the button always acts last, he has the best 'position'. However, the phrase can also mean simply that you act after a particular opponent. If he plays before you, you are said to have 'position' on him.

Pot Odds: A phrase used by many an amateur to display his great understanding of the game. But in truth, pot odds are misleading, at best. This is because pot odds only matter on the river, when you're trying to decide if it's appropriate to call or bluff. It is the ratio of the amount of money in the pot to how much it costs for you to play, but on all streets other than the river, the important odds are *implied odds*.

Rainbow Flop: A flop of three different suits. The significance of a rainbow flop is that the flush draws can usually be chased out of the pot for a single bet, so that you don't need to worry quite as much about anyone making a flush. A rainbow *flushes out* the table.

Runner-Runner: It's good strategy to loudly holler this whenever you lay a really bad beat on someone. If you 'hit perfect' on the turn and the river, you've hit a runner-runner. For example, perhaps you need two hearts to make a flush, also called a *backdoor flush,* and the turn and the river both bring a heart. Start hollering.

Semi-Bluff: A partial bluff. You hold the worst hand, but you have a good draw to make the best hand. Let me clue you in up front: A semi-bluff is an *incredibly* powerful play in poker. This time I'm not joking.

Set: A set really just means three-of-a-kind. However, hold'em players have taken this a step further, and redefined a set to mean a pair in your hand, and a third card of the same rank the table. Thus, a 'set' is much more valuable than 'trips', not only because no one else will have the same three-of-a-kind, but also because your own three-of-a-kind is better concealed.

Street: A betting round. The four 'streets' in hold'em are pre-flop, flop, turn, and river.

Suited Hand: If the two cards in your hand are of the same suit, it's said to be a suited hand. An A-J suited hand will be abbreviated A-Js. Suited cards are more valuable than many good players believe, but not nearly so valuable as most amateurs believe.

Top Pair: If you pair with the highest card on the board, then you have top pair. For example, if the flop contains 9-8-5, then anybody with a nine in their hand holds top pair.

Trips: Three-of-a-kind, with a pair showing on the board (the third in your hand).

Under the Gun: The position just to the left of the blinds. The 'under the gun' player is the first player to act after the cards are dealt.

Underpair: A pair in your hand that is *not* an overpair. In other words, it's lower than the top card on the table.

Value Bet: A bet or raise that is made because your odds of winning the hand exceed the number of players contributing to the pot. For example, if you are a 3:1 dog to lose a hand, but there are four other players, then anytime all five of you put money into the pot, it favours you. Such a bet, with the hope of being called by everyone, is a *value bet.*

OK. We're ready to begin.

Chapter Two

Counting Outs

'If you're going to deviate from the correct play, you better first know what the correct play is.'

Chris Ferguson, World Series of Poker Champion 2000

Did I promise you'd never have to learn any numbers? I hope not. This is where we begin. Counting outs will always be an important part of the game. You need to know your chance of hitting one of the cards you want, on the turn and again on the river. However, it's a tricky business at best. Because what you *really* want to know is, what is the chance of the dealer pushing that beautiful pile of chips towards your corner of the table?

That's all that really matters. Getting the money. But it's far from straightforward, because of these two complications:

1) You might hit one of your magic cards and still lose. The flush card you need comes on the turn, but the river pairs the board and someone turns over a full house. You watch dismayed, as those beautiful chips are stacked up by some other lucky schmuck.

2) You might miss all of your magic cards and still win! There's usually more than one way to pull the pot. You could be drawing to a flush, and instead hit two pair, or even three-of-a-kind by the river. Or your opponent may be on a complete bluff. Anything can happen.

TIP: Counting outs always begins by guessing what will win, and what will lose.

Yes, anything can happen, and the poker gods are fickle. You have to make some assumptions as you play about which cards will win and which will lose, and these assumptions will often be wrong. Nevertheless, we must start somewhere, if we are going to lay a solid foundation, and that somewhere is counting outs. We start by guessing what will win, and what will lose.

NOTE: This is the most important chapter in the book. If you aren't willing to invest a little effort learning about outs, to seriously improve your play, then I'm sorry I've wasted your time and money. Put the book aside. The rest of the book won't be of any help without this chapter.

If you *are* willing, then attack this chapter and the next with a purpose. Work through the examples. Understand them. Use a pencil and paper, if necessary. I guarantee that careful study of this topic will make a big difference in your rate of return.

How Much Does A Mistake Cost?

I want to show you right up front how much it costs you, every time you misplay a hand.

Every mistake costs you money. Every time you call when you should fold, you're giving away money. Every time you fold when you should call or raise, you're giving away money.

WARNING: Every time you call when you should fold, you're giving away money. Every time you fold when you should call, you're giving away money.

That's why you're learning to count outs. This entire chapter will be devoted to learning how to count outs. An 'out' is simply a card, hopefully the one that the dealer is about to lay out on the table, that will turn your hand into a probable winner. The value of every drawing hand can be measured by how many outs it has.

Wait a minute! *Did I say that it costs you money to fold when you should call?*

Damn straight! You paid good money to play those cards, and you shouldn't give that money away without a fight. If you fold now, when you should call, you're just giving away money.

Every mistake you make gives away a little bit more money.

I want you to see exactly how much it's costing you. A little incentive to learn about outs.

This chapter, you're learning how to count outs. In later chapters, you'll learn exactly how many outs you need to have in order to make it worthwhile to continue on with your hand.

Let's say you're playing $10-$20 hold'em, and the flop has just been dealt, leaving you with a hand worth six outs. Let's say a situation comes about that requires you to have an eight-out hand to be worth calling a bet. This means the *expected value* of an eight-out hand in this situation is exactly zero; on average, you'll come out even. Let's say you misread your hand, thinking it's worth more than it really is, and you call.

How much did this little mistake just cost you, to put your $10 into the pot? The answer is 2 ÷ 8 × $10 = $2.50. You needed eight outs; you called with two outs too few; you made a $2.50 mistake. On average, this play will cost you $2.50.

Let's say you need six outs to play a hand, and you have only four outs. You really want to call, because your opponent just got outdrawn on a big hand, and you sense that if you can do it again...suck out and hit your long shot...it'll really put him on tilt. How much is it costing you to go ahead and take the chance?

The answer is, 2 ÷ 6 × $10 = $3.33. Is it worth it? You have to decide.

Suppose you're playing on the turn. Now the bets are $20. You have a five-out hand, and that's exactly what you need. Five outs. You go ahead and call. But the player behind you raises the pot, and you have to put in another $20.

Did you just lose $20? Well, no, it's not quite that bad. But it's bad. If you had known it would cost $20 more, you surely wouldn't have called in the first place. You called with a very marginal holding, and the raise came as a surprise. You screwed up.

Probably, it only cost you about $13, because there's more money in the pot now, so you can play with fewer outs. This will all be made clear in future chapters. But it was still a mistake, and you still gave away money.

Suppose, now, that you have a hand worth ten outs, and only eight outs are required to continue. But you chicken out, maybe because luck just hasn't been on your side, and you fold instead of paying a $20 turn bet. What did this mistake cost?

You gave away two outs for free: 2 ÷ 8 × $20 = $5.

Learn to count outs. Learn how many outs you need in each situation. Learn to make good, mathematically correct decisions, or you'll be giving away money your entire poker career.

An Example Of Counting Outs

Again, an 'out' is simply a card that will turn your hand into a probable winner. For example, if you have two clubs in your hand, and two of the three flop cards are clubs, how many 'outs' do you have to make a flush?

The answer is nine. There are 13 clubs in the deck, and four of them are in play. (There may be other clubs in other players' hands, but these cards are unknown to you, and so cannot be considered in our calculations.)

But what if the two club cards in your hand are the ace and

king, and you estimate that pairing either of these cards will also be enough to win the pot? Then you have six more outs (three kings remaining and three aces remaining) for a total of 15 outs to win.

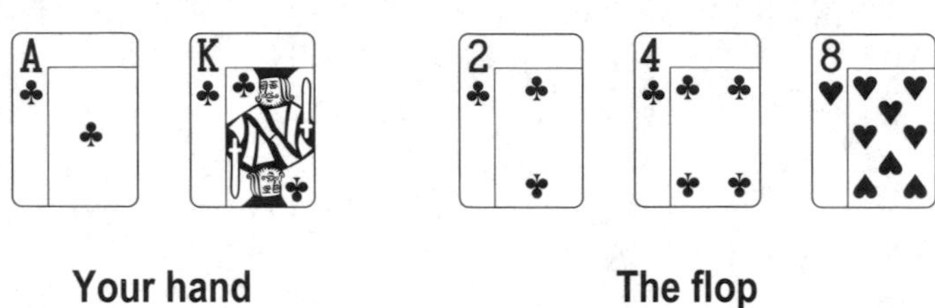

Your hand **The flop**

An A♣-K♣ hand with a flop of 2♣-4♣-8♥ could therefore be said to have 15 outs. But does it really? Who knows? If another clubs comes, will you win? Yeah, probably. But will an ace or a king really be enough to win? If someone is holding A♥-8♠, then the ace in your hand is worthless. Worse yet, what if someone is holding 8♠-8♦? Then you're drawing dead to a club. This means only a club can save you. Even if you pull two more aces on the turn and river, you lose to a full house.

So, the six outs from your ace and king should probably be discounted. Shall we say half-credit? Meaning, if you hit the ace or king, you have a 50% chance of winning? This is not a very scientific estimate, of course; it's more a matter of looking around the table, counting the hands in play, and guessing at what your opponents may have. But half-credit is reasonable. That would mean you should consider the six outs you count for a high pair to be worth, in reality, only three outs. Your 15-out hand has turned, realistically, into about a 12-out hand.

Pot Odds By The Book

Let's continue with our example of an A♣-K♣ hand and a flop of 2♣-4♣-8♥. For now, we're ignoring the possibility that you might still have the best hand. We decided, without too much analysis, to consider this a drawing hand with 12 outs. Fifteen cards in the deck will make you happy, but only nine of those 15 will make you *really* happy. The other six outs we reasonably gave a 50% chance of winning: Half credit. That gives you 12 outs.

Now, calculate the odds. How many cards are unknown? On the flop, only five cards are known (two in your hand, and three on the table), so there are 47 cards remaining. On the turn, one more card is revealed, leaving 46 cards unknown.

Twelve 'outs' among these 46 or 47 cards means you have about one chance in four of hitting a winning card on either draw (either the turn or river). Or we could say the odds are 3:1 against (three chances of losing for every one chance of winning).

The big question is: Do you stay in the pot? Suppose you are playing $5-$10 limit poker. We'll pretend the pot contains $25 after the flop, and the bet to you is $5. In other words, the pot is laying you 25:5, usually written reduced as 5:1. You invest $5 for the chance of winning $25. A pretty good deal, since your odds of hitting a winning card are only 3:1 against.

But what if it's two bets to you? What if it costs $10 for a shot at $25?[1] Now it's a *bad* bet according to the pot odds, right? The pot is laying 2.5:1, for a 3:1 chance of losing. You should fold, right?

Well, it's not quite that simple. For one thing, the poor guy who invested one bet before someone else raised will have to put in another bet to stay in the pot. That will likely bring the pot back to up at least $30, giving you 3:1 pot odds again.

Oh. But what if someone raises again? Now your investment goes up to at least $15, and to get 3:1 pot odds, you'll have to be able to count $45 in the pot (not counting the $15 you put in). Your good bet has turned back into a bad one, if you are raised.

We're forgetting something, of course. We're forgetting that if

---

[1] Yes, yes, astute readers will point out that this is an impossible scenario, given the number of players and the bets already invested. Pretend, with me, for the sake of the example.

you make your hand, you can hope to extract even more money from your opponents on the turn and on the river. That's what's meant by implied odds: you add in the money you can expect to win on all future betting rounds, as well. Now, as you consider future betting rounds, your bad bet has turned back into a good one. In our example, you should call two $5 bets, even if you expect a third bet this round, because of the expected pot size by the *end* of the hand.

The Problem With All This...

...is our basic premise. We started this long analysis by 'guessing what will lose, and what will win'. Not a very scientific process. All of this long analysis is rendered, at best, a rough estimate, because you just don't *know* what your opponents are holding. And you never can know, for sure, until it's too late.

NOTE: Every hand you play has a leader and one or more chasers... Every hand is a study in implied odds.

My goal with this book is to take as much of the counting and mathematics as possible out of the process of deciding whether to play any limit hold'em hand beyond the flop or turn. However, the inescapable fact is that limit hold'em is a game of odds. Every hand has a leader and one or more chasers. Thus, every hand you play is a study in implied odds. I'll show you how to estimate the winning odds of any hand, as accurately as reasonably necessary, to help you make good decisions. Study breeds familiarity, and familiarity will hone your instincts for when you have the proper odds to continue. But before we do this, we do need to agree on the value of each drawing opportunity, by deciding how much each 'out' is worth. Are you ready?

Estimating The Number And Value Of Your 'Outs'

Throughout the rest of the book, we will be calculating the value of several different kinds of hands, by making certain assumptions; in particular, we will want to estimate, as accurately as reasonably possible, the winning chances of each 'out'. Take a look at the chart below:

Draw Type	Outs
Flush	9
Open-Ended Straight	8
Inside Straight	4
Low Pair	5
Overcard	3
Underpair	2

Here are six examples of drawing hands. These are the types of drawing hands we'll focus on in this book. For each type, I've provided the number of outs left in the deck.

Flush Draw: If you have four cards to a flush, then nine cards remain (of the 13 in each suit) that will complete your hand.

Open-Ended Straight: A hand like 9♥-8♦-7♣-6♦ can complete to a straight with any five or any ten. Eight outs left in the deck.

Inside Straight: A hand like 10♥-8♦-7♣-6♦ can complete to a straight only with a nine. Four outs.

Low Pair: By this, I mean the board pairs one of your cards, but it's not top pair. You've paired either the middle card or bottom card on the flop. If you hold 9♥-8♥ and the flop is 8♣-A♦-K♦, you have five outs to make two pair or better (any eight or nine).

Overcard: If you hold A♦-J♣ and the flop is 7♥-8♥-Q♠, you hold one overcard (your ace). You have three outs (three more aces in the deck) to make top pair and a probable winning hand.

Underpair: You hold a pair in your hand, and flop one or more overcards. For example, you hold 6♠-6♥ and the flop comes 2♠-J♣-K♥. This is worse than a low pair, since you have only two outs to work with...the other two sixes.

The problem with these examples, of course, is that you don't *know* whether your outs are any good. You don't even know if you *need* the outs! There are always the same two complications when counting outs:

Complications when counting outs

1) You can make your hand and still lose.

2) You can miss your hand and still win.

Let's cut to the chase then. What we *really* care about in these examples is the chance of winning. We do this by counting outs, but we adjust that count, usually downward, to account for the chance that it won't be enough to win after all. Here are some fairly common examples of how this can happen.

Ways of Improving but not enough to win

- ♠ You can hit your overcard, but lose to two pair.
- ♠ You can make two pair, and lose to a straight.
- ♠ You can make a straight, and lose to a flush.
- ♠ You can make a small flush on the turn, and another card of the same suit appears on the river, causing you to lose to a higher flush. For example, you can have 8♥-7♥ in your hand, and make a flush on the turn with A♥-2♥-6♣-4♥ on the table. Then, another heart appears on the river, and you lose to a hand like A♣-Q♥.

It's just not as easy to count outs as we would like it to be.

From this point forward in the book, we're only going to be interested in something we'll call *modified outs.* For example, let's pretend that you have a hand with exactly six perfect outs. If you hit one of those six cards, you'll always win; if you don't, you'll always lose. Wouldn't life be wonderful if it were that simple?

It never is. If you had 'perfect outs', you would be able to calculate exactly how often you would win the hand. You can't. But we'll use this 'perfect out' standard for valuing any hand you hold.

Calculating 'modified outs' is usually a three-step process:

Calculating 'modified outs'

1) First, you search for and add up your outs in each hand.

2) Then you subtract some of those outs because they are 'compromised' (meaning, you still might not win even if you get the right card).

3) Then maybe you'll add outs for other reasons, such as a three-card flush or straight.

The end result, we hope, will be an approximate measure of the true value of your hand. If, for example, you calculate six 'modified outs' on the turn, you expect the hand to win 13% of the time. Why? Because a hand with six *perfect* outs would win six times out of the 46 cards remaining in the deck. That's 13%.

Let's dig a little deeper now, with modified outs in mind, and consider these examples of drawing hands in more detail.

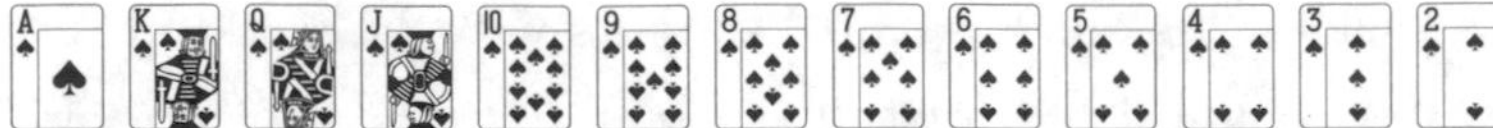

Ace Speaks...

Overestimating the strength of a draw

It is my experience that very few players are capable of counting their outs and analysing the strength of their hand in a correct manner. This is not just at the low limits; even when playing for higher stakes you will find that many players just don't know where they stand in a hand.

For instance, just the other day a hand came up where someone I've known for a very long time (let's call him Dave), complained that 'his premium draws just never got there'. He had J♥-10♥, on a flop K-Q-7 with two clubs. He had gotten into the middle of a raising war, with one player holding K-Q for top two pair, and the other A♣-10♣ for the nut flush draw plus a gutshot. When Dave lost the pot, he claimed that 'every time he had a draw of eight outs or more with two cards to come, he might as well give up immediately, as it would never come.' According to his reasoning, he had eight outs twice – 16 cards total. And with just 43 unknown cards left in the deck, he judged this as a highly profitable situation, where he was a clear money favourite.

But he wasn't. He was probably right to stay in the hand because of the money that was in the middle already and the odds that he was getting, but no way was it good for him that the betting on the flop and turn had gotten extremely heavy. Why? Well, first of all he did not have eight outs. The aggressive postures of both of his opponents should have made clear that there was definitely a flush draw out there, so he couldn't realistically have thought that the ace of clubs and the nine of clubs were outs – in fact, it was almost a certainty that the ace of clubs was not in the deck anymore, but in one of the players' hands. Therefore he probably should have estimated his hand as six clean outs, not eight.

But that's not all there is to it. When analysing the strength of his hand, this player made the common mistake of thinking that completing his draw automatically meant winning the pot. And as we shall see, this is not the case at all. The fact is, that in this hand both of his opponents were drawing to bigger hands than he was. Any jack would give the ace-high flush draw a straight that was larger than the one he was drawing to, any club would have completed a flush, and any king or queen would create a full house for the person who currently had top two pair. This meant that if one of these cards were to appear on the turn, for what is called a 'lockout', Dave would actually be drawing dead with his straight draw. And even if he were to make his nut straight on the turn, then his opponents would still have a bunch of 'redraws' on the river, simply because they were drawing to bigger hands than the one he had just made.

Because of all this, he did not have a premium draw at all. In fact, it was his opponents who were putting in their money correctly by jamming the pot, one of them holding the current best hand, and the other one getting good odds with his premium draw. So, even though Dave actually has years of playing experience, he still did not see (or did not *want* to see) that this situation was not as good as he analysed it to be: that in fact it was his opponents who were making money on this hand – at his expense!

Flush Draws

Not all flush draws are created equal. Suppose you hold 8♥-7♥ and the flop comes K♥-K♣-3♥. You call a bet on the flop, as you should, and the turn brings the 5♥. You've made your hand...but now, you're busy calculating reverse pot odds. Another heart and you're probably toast. A king, eight or five, and surely you lose to a full house...if someone isn't already full.

Yes, my friend, most 'draws' have 'drawbacks'. A normal flush draw has nine outs. Four of the 13 cards in your suit are accounted for, leaving nine...and because, when that fifth flush card hits, it usually doesn't pair the board (only one or two of the cards on the table can possibly be paired when another flush card comes; the others are part of your flush), those nine outs are generally safe. Unless the board is paired, a flush is the highest possible hand anyone can make. But one of the 'drawbacks' to a flush draw is that it's a common occurrence for *another* flush card to come on the river, giving the pot to anyone holding a higher card than you in that suit! Another drawback, of course, is that the board may pair on the river, making a full house possible for someone else.

These are your two biggest fears when playing a flush: A bigger flush, and a full house.

Here, then, is my recommendation for counting outs for your flush draws: Figure between seven and nine outs, depending upon the strength of your draw. On the flop, drop from nine outs down to eight outs if your flush draw is jack-high or lower. If six-high or lower (for example, you hold a hand like 6♣-5♣), then drop down to seven outs. You're now entering the realm where, if anybody else holds a pair of clubs as well, your hand can only bring heartache if you flop a flush draw. Two players drawing to the same flush is uncommon, but far from impossible. For inexperienced players, it is usually best to stay away from suited connecters like 6♣-5♣ and below; your flush draw is low, and your straight draw is often on the wrong end; the *idiot end,* we call it. If you don't know exactly where you're at, small suited connectors can get you into an awful lot of trouble. More on this topic later.

Drop another out if the board is already paired on the flop, and you've got multiple opponents. Say, three opponents or more. If there's a pair on the board, you have to worry about a full house. But I'd never drop a flush draw below seven outs, unless you have some reason to believe someone already has a full house or a higher flush draw.

For example, if you're holding 8♦-7♦ and the flop comes Q♦-Q♣-10♦, give yourself seven of the nine outs on the flop.

After the turn, however, assuming you haven't made your flush yet, you can't be later outdrawn by someone holding a single high flush card. Thus the size of your cards is not so important. Consider all nine of your outs to be valid, unless the board is paired, or you can reasonably put another player on a higher flush draw. If the board is paired, *no* flush draw is worth all nine outs.

A paired board is a danger sign. Look, if someone flops a full house, they're likely to slowplay. You'll never know you're beat until you're hooked. Even if a person only flops trips, they are going to try to play it deceptively. It's often very hard to tell just how good your opponents' hands are, when the flop shows a pair.

On the turn, however, if the board contains a pair and the action begins to heat up, there's a very good chance that you're drawing dead. You don't want to get taken for a ride, putting in four or more bets, on a worthless draw. And you sure don't want to hit your flush if it's already a loser! Discretion is the better part of valour; it may be best to quietly fold your hand. If you decide to play on, the best you can do is try to estimate the chance that you are drawing dead, and adjust your out-count on that basis. For example, if you estimate a 50% chance that someone already has a full house, you have to cut your out-count in half. That would be just 4½ outs for a flush draw instead of nine.

So far, all the examples we have been talking about presume that you are holding two suited cards in your hand, and flop two more. That's a typical flush draw. But there are three other ways to make a flush. Consider these possibilities:

1) The board already contains three suited cards, and you hold a fourth card of that suit. Again, you have nine outs to make a flush. However, it's much more likely now that other players are drawing to the same flush. Unless you have the ace, counting all nine outs just isn't realistic. The second-nut draw usually isn't worth more than eight outs, or even seven outs if several players remain; the third-nut draw is worth maybe five or six outs; worse than the third-nut draw is rarely worth considering. And if the board is paired on the turn, look for indications that someone has already filled up.

2) A three-card flush has value after the flop. You may hold suited cards in your hand, and hit a third card of your suit on the flop. This is called a *backdoor flush draw*. Granted, you have to hit runner-runner flush cards (two flush cards in a row) on the turn and river...24-to-1 odds against...but it's definitely added value. Most experts consider this to be worth one additional out. This sounds about right to me, since you have to hit on both the turn and the river. A normal one-out hand has about the same odds of completing, by drawing two cards (the turn and the river). Count any three-card flush as one additional out.[2]

3) You could also hold one high card (a king or an ace) and have two of the same suit flop, for another kind of backdoor flush draw. In this case, I'd consider it worth one out for the nut flush draw (this usually means you are holding the ace), or the second-nut draw (you probably hold the king). If you're against only one, maybe two, opponents, then the third-nut draw is worth an out. Anything worse than the third-nut draw is probably not worth considering.

---

[2] Some authors recommend counting two outs for a backdoor flush draw, but I cannot find any justification for this. It's simply wrong. One out, only, please!

Open-Ended Straight Draws

You might want to open another beer before diving into this section. Evaluating straight draws can be downright exhausting to the uninitiated. Let's just jump in, discuss the issues, and see if we can come to some conclusions.

The biggest problem with straight draws is the very real chance that you will make your hand, and still lose or split the pot. It happens frequently. Your straight loses to a flush, or a full house, or a better straight.

WARNING: The biggest problem with straight draws is that you will often make your hand, and still lose or split the pot.

But still, an open-ended straight draw is a powerful drawing hand. If you're holding 8♣-7♣ and the flop comes 5♠-6♥-K♣, you have eight outs to the nuts. Any four, or any nine, and you'll take home the money, almost guaranteed.

But all straight draws are not created equal. What if that flop was 5♥-6♥-K♣? The presence of two hearts on the flop makes a huge difference. If the turn brings the 4♥ or the 9♥, then you make your straight, but it could make someone else a flush. You'll wish you'd never made your hand!

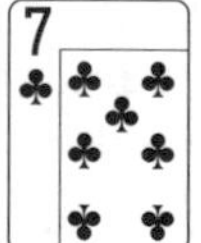
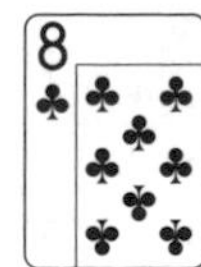

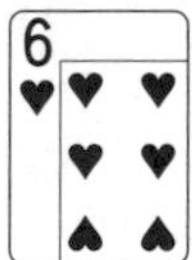

Two of your outs... the 4♥ and 9♥...are compromised, since they introduce a possible flush

And here's something that few players consider:

WARNING: Even if you make your hand on the turn, with a card like 9♣, those flush draws are not going to go away. They'll still be drawing to their flush on the river, and they have a 20% chance of stealing the pot from you even after you make the nut straight.

The bottom line is, if you *know* someone is drawing to a flush, it turns your eight-out hand into something worth only five outs. Because two of the outs will make a flush, and even if you hit one of the six remaining straight cards on the turn, you'll sometimes get outdrawn on the river. It's almost disheartening!

Just how common are flush draws? This is something we need to discuss in detail, because a two-suited flop occurs wel over half the time, and almost every hand you hold will be affected by it. Not just straight draws. If you don't have a full house or better, then two cards of the same suit on the board should make you a little nervous. But when it happens, most players either completely ignore it, or begin to quiver in fear at the flush draws. Neither approach is correct. Certainly, you can't wimp out and throw your hand away every time the flop comes two-suited!

Here's something to consider: One quarter of the playable starting hands are suited.[3] That's right. Only 25%. Look around the table at the next multi-way pot. One, maybe two players are holding suited cards. That's all.

Now, if two hearts appear on the flop, what is the chance that someone is on a heart draw? Most of those players with suited hands will be looking at clubs, or diamonds, or spades. Actually, it's only one chance in 20 that a random playable hand will contain both hearts, if the flop comes with two hearts.

In other words, as you stare across the table at your opponent, there is only about a 5% chance that this double-suited flop on the table gave him a flush draw. What are you afraid of?

---

[3] 20% of the playable hands under average circumstances are pairs; 55% are unsuited; 25% are suited. This comes from my analysis of the opening standards provided by several different authors.

Maybe a two suited flop isn't such a scary thing after all!

Of course, multiple opponents means a greater chance that somebody is on a draw. For the sake of simplicity, we can assume an additional 5% chance for each additional player in the pot. (Surprisingly, this is very close to the true odds, because if one player *doesn't* have a pair of hearts, it becomes more likely that the next player *does*.) Three players in the pot besides you? That's a 15% chance that another heart will cost you the pot...and probably some additional bets, if you *do* make your straight.

Let's look again at our example. You hold 8♣-7♣, and the flop comes 5♥-6♥-K♣. Suppose there are three other players in the pot with you. Unless you can reasonably determine whether or not they are holding a flush draw (how good are your hand-reading skills, *really?*), then you have to assume that about 15% of the time you're up against two hearts.

This means two things:

> 1) Two of your eight outs will actually *lose* the pot 15% of the time. The 4♥ or the 9♥ could cost you the pot, instead of win it for you. There goes about 0.3 outs (two outs times 15%).
>
> 2) If you hit one of the other six outs, anybody with the heart draw will still stick around and try to outdraw you on the river. You'll still lose to a flush about one chance in 33 (one chance in five of the third heart appearing on the river, multiplied by the 15% chance that someone actually *is* on a heart draw.) There goes another 0.2 outs (you had six 'safe' outs, but we have to take away 1/33 of them).

There went half an out (0.3 + 0.2 = 0.5 outs). Thus, maybe we could say that your eight out hand becomes worth about 7½ outs, if there are two suited cards on the flop, and three opponents.

That's not so bad, is it? Ah, but it gets worse, my friend. For one thing, if the 4♥ or the 9♥ appears on the turn, and it *doesn't* give the pot to somebody holding two hearts, then there's always the 22% chance that a fourth heart will appear on the river! Then, you lose to anybody holding even a single heart in his hand. And for another thing, if your opponent puts his money in the pot, you know he's got *something*. Perhaps you glance around the table when that double-suited flop appears, and this time you count four players. That means there's about a 20% chance that someone is on a flush draw. But after the flop betting, you survey the wreckage and find three of the four players still standing. What is the chance that there is someone on a flush draw *now?* You can throw that 20% figure out the window! It's time to re-evaluate.

Follow the logic with me, here. The board came two-suited. Let's assume that, on average, 12 out of every 20 players who see the flop continue on to the turn. I did a study recently that showed just that. You lose 40% of them after the flop. Now, we can assume that one out of 20 is holding a flush draw, and we can assume that *all* of the flush draws stay to see the turn.

Therefore, of the 12 out of 20 that see the turn, on average one of them holds a flush draw. As you are looking around the table *after* the betting on a two-suited flop, you can assume that each opponent has a one-in-12 chance of being on a flush draw. That's an 8% chance if you're facing one player; a 17% chance if you're facing two players; a 25% chance if you're facing three players.

What does all this mean? It means that, for *any* drawing hand that won't beat a flush, you have to compromise the value of your draw, when the flop comes with two of the same suit.

Don't take the wrong meaning, please. I said *compromise*; I didn't say throw your hand away. Too many people go overboard, tossing away good drawing hands and patting themselves on the back, proud of their self-control, simply because the flop came two-suited. This is a serious mistake.

Whenever a flop contains two cards of the same suit, a good rule of thumb is to subtract one out if there are at least three other players in the hand. And I'm assuming we're still talking about drawing to an open-ended straight, where two of your eight outs are compromised because of the chance of losing to a flush. Take one of the two compromised outs away.

TIP: If you have a good open-ended straight draw, but the flop comes two-suited, a good rule of thumb is to subtract one out if there are at least three other players in the hand.

This rule may seem a little exaggerated... after all, the above example might seem to indicate that you should subtract one out for every *six* opponents...but remember, when that third flush card hits, often either the betting dies or you get taken for an expensive ride. Probably taking one out away for every four or five opponents is appropriate. That would be a half out for two or two and a half opponents, right? What if you have three opponents? Hey, let's make it easy. Just round the numbers a little. Take away a full out if you have three opponents or more.

If you haven't made your straight by the turn, you no longer have to worry about being outdrawn after you make a safe straight, since there is only one card to come. Of course, when counting outs on the turn, you must still consider some of your outs to be compromised, because of the chance that the card which makes your hand also makes a flush for another player. But maybe you should subtract one out if there are five or six other players in the hand on the turn, rather than just three? Because you can no longer get outdrawn on a later street?

No. Not if you can see the betting action before it's your turn to act, because if there are any bets this round, you're going to have some casualties again due to normal attrition. The turn betting will chase away even more players. But again, you're never going to chase out the flush draws! So anyone left standing after the turn is even *more* likely to be on a flush draw!

Perhaps on the turn you are able to get a little better read on which opponents may be on a flush draw, but failing this, let's stick with the same rule: Drop one of your two outs in that suit if there are three or more opponents remaining.

An important distinction should be made here. Suppose the

flop comes 2♣-4♥-8♣, and the turn is the Q♥. Technically, now, there are *two* flush draws to be wary of. But unless there was no betting at all on the flop, I would heavily discount the chance of anybody drawing to a heart flush. This is because the flop betting would chase most heart-flush draws out of the pot. Likewise, if the flop was a rainbow (2♣-4♥-8♦) and another club comes on the turn, I would not be concerned, unless there was no betting on the flop to chase the club draws out. What matters most is that the flop itself was two-suited, not that a new flush draw appeared on the turn.

TIP: Unless there is no betting on the flop, don't be terribly concerned about flush draws that appear on the turn. What matters most is that the flop itself was two-suited.

Now, what if the flop contains three hearts? Then, my friend, if you don't have any hearts, there are very few drawing hands that are even worth bothering with. You're now looking at a roughly 5% chance, per opponent, that someone has already made their flush...plus anyone with a high heart (say, a king or ace) will be drawing for a higher flush. You'd better know how to read your opponents well, if you plan to try to figure out how many outs you have.

Likewise, if the turn brings a third suited card to the table, any out-counting process degenerates into an exercise in reading your opponents. This topic is beyond the scope of this book.

Let's return, then, to counting outs for straight draws. Having covered the possibility of having your hand flushed away, there are still three other concerns for every straight draw:

1) You can lose to a higher straight. For example, if you hold 9♥-8♥ and the flop comes J♣-10♦-2♠, you're on shaky ground. Only a seven gives you the nuts. If a queen comes, then even if you haven't already lost to a higher straight, there's a good chance that the river will give someone a better straight than yours.

2) You can split the pot. This is very common when

you're using only one of your cards to make up the straight draw. For example, you may hold J♦-10♠ and the flop comes 10♦-Q♠-K♣. If you make your straight, you share the pot with anyone else holding a jack.

3) If the board pairs, you can lose to a full house or even four of a kind.

Counting outs for a straight draw, then, is seldom 'straight-forward'. Still, there are some good rules of thumb that will help you estimate their value, 'outs-wise'.

Let's talk about four different classes of straight draws:

1) When you hold connected cards on the lower end of the straight (often called the 'idiot end' of the straight, for good reason), it's easy to be outdrawn by a higher straight. I guess I've already told you that. Well, it bears repeating. The 4♣-3♣ with a flop of 5♠-6♦-J♣ is an example of being on the idiot end. If you make your straight on the turn with a 7♦, then someone else could already have a higher straight. Moreover, anyone with an eight or a nine would be drawing to an even better straight. Thus, four of your eight outs (the four sevens) are seriously compromised. Even the deuces in the deck are somewhat compromised, because anybody holding 8-7 will be trying to outdraw you on the river with a higher straight. I would estimate that this draw is worth only six outs. By the way, this is why you seldom want to play 4♣-3♣ or 3♣-2♣; besides the fact that your flush draw is miniscule, you'll often find yourself drawing to the wrong end of a straight.

Class 1: the idiot end

2) You hold unconnected cards in the middle of the straight. For example, 10♣-8♣ when the flop comes J♠-9♦-2♥. It's still a little scary when you turn the Q♦, because you don't hold the nuts, and because plenty of new draws are available for other players to beat your straight. But it's a far sight better than holding the idiot end. I would estimate that this draw is worth seven outs.

Class 2: Unconnected In The Middle

3) You hold unconnected cards on the top of the straight, or connected cards in the middle of the straight. Examples of this are J♣-9♣ with a flop of 10♠-8♦-2♥, and 10♣-9♣ with a flop of J♠-8♦-2♥. Now it's worth all eight outs, or close, because any straight that you make is the nuts...at least until the river.

Class 3: Unconnected On The Top, or

Connected In The Middle

4) You hold cards on the top of the straight. For example, you have 8♣-7♣ and the flop comes 5♥-6♦-Q♣. Any straight you make is now the nuts, and in fact, any straight redraw that appears for you is also probably the nuts. This is clearly the best of all worlds. All eight outs are clear winners.

Class 4: Connected On The Top

So it's all about whether your draw is to the nuts, and how easy it is for someone to make a better straight than you on the river. Sometimes you find yourself with a two-gapper in your hand, and a straight draw on the table. Maybe you hold Q♣-9♣ and the flop comes 7♥-10♦-J♠. How many outs would you say this straight draw is worth? Answer: Only seven outs, because you're not drawing to the nuts. (Later in the book you will learn how to add additional outs for your queen overcard.)

These are, of course, rules of thumb. The more players you are up against, the more likely it is to matter that you aren't drawing to the nut straight.

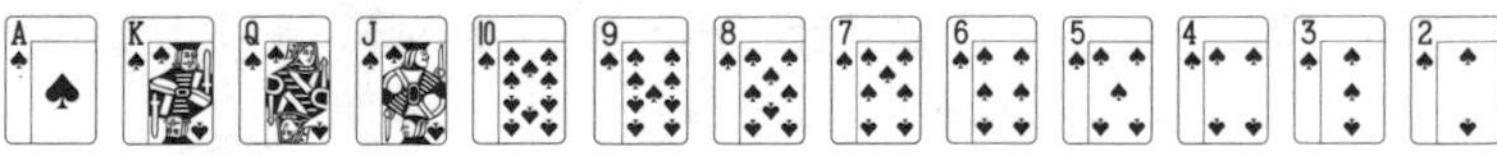

Ace Speaks...

Underestimating the strength of a draw

Earlier in this book, I gave an example of someone who grossly overvalued the strength of his draw. But a while ago, I was criticised myself for allegedly making this mistake.

Here is what happened.

With K♦-Q♦ and three limpers in front of me, I had raised on the button. When both players called, six players saw the flop J-9-2 with one diamond. The small blind bet out, and immediately was raised by the big blind. All others folded to me. Now, while I was contemplating what to do, the small blind had not noticed I was still in the hand, and simply called the raise out of turn. I now decided to cold-call the raise as well, to see the turn for two small bets.

When in the end I won the pot, someone criticised me for calling this raise on the flop. He said: 'You always claim to be so hot with your articles and all, but here you called not one but two bets with nothing more than an inside straight draw. This was clearly a bad play, because no way did you get the proper odds to pay this much with a mere gutshot.'

Again, this player failed to analyse the strength of a hand correctly. After all, my hand was *not* just a gutshot. When the small blind did not three-bet, I thought there was a good chance that he just had a one-pair hand, and the flop raiser didn't need to have better than one pair either – even though of course this *was* a distinct possibility. What all of this meant for my hand, was that there now was actually some chance that hitting a king or queen would also be good enough to win the pot, in addition to the ten that would of course give me the nuts. What's more, I also had a backdoor flush draw, to give my hand some more added strength.

Now, if I had not known that the small blind would just call, I might actually have folded, for two reasons:

1) The pot could get raised again, meaning I would have to pay three, possibly four bets to see the turn.

2) If indeed I were to call the two bets cold and then the small blind were to pop it once more, then I would know that hitting a king or queen

> on the turn would almost certainly *not* be good enough to win the pot, meaning that in that case I would have put three or four small bets in the pot with not much more than a gutshot – a play with a clearly negative expectation.

But now, the mistake that this player made by prematurely showing his intentions, actually helped me in making a profitable call by correctly analysing what my opponent's call may have meant for the strength of my draw, or more specifically for the strength of my overcards. The fact that there were already 12 small bets in the pot before the flop, and that on the flop I called two bets for a total pot size of 18 bets, meant that folding the hand at that stage would have been an absolutely horrible decision – yet to the player who criticised me, it seemed that this would have been the proper play.

An interesting sidebar, here. Some players will routinely play a hand like 9♣-8♣ but will throw away 9♣-7♣ under the same circumstances, because the cards are not directly connected. Others scoff at this, because of the following logic:

9-7 will make fewer straights than 9-8. 9-7 can make a straight with 8-6-5, 10-8-6, and J-10-8. 9-8 can make a straight with 7-6-5, 10-7-6, J-10-7, and Q-J-10. So the connected cards will make a straight 33% more often. That's significant...except that, if you happen to hold 9-8 and flop something like J-10-2, you're often going to have to throw the hand away. You've flopped the idiot end of the straight, often not worth playing. So one of those four straight possibilities is not worth considering seriously.

TIP: Simply put, connected cards make nut straights. They make the nut straight three times as often as one- or two-gappers.

The difference, however, between 9-7 and 9-8 is that unless you are on the idiot end, *connected* cards in your hand almost always make the nut straight! There are, in fact, three times as many nut straight possibilities with 9♣-8♣ as there are with 9♣-7♣ (only 8-6-5 makes a nut straight for the latter).

Connected cards really are much more valuable than one-gappers!

Anyway...back to our discussion of counting outs. In the types of draws given above, you used both of the cards in your hand to make the straight. This is obviously desirable, since it lessens the likelihood of someone else making the same straight.

If you're using only one of your cards, it's very common to have to share the wealth. For example, if you hold A♣-9♣, and the flop comes 7♠-8♦-10♥, you have a good straight draw...but so does anyone else holding a nine. If a six or a jack comes, you split the pot. If someone *does* have a nine, the value of your outs are cut roughly in half, since you'll be sharing the pot. In fact, the true value is less than half, since any further bets *you* put into the pot are also split...bets that we usually assume will find their way back to you in one piece if you win.

If you are using only one of your hole cards, decrease your out-count by one for the likelihood of a shared pot.

Let's summarise, then, the rules of thumb we've come up with for counting outs in an open-ended straight draw. Remember that these are just general guidelines.

Guidelines for counting outs in an open-ended straight draw

1) Begin with all eight outs.

2) Subtract two outs if you are drawing to the idiot end of the straight.

3) Subtract one out if some of your outs don't give you the nut straight.

4) Subtract one out if only one of the cards in your hand is being used, because you may have to split the pot.

5) Remember to subtract one out if the flop comes two-

suited, and there are at least three other players.

6) And remember to subtract another out if the board is paired, and you have three or more opponents, because of the possibility of someone having or drawing to a full house.

Complicated, yes, but with just a little practice, it'll become second nature to take all the complexities of your straight draw into consideration when counting outs.

Inside Straight Draws

Remember that there is a considerable difference between an open-ended straight draw (with eight outs) and an inside straight draw (with only four outs). Some inside straight draws are hardly worth considering. As an extreme example, if you hold A♣-7♣ and the flop comes 9♦-10♦-J♠, you technically have an inside straight draw, but of course it's totally worthless. If you were to count the outs using the techniques discussed above, here is what you get: You have four outs (four eights) to the idiot end of a straight (drop a couple outs) with only one of your two cards participating (drop another out) and the board contains two diamonds (drop another out if three other players are in the hand). You are essentially playing with a zero-out hand!

If there is any good news about inside straight draws, it's that you have fewer outs that may be compromised.

Eh? That's good news?

What I mean is, you shouldn't subtract an out for a double-suited flop, unless there are *lots* of players in the pot, because you only have one out in that suit to give away! Suppose you need a seven and there are two hearts on the flop. Only one of your four outs (the 7♥) is compromised. To subtract an entire out because of a possible flush draw would mean that you *know* somebody is on a flush draw and that one out is totally worthless!

Nor should you be so generous in giving away your precious few outs if the board is paired, or if you aren't drawing to the nut straight.

A realistic set of rules follows for inside straights

1) Begin with four outs.

2) Just say no to the idiot end of an inside straight. Or at least use your judgment; if you're against just one or two opponents, maybe you can give yourself an out or two for this clunker.

3) Take away an out if you are facing *multiple* drawbacks from the following list:

a) A double-suited flop with three or more opponents.

b) A paired board with three or more opponents.

c) You are using only one of your two cards in the straight draw.

Getting Counterfeited

Did it sound a little harsh when I made you take away an entire out if you weren't drawing to the nut straight? Well, actually, it's just the opposite. I'm being a little too generous in giving you all eight of your outs even when they all make the nuts.

At least, I am being too generous on the flop. Maybe not on the turn. Here's why. A common frustration in dealing with straight draws is that your hand can easily be *counterfeited.*

That means that you make your straight on the turn, and then on the river, one of the cards in your hand pairs. The extra pair doesn't help you one iota, of course. All it does it give everybody else a better chance of making the same straight or possibly an even better one.

TIP: No straight draw is really worth all eight outs on the flop, because any straight can be toppled or counterfeited by an unfortunate river card.

Let's say you hold K♣-Q♦ and the flop comes 6♦-10♣-J♥. What a wonderful flop! An open-ended straight draw and two overcards! Then, an ace comes on the flop, and it gets even better! You've got the nuts.

Now the Q♥ comes on the river. Your own queen has been counterfeited, and you share the pot with anybody holding a king.

It's far from a rare occurrence. No straight draw is really worth all eight outs on the flop, because any straight can be toppled or split. If you want to consider all straights against three or more players to be worth no more than seven outs, go right ahead.

The queen on the river counterfeits your own queen, and you share the pot with any king.

Three-Card Straight Draws

Finally, it's quite common to flop a backdoor straight draw. This means you need two more cards, after the flop, to fill your straight. For example, you hold J♣-10♣ and the flop comes 2♣-9♠-A♠. You have a three-card straight, with J-10-9, and need two more cards to fill your hand.

Surprisingly, a three-card straight is more valuable than you might think! Let me give you some odds:

Chances to fill a three-card straight draw

1) **Q-10-8** will fill to a straight once every 68 hands.

2) **J-10-8** has two ways to fill: Either with 9-7 or with Q-9. It therefore has twice the opportunities of the first hand, and will fill once every 34 hands.

3) **10-9-8** has three ways to fill: 7-6, J-7, and Q-J. It will fill once every 23 hands.

Runner-runner straight draws are deceptive. Suppose you hold 9♠-7♠ and the flop comes 4♦-5♠-J♥. This is a total throwaway hand, right? You hit nothing. Does it surprise you to know that there are three ways to make a straight with this hand? You can fill to a straight with 6-3, with 8-6, and with 10-8. It will fill once every 23 hands. You will also make a flush with runner-runner spades one chance in 24 hands. So you'll make a hand about once out of every 12 hands...about the same odds as playing a two-out hand through to the river.

Of course, you're going to have to pay on both the flop and the turn to get to the river card. We'd better look a little deeper into the hand. If the turn brings a three, a six, or a nine, all you've done is turn a garbage hand into an inside straight draw. That's rarely worth continuing past the turn. An inside straight draw is only a four-out hand, and usually doesn't bring strong enough odds to warrant paying a double-sized bet on the turn. In fact, looking at the above example, only an eight on the turn transforms your hand into a legitimate straight draw...because now you have a two-way straight draw (any six or ten makes a straight).

Therefore, when evaluating the value of a three-card straight draw on the flop, it's relatively unimportant how many different kinds of straights you can make. What's important is how many *two-way* (open-ended) straights you can make on the turn, which will elevate the value of your hand to a draw that is worth continuing on to the river.

If you can't find two cards that will turn your three-card straight into an open-ended straight draw on the turn, or a double belly-buster, your three-card straight is worthless. (A double belly buster is a hand like 9-7-6-5-3, where you are essentially drawing to two different inside straights.)

Of course, you also want to make sure that any straight draw which materialises uses both of the cards in your hand.

Let's look at some examples. In each case, I'm assuming that two of the cards are in your hand, and the rest on the table.

10-9-8

Any seven or jack turns your hand into a legitimate straight draw. It's important, here to have the top card of the three-card run (the ten) in your hand. If you don't, then a jack on the turn puts you on the 'idiot end' of the straight draw. It's true that a queen on the river fills your straight, but your 9-8 can then lose to anyone holding K-9 or A-K.

J-9-8-6

Any seven or ten turns your hand into a legitimate straight draw. But again, it's much better to be on the top end of the straight. Holding 8-6 is nearly worthless as a straight draw. 9-8 is better, though a ten on the turn puts you on the idiot end. J-9 is best, with J-8 a close second.

A-Q-10-8-6

Any nine or jack elevates this hand to a legitimate straight draw. Which two cards do you need to be holding? Q-10 is best...most any other two cards are far too compromised, meaning someone else will often make the same straight or a bigger straight at the same time you do.

Are you getting the idea? Three-card straight draws add value to your hand, but like four-card straights, they are not all created equal.

- ♠ You need eight outs that will create draws to *two-way* four-card straights, such as an open-ended straight, so that it will be worth continuing to the river. The above examples all show eight outs, and all eight outs provide a two-way straight.
- ♠ You need to hold the top card or cards, so that you don't cost yourself a lot of money when you hit your straight and lose to a bigger straight.
- ♠ You want to use both of your cards. If you don't, anyone else holding the same card you have will share the pot with you.

It should be pointed out that if you hold a pair in your hand, it's much less likely that anyone else holds the same card. An example is if you hold 10♠-10♦ and the flop comes 8♦-9♣-A♠. It's much less likely that anyone else holds a ten in their hand, if you hold two of them. This is an example where the three-card straight certainly adds value to your hand, even though you hold only one of the straight cards.

NOTE: If you took all the fives and tens out of the deck, nobody could make a straight.

You may have heard it said that every straight contains a ten or a five. If you took all the tens and all the fives out of the deck, nobody could make a straight.

Another interesting observation is that if you hold a ten or higher, you're drawing to the nut straight. No one can beat your straight unless they *also* have the same card you have.

This makes 10-10 a rather special pair to hold in your hand. It will participate in straights as often or more often than any other pair (it's more likely to make a straight than, say, J-J) and if it *does* make a straight, you can't lose to a bigger straight unless someone else holds a ten...a rather unlikely possibility, since you hold half the tens in the deck.

But let's get back to the topic. A reasonable 'draw to a straight draw' adds value to your hand, worth about one additional out.

This is for the same reason that a three-flush adds one out: It succeeds in filling to a runner-runner straight about as often as a one-out hand would fill by the river.

It's like flopping a three-card flush. A three-card straight surely can't stand on its own as a playable hand, but it can sometimes add enough benefit to turn an otherwise bad call into a profitable one.

I can hear what you're thinking. 'All this effort searching for three-card straights to garner only one out?' You're going to find, in chapter five, that one out can make a tremendous difference, quite often turning an unplayable hand into a playable one. *Find those extra outs!*

Whew! Enough about straights for now.

Low Pairs

Remember that I'm using the phrase 'low pair' to describe middle or bottom pair. You have unpaired cards in your hand, and one of them paired on the board, but it's not top pair. In a ring game (nine or ten players), top pair is the hand by which all other hands are judged.

TIP: In hold'em, top pair is the hand by which all other hands are judged.

Yes, there *is* a difference between flopping bottom pair and flopping middle pair. Middle pair is obviously better than bottom pair. But neither of them is *top pair,* so both of them are probably drawing hands.

When you hit middle or bottom pair on the flop, and there's a bet and a call ahead of you, it usually means you're beat. If you stay in the hand, you're hoping to make trips or two pair. That's five outs: two outs to make trips, and three outs to make two pair.

It is not *always* the case that you are beat. You have to decide, now, whether to treat it like the best hand or whether to play it like a drawing hand. It often comes down to your board-reading and player-reading skills.

Many poker books tell you that it's already time to give up your low pair, as soon as someone bets into you. And many times they're right. Drawing to improve has a low success rate, with only five outs, and often two pair isn't enough to win anyhow. Someone could already have a set. You never know.

But the books are not *always* right. It's often correct (pot odds-wise) to make that call on the flop, especially if the pre-flop betting was raised. And there remains the possibility that your low pair really *is* the best hand. Perhaps the betting will cease on the turn and river, and you'll flip over your cards to the pleasant surprise that you hold a winner. It's just not a clear fold.

So, let's address the situation. Let's work through the logic, like we did with straight draws. When you flop low pair, you must decide whether to play as if you hold the best hand, or whether it's time to slow down and play it as a drawing hand. But even if you slow down, on the assumption that you're beaten, you should still add marginal value to your hand on the off chance that it really *is* best.

Suppose you hold 10♣-4♣ on the big blind and get a free play. Now, the flop comes 6♦-10♠-A♥. Here's an example where, if anyone bets, you're probably beat. There just aren't many ways a person could be semi-bluffing with the flop like that. A raise to 'find out where you're at' isn't likely to have very pleasant results. So do you call? You have five outs to beat a pair of aces: two tens, and three fours.

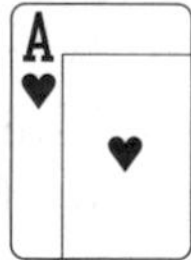

You have five outs to improve: any ten and any four

The most important consideration when counting outs for a bottom or middle pair is to decide whether any of your outs are likely to improve anyone else's hand. Here, it's unlikely. Another ten won't improve a hand that doesn't already have a ten, and it's hard to imagine a four helping anybody that sticks around with this flop. So, all five of your outs are probably good; no reason to think any of them are compromised.

What if your hand is J♣-10♣ instead of 10♣-4♣? The problem is that a jack is much more likely to help another player than a four. Since a jack doesn't beat the ace on the table to make top pair anyhow, you're actually better off holding 10♣-4♣ than J♣-10♣. Suppose a jack *does* come on the turn. Someone with K-Q has just made a straight. Someone with A-J has just made a higher two pair. A-J is a much more common hand than A-4.

So how much do you discount your outs for a hand like J♣-10♣ when you flop 6♦-10♠-A♥? That's not an easy question to answer. It depends greatly upon the playing styles of your opponents and how well you can read them. Drawing to two pair is a five-out hand at best, and about a three-out hand at worst. It will sometimes take all of your skills to figure out what bottom or middle pair is really worth. In fact, there are so many things that can go wrong when you draw to two pair, that I *never* recommend giving yourself all five outs. We'll get back to this idea shortly.

In this example, I'd give you between three and four outs, depending mostly upon the number of opponents. Because the more opponents there are, the better hand you must have to take home the money.

Now consider this example: You have J♣-10♣ again, and this time the flop comes Q♥-J♦-A♥. The good news is, you've picked up an inside straight draw. Add three outs or so for the chance of hitting a king. (Remember, if a king comes, you'll share the pot with anyone else that holds a ten, so you can't count all four outs to your inside straight). But what else is there to hope for? Another ten? Your two pair will lose to anyone holding a king for a straight. A jack? Well, the J♠ is probably good, but the J♥ puts a three-flush on the board.

I would say the J♣-10♣ in this case is worth no more than five outs...the value of which comes mostly from the inside straight draw, rather than the pair!

That does bring up a point to be considered, though. Let's go back to 10♣-4♣ again, and pretend that this time the flop comes 9♦-10♥-Q♥. The difference here is that it's possible, even when there is betting on the flop, that your pair of tens is the best hand. Not likely, but very possible. Why? Because who knows what the other players are betting and calling with! There are draws galore out there. *I would add one out to your count for the possibility that you already have the best hand.* If you *do* have the best hand, and blanks hit on the turn and river, the betting is likely to slow to a crawl, letting you cruise to a won pot.

Is the 4♥ on the turn a good or bad card for you?

So, you're thinking about the 10♣-4♣ under your card-protector, staring at the 9♦-10♥-Q♥ on the table, and trying to figure out how many outs you have. Low pair is a five-out hand to improve, but you've added one out more out for the remote chance that you're calling with the better hand. Do you need to discount any of those six outs? Are they compromised? Any ten looks good, but what about the 4♥? Normally, you wouldn't be very concerned if only one of your outs put three hearts on board. It's like when you have an inside straight draw: there aren't enough 'heart outs' to consider taking one of them away. But here, the 4♥ looks even worse than usual. Just what *are* these guys betting with, if not a heart flush? Probably either a heart draw, a jack for a straight draw, or another queen. Which means either the 4♥ is a probable loser for you, or you can forget about the chance that you're already best. It's best to figure that at least one out is dead. Or maybe somebody is betting with a made hand? Something like K♣-J♥? Yes, I'd bet out, myself, if I were in that position with K♣-J♥, just to make the higher straight draws and the flush draws pay to see the turn.

Bottom line is, you'd better not consider this more than a five-out hand *at best*. Four outs for the 10♦, 10♠, 4♦, 4♠, and maybe one more out for the pair in hand, hoping that it's already best. And if I thought I could put anyone on K-J, I sure wouldn't bother counting outs at all. I'd be outta there.

WARNING: Never, ever, count all five of your outs with a low pair. Too many things can go wrong.

Want my advice? Never, ever, count all five of your outs with a low pair. There are just too many ways you can be beat, even when you make two pair. Have I said that before? Someone could show down a set. Straights often appear like magic, to rob you. And if the board pairs, it often counterfeits your own pair.

Here's what I mean. Suppose you're staring at a flop of 6-7-J, and you notice that it pairs one of your cards. Hooray! Maybe you have A-6 in your hand. You're beat by anyone holding a jack or a seven, but you have a draw to aces up, or trip sixes; both very good hands.

Suppose you hit that beautiful ace on the turn. You're celebrating, tossing money happily into the pot. But if another jack or seven comes on the river, your pair of sixes is completely worthless. *Completely.* Three pair is no better than two pair. Anybody with an ace and a reasonable kicker beats you.

Please, folks, if one of the holes in your game is a weakness for playing 'any ace', plug that hole immediately. A hand like A-6 is so much toilet paper in ring games. What are you hoping to flop? An ace? Someone will out-kick you with a better ace. A six? What the heck is a pair of sixes worth against nine other opponents? Two pair? Hey, that's great! Now you can put a lot of money in the pot before the river breaks your heart! And it'll happen more often than you think. Facing several players, I'd rather play 7-6 than A-6. At least my cards work together.

Anyway, back to this 6-7-J flop. It's definitely better if you have middle pair. A-7 won't be counterfeited if a six comes on the river. Do you see why?

Having an overcard in your hand is definitely an advantage, too. A-7 is better than 10-7. Why? Because if 10-7 improves to two pair...tens and sevens...you *again* lose when the board pairs with another six. Why? Because anyone with a jack has just made jacks over sixes.

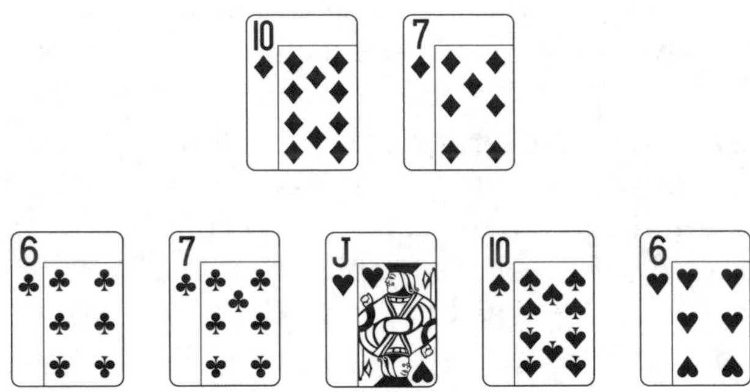

You lose to anyone holding a jack

TIP: Let me give it to your straight: Little cards suck. Little pairs are nearly worthless, and little two-pair hands are fragile as glass.

This may seem obvious or fundamental to more advanced players, but it seems like every player has to get through this learning curve, so let me say it bluntly: Little cards suck. Little pairs are nearly worthless, and little two-pair hands are as fragile as glass. If the board pairs, it's like tossing a rock at the glass.

I see this happen even in middle-limit games: A person will flop two low pair, and it just looks so damn pretty – 'Look, ma, both of the cards in my hand match the table!' – that they put on blinders and happily ram and jam the pot through the river without a care for what else is developing. The board pairs, counterfeiting their second pair, and they don't even seem to notice it. They stare blankly as the dealer pushes 'their' pot to somebody else. *What happened? I flopped two pair!* Yeah, two little ones, dummy.

Enough said. Let's talk again about fighting those pesky flush draws. If the flop comes two-suited, the flush draws are going to hang around to the river, raising your blood pressure even if you do make your hand. Trips and two pair lose to a flush almost as easily as a single pair does.

So, here we are again, with these two issues:

Problems When Flush Draws are out there...

1) You can make your hand, and then lose on the river to a flush.

2) You can make your hand with a compromised out, which gives another person a flush at the same time.

TIP: The first thing you must do, whenever the flop comes two-suited, is make a mental note of which of your cards match that suit. It doesn't matter WHAT hand you have, if you can't beat a flush. You've got to know how many of your outs are the same suit as the possible flush draw.

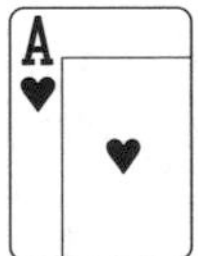

Your outs are heart-free; here the flush draw is not so scary

It isn't so much that you are trying to make a flush yourself. You just want to make sure that your outs aren't compromised. If the flop comes A♥-7♥-3♣ and you hold 8♥-7♣, you aren't nearly as concerned about the presence of two hearts on the flop. Why? Because the flush won't come at the same time that you improve! You are looking for another eight or another seven; you hold the eight of hearts, and the seven of hearts is already on the table! All five of your outs are safe from a flush. No hearts among them.

What if you hold 8♣-3♦ with this flop? Besides having a horrible draw to two pair...you hold low pair without even an overcard...two of your five outs are hearts. This hand is almost worthless.

Counting outs when you flop a low pair is not an exact science. It'll make you think more than any other draw. Here are the mental steps you should go through when counting your outs:

1) Start with four outs. Never give yourself more than four outs for this draw. *Too many things can go wrong.* Have I said that enough?

2) Is it possible that you have the best hand? I'm assuming that you believe you don't, or else you wouldn't treat it as a drawing hand. But look closely at the board to see if anyone that bets could be semi-bluffing with a draw. If it seems reasonably possible that you're best, add an out. Who knows; the betting may die on the turn and you can slide into the river for free with a possible winner.

3) Subtract an out if the board is two-suited and there are three other players in the hand, *and* two of your outs are of the majority suit. Does that make sense? If the flop contains two diamonds, and two of your outs to make two pair or three-of-a-kind are diamonds, then start counting players.

4) If you paired the bottom card (instead of the middle card), or you have no overcard, you can be easily counterfeited. Subtract up to one more out. Actually, dropping ½ out would be about right.

5) Look very carefully at the board to see if the card you need to make two pair will likely fill someone's straight. Drop an out if it does, using your own judgment for how likely it is that you would lose to a straight.

This sounds like a lot of work. Here is what I usually do: I consider my draw to be worth four outs if it's nearly perfect (no obvious compromises) and three outs if I can see some problems. Sometimes I drop down to three outs because I can see several little things that add up. If the board pairs, and my cards are little, I begin to panic and take my count down to as little as two outs. Finally, I give myself another out if I think it's possible that I may have the best hand.

Overcards

Overcards are similar to low pairs in one respect: After the flop, you must decide whether to play as if you have the best hand, or whether to slow down and play it as a drawing hand.

Overcards are dangerous business. The reason is, you're only drawing to a pair. Who knows if that will be enough to win? For example:

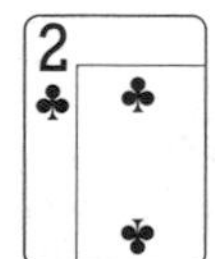

How many outs are the overcards worth?

- ♠ You hold A♥-K♥ and the flop comes 2♣-7♣-J♥. You decide to continue on with your overcards, and the A♦ comes on the turn. But the same card that gives you high pair gives someone else two pair. You lose to A♣-J♠.
- ♠ This time when you hold A♥-K♥ and the flop again comes 2♣-7♣-J♥, somebody is sitting on pocket sevens, and you're drawing nearly dead. Your only hope is the backdoor flush; overcards are worthless against a set.
- ♠ The next time you hold A♥-K♥ and the flop comes 2♣-7♣-J♥, you snag a king on the turn. Then another club falls on the river, and you lose to a flush. Sigh.

The point is, you seldom know if hitting one of your overcards is enough to win. Some experts have suggested that you count each overcard as 1½ outs, rather than three. Others tell you to call with overcards if you can find additional value in your hand. For example, K♦-Q♠ with a flop of 5♠-9♦-10♣ is a good draw, because of the additional inside straight draw.

One way to do it is this: Give yourself two outs for each overcard if you are against a single opponent, and work your way down to one out per overcard if you are against five or more opponents. In other words: two opponents might be 1¾ outs per overcard, three opponents 1½ outs, four opponents 1¼ outs, and five or more opponents one out per overcard. Then, look hard to find additional value in your hand.

Actually, I don't usually count partial outs. You shouldn't either, at first. It becomes a chore, then, to stay on top of the count...and one goal of this book is to take some of the work out of calculating odds, so that you can concentrate more on playing the players rather than playing the cards.

TIP: Overcards are tricky. A-K is best in a tight game, but K-Q may be better in a loose game.

I will usually consider one overcard to be worth either one or two outs, and two overcards to be worth between two and four outs. A good rule of thumb is, one or two opponents means your two overcards are worth four outs; three or four opponents, and they're worth three outs; five or more opponents, and they're worth only two outs.

Of course, the overcards you hold makes a difference, too. A-K is clearly best in a tight game, but K-Q may be better in a loose game. This is because, in a loose game, some players will commonly play hands like A-8 or A-4s. It may be best to *not* have an ace in your hand, if it's likely that hitting an ace will just make two pair for another player. But at the same time, if your cards are something like Q-J, you can too easily be dominated by hands like K-Q and A-J. If the flop comes something like 2-3-6, I'd rather be holding overcards like 9-8 than Q-J, simply because it's less likely that someone else is holding a nine or an eight.

Finally, as always, when the flop comes two-suited, be aware of whether you have any cards of that suit. If you don't have either card of that suit, then drop your out count by one if you have three or more opponents.

It's very hard to quantify the value of overcards by a series of rules, like I did with other types of drawing hands. As is so often the case in hold'em, I can only warn you to use a little good judgment. Don't always fold when you hold nothing but overcards; but don't always play them, either! Don't let your game become too predictable.

Underpairs

Small pairs may be the easiest of all hands to play, for the simple reason that if you don't hit the flop (improving to a set) you usually fold immediately. This is because, with nothing but a pair in your hand, it's very hard to improve.

The rule is, on the flop with a small pair: 'Fit or fold'.

You have only one chance in eight of making a set on the flop, and unfortunately, if you miss, there are only two outs left in the deck to help you.

Two outs. Or, going on the same logic as the way we valued a low pair, you may wish to add another out for the possibility that you are actually hold the best hand...and will continue to hold the best hand with your little pair through the river.

Suppose you hold 8♥-8♣, and the flop comes 2♠-6♥-J♣. There's a very good chance that you hold the best hand on the flop, with your pair. But if there's a bet and a call ahead of you, it's time to modify that analysis; somebody out there has a jack or a better pair. Get out now!

But now suppose the flop comes 6♥-7♥-J♣. Here, if there are bettors and callers, I'd be more inclined to believe that I might...just might...still have the best hand. Why? Because there are potential draws on the board with the 6♥-7♥. If there's a bet and a call ahead of me, I'd play this hand as a drawing hand, still, but I'd treat it as if it has at least three outs. I may be winning and don't know it.

 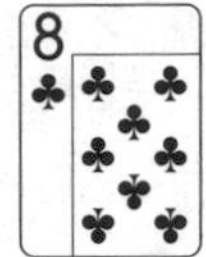   

You may still have the best hand, even if there is betting on the flop

What if the flop comes 9♥-J♥-Q♣ to your 8♥-8♣? Yes, there are lots of drawing possibilities for other hands, so there's no way to know what they are betting with, but so what? Get out of there.

The Basic Rules For Counting Outs

Let's rebuild our outs chart then, with what we now understand. This is by no means an exhaustive analysis, but it's a good starting point.

Draw Type	Outs
Four-Flush	Between 7 and 9 outs, depending upon the strength of your flush and whether the board pairs.
Open-Ended Straight	Between 5 and 8 outs, depending upon the make-up of your straight draw, whether you are using both of your cards, and whether the board pairs.
Inside Straight	3 or 4 outs, depending upon the make-up of your straight draw, whether you are using both of your cards, and whether the board pairs.

Draw Type	Outs
Low Pair	3 or 4 outs, depending upon how many little problems you might see with your outs. If the board pairs, look out.
Overcard	1 or 2 outs per overcard, but when drawing to only overcards, consider carefully the chance that you are already drawing dead.
Underpair	2 outs. No more, no less.
Other Outs	If you have a three-card flush, or a good three-card straight, add 1 out. If there is a reasonable chance that you have the best hand, add 1 out.
Two-Suited flops	If you have a hand where two of your outs put a three-card flush on the board, then take away one of the two outs if there are three or more opponents.

Ace Speaks...

Counting outs as a starting point

As readers of my work will know, I am not a big advocate of hard-and-fast rules, and I don't like point counts much either. They tend to let people focus on alternate counting processes, rather than on what matters most: Making the best decisions based on good analysis of all relevant circumstantial factors.

Having said that, when counting outs becomes necessary, Dew's system works extremely well, for the following reasons:

1) Because it's a simple system.

2) Because it takes into account at least some of the relevant circumstantial factors mentioned above.

3) Because it leaves room for interpretation.

Please note that this system is merely a guide though, it is not gospel. It will be very helpful if you use this as a *starting point* to correct analysis of the (possible) strength of your draw, in combination with what you read your opponents for, and taking into account their pre- and post-flop habits. It is *not* meant to be a system that gives you automatic answers without requiring any additional thoughts on your part. If that is what you are looking for, you have probably picked the wrong book, because that is *not* what we will be providing.

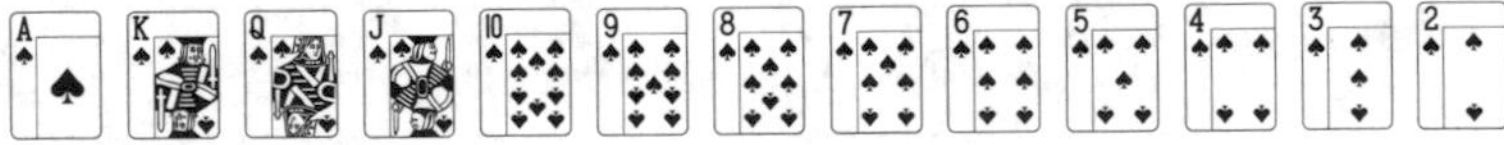

Why Do We Sometimes Add One Out For The Possibility Of Holding The Best Hand?

Honestly, I don't have an easy answer to the question. It's clearly a very subjective thing. Basically, my instructions to you are 'if it looks like you have the worst hand, you have to consider it a drawing hand; but when doing so, if it's possible at all that you *might* have the best hand, give yourself an extra out.'

Clearly, you should give yourself *some* credit for the remote chance of having the best hand. But exactly one out? Where did that idea come from?

Am I trying to convince you that the chance of you having the best hand is approximately one chance in 46 or 47? That's what one out is worth. But it's not what I mean to imply.

Let me ask you this: If you don't improve, are you planning to fold to any bet on the next street? If your answer is no, then why are you bothering to count outs? If your answer is yes, then it just doesn't make sense to give yourself several extra outs for the possibility of holding the best hand. And if you don't *know* the answer to this question, you're playing like a fish.

NOTE: What this extra out *really* represents is the chance that nobody else thinks they have the best hand, so you may get a free card on the next street.

What you're really adding an out for, is the possibility that you might get through the next street without having to pay. And that means nobody else thinks they have a better hand than you. This 'extra out' represents the chance of a free card, plus the chance that you really are best.

The point is, you may be best, but for you to cash in on that best hand, several things must happen:

1) First, we have to assume that you'll still be best at the river, after one or two more cards have come. Who knows what the odds are of that.

2) Has the flop just been dealt? Then unless you have a pretty good draw, you're planning to fold on the turn. It doesn't matter that you actually had or have the best hand; you're folding because you don't believe it to be the case. It just isn't worth paying two or more big bets over the turn and river to learn that you're beat. Thus, since we're assuming that the turn card doesn't help you, for you to continue on to the river with your 'currently best hand', the turn must come and go without anyone placing a bet.

3) Unless you're heads-up and the table provides a bluffing opportunity for your opponent, you're likely to fold to any bet on the river as well, again under the assumption that you aren't best.

What you really want, of course, is for the betting to entirely cease and for you to coast on through the river still holding the best hand. Or at the very least, you're hoping for a free card; another chance to hit your outs. If it doesn't happen that way, then it can be an expensive lesson to learn that you're *not* best.

So why one out? Because you've already made the decision to treat it as a drawing hand, or you wouldn't bother counting outs. Basically, all we want to do is just bump your hand up in value a little bit. Just enough so that the borderline decisions are influenced in the proper direction. No more.

Now, let's add some common sense. The more players there are, the less likely it is that you have the best hand. More to the point: The more players there are, the more likely it is that someone will bet the next street, even if they are on a drawing hand, and you will have to fold, even though you aren't sure you are losing.

Therefore, it makes sense to be more inclined to give yourself this extra out if there are fewer players.

Partial Outs And Borderline Decisions

You'll notice that I've tried hard to keep everything in whole numbers. No partial outs. That's because it's the way *I* keep track of outs. But at the same time I'm keeping a count of the outs, I'm making a mental note of little issues to be aware of, and then I tend to 'lean' one way or the other after coming up with my count. It helps me to make borderline decisions.

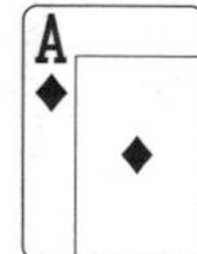

A typical big blind scenario

Let me give you an example of my thought process throughout

the play of an off-the-wall hand. I'm in the big blind holding 7♠-5♣ and get a free play. Let's say the flop brings me an open-ended straight draw: 6♠-8♠-A♦. Eight outs for a two-way straight draw. I'm not drawing to the nuts, though, because my cards aren't connected (I have a one-gapper) and I don't have the high card on the straight. Seven outs, then, I guess, instead of eight. But, hey, it's a little straight...how many people are going to make something out of cards that little? A six and an eight? It's not too likely that anybody else will share that draw with me. It's got to be worth a little more than seven outs.

I'm liking that ace on the flop! It may keep some people in the pot, and it's a long ways from the straight draw. If we're going to get a big card, it may as well be an ace. Everybody likes to play aces.

Oops, there are two spades sitting out there. Damn, I can't remember if I have any spades. Gotta peek. I hate that; now everybody who saw me peeking knows I'm not on a flush draw. I'd surely be able to remember my suits if they were both spades. I should have waited and peeked after my turn to act.

'What'd you say, dealer? Oh, I check, I got no aces, ha, ha, just forgot my cards for a minute, ha, ha.'

Hmmm. The action went bet, call, fold, call, call, back around to me. Four other players. I guess I'd better be a little worried about somebody being on a flush draw. There goes at least one more out, maybe more. Naw, one out is plenty, 'cause I've got one of their precious spades. That takes one of their flush cards away.

That leaves me with six outs, probably a little more. Plenty for now, but probably not enough to play on the turn, if we don't get some money in the pot. 'Yeah, I call.'

5♦ on the turn? That's an interesting card, but it's no winner, by a long shot. At least now I have a pair. 'Check.'

A little under ten outs

Hey, I just noticed that put another diamond on the board. Should I be concerned about a diamond flush now, too?

No. There was a bet on the flop, so the diamond draws were probably chased away. They wouldn't have hung around for a runner-runner.

My straight draw is still hanging in there. I think I'll bump up my outs up a bit, now that there's only one card left to come. I can't be outdrawn after I make my straight. What would they have to have, now, to beat my straight with a better straight? A 10-7? Nobody here is playing that kind of trash. I'd say I'm pushing seven outs with this hand, now, eh?

Aw, heck, I forgot that my five in the middle of my straight draw got counterfeited. Anybody with a seven now shares the pot with me. There goes a whole out, sigh. I'm down under six.

Bet, call, call, the button's still thinking, nobody seems to want to give this pot up, so I'd still better continue to subtract a full out or more for the two spades sitting out there. If we'd lost a player or two, I could at least recover a portion of my outs.

The button calls. Back to me. I'm not ready yet. What should I do?

Did that five give me any more outs? Yes, it did! It counterfeited my straight a bit, but it gave me a pair! A low pair is usually worth four more outs! That puts me up to almost ten! Get some chips in my hand, I wanna check-raise! I can bet for value on the turn with ten outs and this many opponents. It'll be too late to check-raise on the river, since if I make my straight, there will be so many low cards on the board that *everyone* will be terrified of me sitting here in the big blind. They know I could be holding any two cards. I have to raise *now!*

Unless, of course, those four new outs are compromised. There's those two spades on the board, but I've already considered them, it doesn't matter if they compromise my new draws. I'm not about to take any *more* outs away for somebody else's flush draw, just because I now have additional draws to two pair and three-of-a-kind. But what *else* could happen if a five or a seven comes?

Another five looks pretty safe. Trips will win this hand, I reckon. What about a seven, for two pair?

Oh, that would put 8-7-6-5 on the board. Ouch, that bites! Could any of these bozos get this far with a four or a nine in their hand? Well, yeah, a flush draw could have *anything*. I sure wouldn't muck my hand if I held A♠-4♠ or 10♠-9♠ before the flop, not with this many players in the pot.

OK, well, I didn't quite have ten outs anyway. I need ten outs to bet for value. I'm not sure what the odds are of somebody holding a four or a nine, but I sure can't give myself a full four outs for my little pair of fives.

That makes my decision easier. 'Call.'

Common Sense

Like most poker authors, I hesitate to build charts like the one I gave you earlier. I don't want you to read the chart, and trust in it as if it were the Holy Grail. Poker isn't like that. Exceptions abound for every rule.

That brings me to my next point.

In all cases, when counting outs, use a little common sense! Don't be afraid to think! Which do you think is more likely:

1) That a person will fill up (make a full house) after a flop of J-10-10, or after a flop of 2-2-7?

2) That you'll share a pot with another straight when you hold an ace and the board shows K-Q-J-10, or when you hold a five and the board shows 6-4-3-2?

3) That one of your three opponents is on a flush draw if they all call a bet after a flop of 2♠-6♦-K♦, or a flop of 10♠-J♦-K♦?

Clearly, no rigid set of rules can guide you in every situation that comes up. For example, suppose you're holding Q♣-9♣ and the flop comes 9♠-10♦-J♦. You missed your club suit completely, but you've still flopped a pretty good hand, having hit a pair and an open-ended straight draw. How many outs do you have?

Roughly eight outs, but it's so complicated, who really knows?

Well, let's see. A king gives you a straight, of course. As long as it isn't the king of diamonds, which compromises the value of your made straight because there will be three of the same suit on the board. The good news is, the board is so coordinated that the chance of someone staying because of a flush draw is diminished; there are too many other possible hands that your opponents could be playing.

Of course, you're holding only one card to the straight, so anyone else holding a queen will split the pot with you if a king comes...and anybody holding A-Q will scoop the whole pot.

You could turn a queen. But that would certainly be a mixed blessing, with the table showing Q-J-T-9. How likely is it that your two pair will win? I'd be squirming in my seat.

You could hit a nine, giving you trips. But the 9♦ again puts three diamonds on the table. If you aren't beat already by a flush after the 9♦, someone's going to be drawing on the river with their four-flush. So only one nine (the 9♥) is very safe.

You could already be facing a straight, of course. Everybody likes to play K-Q, and if somebody *does* have this hand, they're going to make you pay through the nose to stay in the race. You could make *any* of these hands, and still lose to a full house when another ten or jack hits on the river. J-10 and J-9s are pretty common hands.

The only *good* thing about this hand is that your pair of nines may already be a winner. It's very possible that your opponents are all on draws!

So how would I value this hand? The straight draw is severely compromised (I'd give it five outs instead of eight), and the low pair is compromised (I've give it two outs instead of the usual four) for a total drawing value of about seven outs, maybe a bit more. Then I'd add one more out for the chance that my nines are currently best.

My point is, you still have to think. Nobody ever said that you could master the game of hold'em without having to think. Every hand is unique, and many hands have hidden pros and cons that you have to train yourself to recognise. Add up your outs when playing any hand on the come, but don't be afraid to modify that out-count with a little common sense, and a good read on your opponents.

One of the most important adjustments you can make, by using a little common sense, is to realise that the fewer opponents you have, the more outs you have. I've given you rules of thumb about what to do if the board pairs, and how to adjust your count if your straight draw isn't to the nuts, and how to estimate your outs when drawing to improve a small pair, and so on. But most of the time, I've just given a few rules of thumb without discussing the number of opponents.

It's a catch-22. You often need multiple opponents to make it worthwhile to continue with a drawing hand, but the more opponents you have, the less likely your outs are to be good.

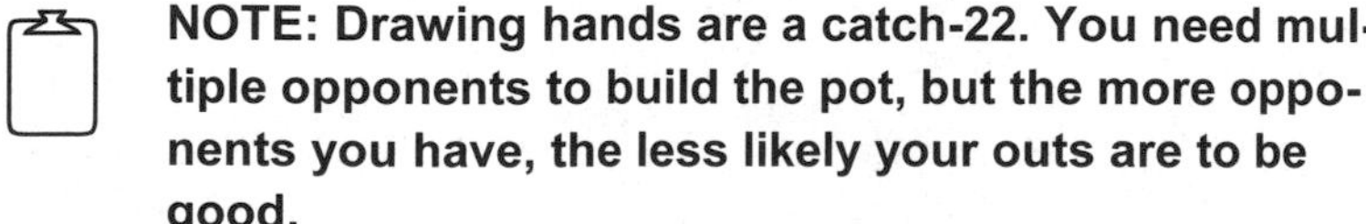

NOTE: Drawing hands are a catch-22. You need multiple opponents to build the pot, but the more opponents you have, the less likely your outs are to be good.

What to do? Understand that most of my recommendations about compromising your outs assume you have two or three opponents. Such as my suggestion that you drop one out on a two-suited or paired flop if there are three or more opponents. If you have fewer than that, you can consider your outs to be worth a little more; if you have more opponents than three, consider your outs to be worth a little less. It's less likely that the pair on the board will give someone a full house by the river. It's less likely that someone is drawing to a bigger straight. It's less likely that somebody has an A♥ hovering over your heart flush, waiting for the river to bring another heart.

Use the rules of thumb, but learn to temper your hand valuations with a little common sense.

Chapter Three

Practice Counting Outs

Poker is a strange and wonderful game. No one ever said it would be easy to master. Counting outs properly will never be an exact science, and never will two experts be in exact agreement. There is simply too much to consider, and each hand is different. Furthermore, your ability to read players will hopefully assist you in counting outs.

Nevertheless, it is worthwhile running through some sample drawing hands, and discuss how we could arrive at a reasonable modified out-count. Here are ten practice hands. I've purposefully chosen a few examples that entail complex decisions, to make you think. You may not agree with me on all examples, and that's OK. I suggest you work through the examples like this:

1) Formulate a quick opinion, taking no more than five seconds or so, by trying to memorise the rules presented in the outs-counting chart I gave you.

2) Then take time to think through the complexities, perhaps to arrive at a different answer than your first opinion.

3) Then read through the solution I provide, to see if we agree.

In any case, I want you to formulate your own opinions about each hand. The games that you play in are different to the games I play in, and my answer to each problem may not be appropriate for your game.

Hand 1: K♠-9♥, flop 10♦-6♦-7♥, four other players

Two strikes against your gutshot straight: There are two diamonds on the board, and you're only using one of your cards. The straight draw is worth only three outs. The king overcard is worth only one out with this many players. Total: Four outs.

Hand 2: 6♦-5♦, flop 8♣-9♦-10♦, four other players

The gutshot to the idiot end of a straight is worthless, and the flush draw is worth only seven of a possible nine outs, because your cards are so low.

Hand value: seven outs.

Hand 3: K♠-K♥, flop A♣-3♥-9♦, two other players

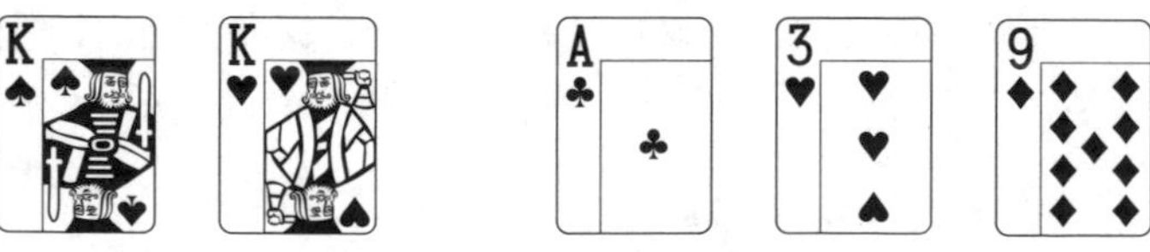

Two outs, pure and simple. A pair of kings is like an ace magnet, and it has happened again. If there's a bet and a call ahead of you, you're beat by a pair of aces; there are simply no draws on the board. Throw your hand away.

Hand 4: A♦-4♦, flop 3♦-2♦-J♥, three other players

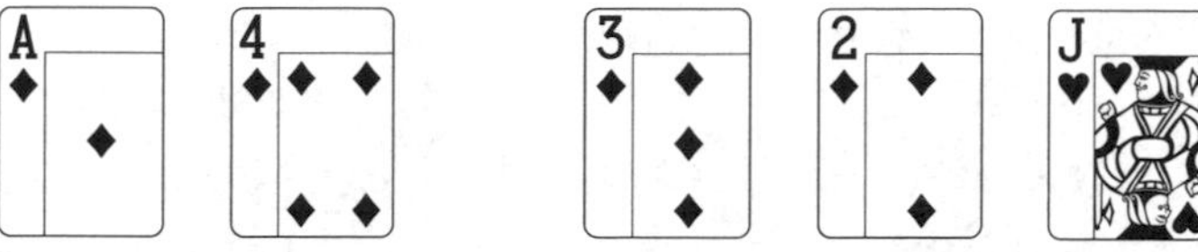

You have all sorts of goodies here

- The flush draw is ace-high with no paired board: Good for all nine outs.
- Your one-way straight draw buys you three more outs. Why not four? An inside straight is worth four outs, isn't it? Not this time: You'd be counting the 5♦ twice (it makes a straight flush!)
- Your ace overcard is worth one out. That's all. If you had fewer opponents, or a better kicker, it might be worth more.

Total out-count: 13 outs.

Hand 5: 8♠-6♠, flop 4♥-7♥-10♦, four other players

Did you see that you flopped a double belly-buster? You have two ways to make a straight.

A nine, however, does not give you the nut straight. So your straight draw is slightly compromised: seven outs instead of eight.

The presence of two hearts on the board further compromises your straight, because there are three or more players.

Final hand value: Six outs.

OK, let's do some that are a little more difficult.

Hand 6: A♣-K♣, flop 10♠-J♣-J♦, three other players, pot is raised on the flop

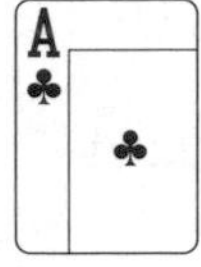

How many outs? I would give you four outs for any queen, one out for the ace-high backdoor flush possibility, and two more outs for your two overcards...unless you can reasonably read other players as *not* having a jack. If nobody has a jack, then your overcards would be worth more.

Hand reading is a learned skill. If the betting before you goes bet, raise, do you put the raiser on a jack? Perhaps not... many players would slowplay their jack. But the board is coordinated, and player holding a hand like A♥-J♥ could indeed be nervous about straight possibilities. His raise could be for the purpose of chasing out any inside straight draws.

Therefore, you'd have a tough time reading the raise to determine if the raiser has a jack, a ten, or a straight draw trying to buy a free card. Likewise, you also would be unable to read a cold call. You just don't know *what* your opponents may be holding.

Playing overcards against a pair on the table, like this, is a two-edged sword. If someone holds a jack, your overcards are nearly worthless. But if no one has another jack, then the pair definitely helps you, since you can now beat someone's two pair! In other words, if anybody holds K-10 or A-10, the presence of the two jacks counterfeits their ten. You still win when an ace or king comes.

Finally, note how easy it would be for the same card that gives you top pair (an ace or a king) to give someone else a straight.

Conservatively, I'd count your two overcards as just one out apiece. But it's close.

Why all four outs for the inside straight? After all, the board is paired and coordinated; shouldn't that concern you?

Yes, it should. Lots of people play hands like J-10, which would make a full house...and if a queen comes to fill your straight, then somebody holding Q-J (another common starting hand) also holds a full house. However, we've already compromised your out-count for the pair on the board by counting only two outs for the overcards, instead of three or four outs.

That gives you a drawing hand worth seven outs. Still not a bad draw.

Hand 7: A♣-J♦, flop 2♠-J♣-K♦, four other players, no pre-flop raise

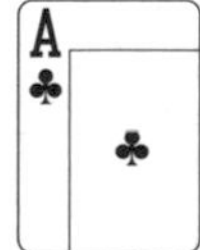

These are the hardest hands of all to analyse, because you usually must decide whether you are drawing, or whether you hold the best hand.

We can assume that at least one person has bet into you, or you'd have no reason to believe you aren't already winning.

So...how many outs? Five, for the remaining jacks and aces in the deck? The fact that there was no pre-flop raise indicates that probably no one is holding A-K. That means that any ace and any jack is likely to give you a winner. Five outs, then?

No, that's too optimistic. As a rule of thumb, *never* consider all of your outs with a low pair to be good. Say it with me, now: *Too many things can go wrong.*

Can you tell by the betting, for sure, that your pair of jacks with top kicker isn't actually the best hand? Do you *know* that somebody has a king? Of course not. They could be testing the waters with a jack, or betting with a draw. It's very possible that you have the best hand.

Suppose, now, that there's both a bet and a call ahead of you. Is it safe to assume that one or the other is holding a king? One of those two may be holding only a jack, but it's unlikely that both do. Could either be on a draw? Yes, that's possible...a hand such as A♣-Q♠ or A♦-10♦ may want to stick around for the inside draw on the strength of their overcard ace or runner-runner flush draw. Q♣-10♣ is also a likely hand, though not especially one that you want to be up against, since it negates the value of your ace. In fact, if an ace comes on the turn, you could lose a lot of money to Q♣-10♣!

The bottom line is that it's logical to add *at least* one out to your modified count on the possibility that your jack is the best hand, but not to get too carried away with the idea that you may be best. I'd value this hand at five outs.

Let's talk about one more thing. What happens if you *do* hit your ace on the turn? Is it enough to win? Remember, there are always two difficulties when calculating modified outs:

1) The possibility of hitting your outs and still losing.

2) The possibility of missing your outs and still winning.

Right now, the *only* way you win without hitting your calculated outs is if you are already winning. Well, I suppose a runner-runner ten-queen to give you a straight is possible, but it's unlikely, and it would probably be a shared pot anyway.

So the only way you should modify your out-count, by factoring in the unexpected, is to go downward, not upward.

We're back to that question of what happens if you hit your ace on the turn. What happens is, anybody with a hand like Q-J or K-Q or A-Q is probably getting proper odds to stick around and try for trips or an inside straight after the ace hits. *It's still very possible to lose after making two pair,* because, in this case, your second pair (the pair of aces) makes the board more coordinated. An ace on the board can too easily help other players even more. That's usually the problem with drawing to overcards or a low pair: After you make your hand on the turn, anything unexpected that happens on the river is more likely to be bad than good.

Your first reaction when you flop a low pair should be that it's a five-out hand: Four outs to improve, and one out because you might be best. After all the checks-and-balances, there remains no reason to deviate from that assessment with this hand. It's a five-out hand.

Hand 8: 4♦-7♥, flop 3♥-4♣-6♠, three other players, heavy flop betting

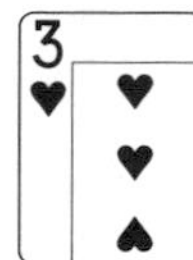
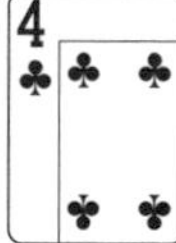

This is very good hand. It looks like a big blind special! The type of pleasant surprise that often comes your way when nobody bothers to raise you off your big blind. You have middle pair and an inside straight draw.

You'll usually play this hand by betting on the flop. You'd like to win it outright, but you're not disappointed if you get callers. You'd like even better to check-raise, but who knows if you can get away with it? It's far from certain that anyone else will bet this flop for you!

It helps that the flop is a rainbow. Nobody is on a flush draw.

Let's suppose you bet out, and you suddenly find yourself raised and re-raised. Things aren't so wonderful anymore! You can probably assume you're beat by an overpair. It's time to start counting outs.

You have five outs to make two pair or trips, and four outs to make a straight. But the two pair doesn't look like a sure thing at all; it's certainly possible that someone has a set. Would anyone in your game play 3-3, 4-4, or 6-6 with only three other players? If so, you could be drawing dead to a five.

Moreover, a seven (giving you two pair) is vulnerable to anyone holding a five. It's possible that someone holds something like A♥-5♥, for a straight draw. But four players (counting yourself) is not usually enough for a knowledgeable player to call pre-flop in limit hold'em with A♥-5♥. How about the players in *your* game?

It would be reasonable to drop those five 'low pair' outs down to three. And if your inside straight comes, you're going to split with anybody else that holds a seven, so you must drop another out, for that reason.

Realistically, you're probably holding a drawing hand (meaning you're beat if you don't improve) worth about six outs.

Hand 9: 8♥-8♠, flop 7♥-9♠-10♠, one other player, who bets into you

You first task, again, is to decide if it's possible that you are holding the best hand. Let's fill in some more details. Suppose the under the gun player raised, you called from the button, and the blinds both folded. Now, he bets into you on the flop.

That wasn't very smart, by the way. Just calling pre-flop, I mean. Raising before the flop was a no-brainer. You don't want the big blind limping in for one more bet with a hand like Q♦-10♠. You want to serve notice to both blinds that you're challenging the under the gun player, and it's going to get hot 'n' heavy.

But you didn't raise, and it worked out OK. The question is, what now? What can your opponent have, to make him open with a raise from early position? The most likely hands are A-A, K-K, Q-Q, J-J, 10-10, 9-9, A-K, and maybe A-Q.

If he had pocket nines or tens, would he slowplay this flop? Yes, probably. The flop isn't that terribly scary when he has only one opponent. Remember that *you* called a single player for a raise, so he's not going to put you on a lone eight or even a spade draw. He figures you've got big cards.

That leaves A-A, K-K, Q-Q, J-J, A-K, and, shall we say, a 50% chance that he would raise if he held A-Q under the gun? You know your opponents better than I do. These hands, plus 50% of the A-Q hands, will have to do for now.

A moderately aggressive player would come out betting on the flop with any of these hands. Even A-K and A-Q. I sure would. I'd want to know where I stand.

TIP: Half the time, in a typical middle-limit game, an early position raiser is holding a high pair in his hand.

So... the odds that he has you beat (with an overpair) are 24:24, or 1:1 (there are 24 combinations of high pairs, and 16 combinations each of the two ace-high hands. But we'll cut the odds of him holding A-Q in half, giving 16 + 8 = 24 combinations of ace-high).[4]

---

[4]I once did a study of the general raising standards of middle-limit players from early position. Considering some of the other reasonable raising hands...8-8, 9-9, 10-10, maybe even A-J...my conclusion was that it is almost even-up odds that a knowledgeable early position raiser has a high pair (nines or higher). Since then, it has become more fashionable to occasionally limp in with A-K or A-Q, so the odds of a high pair go up even more. However, on the other hand, quite a few players will occasionally just limp in with the big pairs, A-A and K-K, as well, so you must take this possibility into account. Also, when playing at the limits, say, $15-$30 or higher, lots of players will bring it in for a raise with *any* hand they intend to play, and this means under the gun raises may sometimes be done on hands as weak as A-10. Aggressive players will raise with K-Q so that they can *represent* an ace if

If it's even-up odds that you're best, you're sure not folding your hand! You're in there raising, finding out *exactly* where you stand. You don't even count outs, not with the pair and the straight draw.

So let's take this hand to the turn. Now, the A♦ hits, and he bets out again.

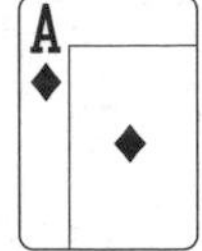

There is virtually no chance that you are still winning against an early position raiser

It's almost certain, now, that you're losing. If you didn't count outs before, it's time to do it now. You can make your straight with any six, or any jack. That's eight outs. You can make a set with an eight. That's two more outs, for ten total.

Are any of your outs compromised? There's a flush draw, but against just one opponent, it isn't significant. Are the two eights left in the deck compromised? Yes, if your opponent is holding J-J or possibly A-J. Should you subtract an out because an eight puts a four-straight on the table?

No. Here's why. You're only getting two outs from the eights; only two of them are left in the deck. To subtract one of those two outs means you figure there's somewhere around a 50% chance that the eights are no good. Of course, that just isn't so. There isn't nearly a 50% chance that he's holding a jack in his hand.

You have a drawing hand worth ten outs. None are compromised enough to matter. No way do you fold with a ten-out hand.

---

one comes on the flop – it's like playing with three cards in your hand. In these types of games, the odds of an early position raiser holding a big pair actually go *down* quite a bit.

Here's a question for you. Let's revisit the flop, for the sake of argument. It comes with two spades, and you hold a spade in your hand. Does the chance of making a flush with runner-runner spades benefit your hand?

It's a good question! Suppose two more spades *do* appear on the turn and river. With five spades accounted for, what are the odds that your opponent holds a spade? The answer is, 2/3 of the time he'll hold no spades with a random hand.[5] If he *does* hold a spade, it surely beats your eight, but if he doesn't...well, runner-runner spades has to be considered a winner. So it's worth an out, right?

No. You're trying too hard to find outs. For one thing, if runner-runner spades do come, then that compromises *all* of your other outs. Your straight draw is worth nothing, and your pair of eights is worth nothing. The hand degenerates into a contest of who holds the highest spade.

Worse yet, what if your opponent holds *two* spades? There's about a 5% chance that a random playable hand will hold two spades, if there are a couple more on the table. On the other hand, you're not staring across the table at a 'random playable hand'; half of those probable hands are pairs, we decided, so they can't be suited. In 12 years, I've never seen a suited pair. But we don't *know* that he doesn't hold a hand like A♠-K♠.

The bottom line is, I guess if I were in your shoes, I wouldn't mind seeing a spade come on the turn, but it's a very close call. It's almost as likely to hurt you as to help you. So you don't want to add an out on the flop for a backdoor flush.

By the way, this is off the topic a little, but it's very common to see four of a suit on the table by the river, and we just stumbled over something very useful: Two-thirds of the time, a single opponent won't be holding a card of that suit. Well, not quite two-thirds of the time. If you don't hold any spades in your own hand, the chance is about 63%. Should you bluff in a

[5]After the river, there are 45 unknown cards remaining. Eight of those cards are spades; 37 of them aren't. The odds of your opponent holding *no* spades is $(37 \div 45) \times (36 \div 44) = 67\%$, because he holds two cards. So the odds that he holds one or two spades is $1 - ((37 \div 45) \times (36 \div 44)) = 33\%$.

situation like this? Note that against two opponents, there's a 39% chance that neither of them hold spades. Three opponents? 23% chance. Four? 13%.

I find this totally amazing, don't you? Suppose someone bets into a four-flush board, and there are four other players in the hand, counting you. Five, total. He's representing a high flush card. Don't you throw your straight away without a second thought? Of course you do! Who wouldn't? What kind of idiot bets into a four-flush and four other opponents without the nuts? You believe him. But *should* you?

TIP: *Always* think about bluffing into a four-suited board. The odds are better than you think that nobody has a card of that suit.

Suppose you're the first to act of five players, and the river has just brought the fourth heart. You have no hearts. Instead of sighing loudly and rapping the table in disgust to check your hand, try betting! There's a 13% chance that nobody else has a heart! That's one chance in seven or eight! Will they all fold if they don't have a heart? You show me a five-player pot that isn't laying you better than 7:1 odds on the river!

If you have 'em, you don't need 'em. The nuts.

Always think about bluffing into a four-suited board, unless you read an opponent as unbluffable or as having a high flush card. And if there are bluffers at your table with any kind of knowledge of odds, consider seriously the chance that *they* might be bluffing when they do the same.

Sorry, I guess my mind has wandered. On to the next hand.

Hand 10: K♠-9♠, flop 2♦-10♠-8♥, four other players, no pre-flop raise

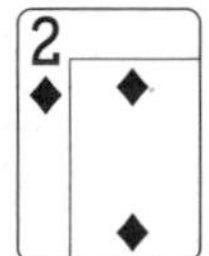

It completely missed you. This looks like a hand only a fish would play. Throw it away without looking twice, right?

Wrong! You may have enough to call, if you can stay in for a single bet! It depends upon how well you know your opponents. Are they just a little too tight?

Give yourself one out for the three-card flush, and give yourself one out for a three-card straight (note that if a jack comes, you're still drawing to the nut straight, using both your cards!). Now add a couple of outs for your king, figuring that the K-J and K-Q hands have to fold. They don't, necessarily, but let's not tell them. Probably nobody has A-K, since there was no pre-flop raise.

Does anybody play K-10 at your table? That could be painful! Let's hope not. The bottom line is, if you know your opponents well enough to believe the betting will chase out the K-J and K-Q hands, your king is a pretty safe overcard. But of course you can't add *three* outs for your one overcard; that would be a bit too optimistic against four other players.

You have a hand worth four outs. Maybe just a teensy bit less, but not much less! And you'll soon learn that four outs is enough to call against this many players! It's very close, and I myself would probably throw the hand away if I didn't know my opponents at all, but I'm not going to be the one that tells you not to play it!

How ironic. The knowledge that your opponents won't usually play some of the better hands than yours (K-Q, K-J) means that, with a little help from backdoor draws, your own pitiful hand squeaks into contention.

Don't look at me that way. I don't make this stuff up! Poker is a strange and wonderful game.

Chapter Four

Some Important Concepts

Let's take a short detour now, and make sure we are in agreement on a few things. Here are ten concepts that are key to understanding drawing hands.

Concept 1

Draw Odds Are Meaningless Unless They Measure The Chance Of Winning

There are a lot of 'knowledgeable' poker players out there, who rigorously calculate drawing odds with each hand, and invariably come to the wrong decision, because they are measuring the chance of making their hand, instead of the chance of winning the pot.

For example, an open-ended straight has eight outs to fill. Many players blindly play their straight draws as if any of these eight outs will actually *win*. But if someone makes their flush, they'll wish they never made their straight!

You know this by now, but I can't reinforce it enough. *Count your outs with an eye towards winning the pot, not making your hand.* We only care about modified outs.

Concept 2

Money In The Pot Belongs To Nobody... Yet

Money in the pot when it comes your turn to act is just that: Money in the pot. It makes no difference how much of that money came from your own chip stack. In other words, the amount of money you invested in prior betting rounds is now completely irrelevant; it belongs to the pot now, not you. How much you've invested prior to the current decision should have no bearing whatsoever on what you choose to do *now*.

Once you've put money in the pot, forget about it. It's no longer yours.

Well, don't forget about it. Just forget where it came from. It's now money that you can try to win. It counts towards your prize just as much as if somebody else had put that money in there.

Concept 3

Each Betting Round Generally Stands On Its Own

Don't be confused by this statement: I'm not discounting such strategies as setting up a bluff, or preparing for a check-raise, on a future betting round. Our primary goal with this book, however, is simply to decide whether, mathematically, any given hand is worth playing on any given betting round. And for that isolated purpose alone, this statement stands pretty much true.

Each round of play brings its own unique playing odds. What I mean by this is, if you decide to take your chances and try to hit your winning card on the turn (by calling or raising on the flop) then you should usually be doing so because of the odds of hitting *now*, not based upon what may happen by the river. This is because in every example we look at in this book, we will always be looking at *implied odds*.

Let me give you an example. Suppose after the flop comes, you have an inside straight draw. Your odds of hitting on the turn are approximately 11:1 against (four outs). But since you have two chances to hit your straight, your odds of hitting the magic card by the river turn into approximately 5:1 against.

So, when drawing to an inside straight on the turn, which odds should you be considering? The 11:1 odds against hitting the straight *immediately*, or the 5:1 odds against hitting the straight by the end of the hand?

The answer is, you should think of it as 11:1 odds, and worry about what to do on the turn when it comes.

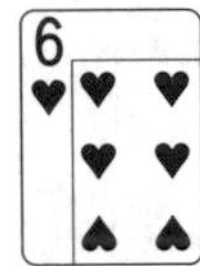

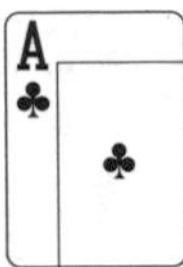

The odds are 11:1 against making a straight on the turn

Here's why. You're in the big blind, playing \$10-\$20 limit hold'em, and everyone folds to the small blind, who makes a play at you with a raise. You call with 8♠-7♠. The flop comes 6♥-10♦-A♣, giving you nothing but an inside straight draw, and he bets again. You decide he has you beat so far; certainly a reasonable assumption. Now there's \$50 in the pot, and the bet to you is \$10. You're on an inside draw...only four outs (let's assume for simplicity that any nine wins for you, and any other possibility wins for him; it's not that simple, but it's close enough to the likely truth). Do you call?

No. What are the implied odds? Shall we assume that you could win \$90, on average, with a winning hand? (This counts hopefully another single bet on the turn and river...granted, this is an assumption, but not a bad one). Then the return on investment to try for a straight on the turn is 9:1 (\$10 to win \$90). Since it's less than the 11:1 odds against hitting the straight, it's a bad decision.

But, you say, you get *two* chances to hit your straight. The turn card and the river card. That's only 5:1 odds against. So let's look at it this way. Are you saying you're willing to pay a small bet on the flop, and a large bet on the turn ($30 total) in order to try to win that same $90? (Let's assume for simplicity that there will be, on average, a single turn bet as well...whether or not you hit your straight). Now you're paying $30 to win $90, a 3:1 return-on-investment, with 5:1 odds against. Nope. Don't do it.

If it isn't a good deal on the flop for a single bet, it isn't a good deal on the turn, either. This means that you don't call a flop bet purely on the basis of having two cards to come; if the cost of playing on the flop makes you stop and think, that last card after the turn will almost always be too expensive to consider.

What's the point of this long discussion? It's that most of time, you will base your decision of whether or not you belong in the pot after the flop on three considerations only:

1) How much it costs to stay in the pot.
2) How much you can win in the end, after river bets.
3) The odds of making your hand *now*, on the very next card.

For example, if you estimate that it will cost you $10 to stay in on the flop, you think you can win $90 by the river if you hit your card on the turn, and you have a better than 10% chance of hitting a winning card on the turn, you pay and pray. If your chances are less than 10%, you get out. It's really that simple.

Concept 4

But Flop Odds Change If You Are Committed To The Hand

We're going to discuss this concept again in more detail a little later, but here is the idea. Suppose it costs you two bets to call, with your drawing hand, on the flop, but that it costs only a single large bet to call on the turn.

Suppose further that the implied odds you are receiving on the flop are marginally too low, but that by the turn, the implied odds are correct. Maybe you have an eight-out hand, but the flop calculations show you need nine outs to call two bets cold. However, when the turn arrives, you need only seven outs to call a single bet on that betting round.

Do you understand how this can happen? *It's because by the turn, there are more bets in the pot to consider...the ones you, yourself, put in on the flop!* If this idea is confusing, don't worry. It'll hopefully become more clear as we continue.

TIP: If, by calling on the flop, you are committing yourself to call again on the turn, then you actually need a little *less* of a hand to make it worthwhile to call on the flop.

Implied odds also change marginally between the flop and the turn because the number of unknown cards remaining in the deck changes from 47 to 46. If you have eight outs, then you have an 8 ÷ 47 = 17% chance of hitting on the flop, and an 8 ÷ 46 = 17.4% chance of hitting on the turn.

The concept I want to explain, however, is this. If it costs as much or more to continue on the flop as it does on the turn (such as our example where it costs two small bets on the flop and one large bet on the turn), then you are more than likely committing yourself to the turn bet when you call on the flop. In other words, by calling on the flop, you've made the decision to call on the turn as well.

Let's call this *committing* on the flop. When this happens, your flop odds change. They become *better. If you anticipate that it will cost no more to continue drawing after the turn than it costs to continue now on the flop, then you should be a little more inclined to go ahead and call on the flop.*

Concept 5

Your Number Of Outs Can Change Between The Flop And The Turn

Actually, this should be rather obvious. You may count nine outs for a flush on the flop, and then pair one of your cards on the turn. Suddenly you're playing with up to 14 outs (drawing to two pair, trips, and your flush).

What's not so obvious is that your out-count is as likely to go *down* as it is up. The board may pair, an overcard may appear, your straight card may be counterfeited, or the straight opportunities on the board for other players may become scarier.

Likewise, any time you add an out on the flop for a three-card straight or flush possibility, that out goes away on the turn, unless it turns into a legitimate draw.

Some hands are more likely to increase in number of outs, and some hands are more likely to decrease. Let me explain.

Any turn card besides a queen or jack is bad for you

If you hold Q♣-J♣ and the flop comes 2♦-6♠-7♥, you have six outs: Any queen and any jack (actually, with just two overcards, I would estimate that you have a hand worth three or four *modified* outs, depending upon how many other players are in the pot).

Are there any cards that could come on the turn that can increase your outs? Nope, not a one. Are there any cards that can *decrease* your outs? Yes...any ace or king, and you're no longer drawing to top pair. Any two, six, or seven and the board pairs, creating chances for trips or even a full house. Any other card below a jack, and straight possibilities appear. Amazingly, unless you hit a jack or a queen on the turn, *any other card that appears is bad for you!*

So, if you miss on the turn, life isn't going to get any rosier. If it costs two bets to stay in the hand on the flop, and by some miracle the pot odds on the flop make it even a marginal call, I'd lean towards folding this hand rather than calling.

But suppose you are holding 7♣-6♣ and the flop is 4♣-Q♦-A♣.

You have nine flush outs...which we would usually estimate at eight *modified* outs because your flush draw is small.

 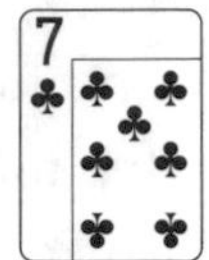   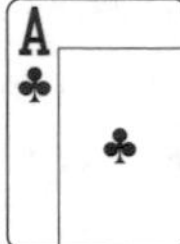

Most turn cards make your hand better!

What can happen on the turn? There are nine cards that can make your draw worse...any four, queen or ace. But there are actually 18 cards that can enhance your draw! A six or seven gives you about four more outs. And with any three, five, or eight you've picked up a straight draw.

The point? If I'm playing little cards, and I don't expect the turn to cost any more than the flop to call (in other words, I'm paying at least two bets to call on the flop), then these 'hidden' outs that may come on the turn are sometimes enough to turn a marginal call on the flop into a profitable call.

I said 'little cards' on purpose. Yes, it's true! The turn is more likely to improve your draw if you have little cards than if you have big cards! But this is a statistical anomaly—little-card hands like 7-6 make easier straights, and don't have to worry about overcards taking away their outs—don't let this freaky fact talk you into playing little cards.

Now I want to remind you of four common ways that the number of modified outs can change between the flop and the turn, mostly because after the turn there is only one card yet to come:

Four ways the number modified outs can change between the flop and the turn

1) If your three-card flush or straight doesn't improve, that out is gone.

2) Straight and flush redraws are gone. For example, if you're looking at a two-suited flop, then you no

longer need to worry about making your hand on the turn, and then later losing to a flush on the river. Most flush draws are worth more outs on the turn, and many straights are also worth a little more, simply because they can't be outdrawn on a later card.

3) Normal attrition through betting will knock out a few players, and as this happens, your own outs become safer. The more opponents you have, the more compromised are your outs.

4) The betting pattern, when the bets turn 'serious' on the turn, may change your mind about how many outs you had in the first place. Rolf has already cautioned you about the evils of point-count systems, and how they make a person lazy. Never stop watching and thinking! If a perfectly innocent card comes on the turn, and suddenly the betting goes crazy, you might want to rethink the situation. Somebody out there may have a monster.

Please be aware that when I reference a six-out hand, I mean, literally, that you have six perfect outs. Exactly a 13% chance of winning. I don't mean that you have added up your outs according to the rules of this book, and they added up to six. *I mean I expect you to win 13% of the time.* You'll see statements often in this book, such as 'never, ever, fold a 10-out hand', Well, if you really do have ten outs, this statement is correct! But if your ten outs are all dead—perhaps because you are drawing to a flush and the betting indicates that someone has already filled up—well, you get the point. *Think.*

Just simply be aware that the situation often changes after the turn card is dealt, and you may need to recount your outs.

Concept 6

Aggressive Play Can Manipulate The Implied Odds

I said that the decision to play each street 'generally' stands on its own. Here is another exception. You're playing $5-$10 in the big blind, and the small blind limps in. Just the two of you. You're holding something like 6♦-3♦, and the flop brings a diamond flush draw, nothing else. The small blind bets into you. You're clearly beat.

You call the bet with your flush draw, and the small blind bets out again when a blank comes on the turn. Now you're a 4:1 dog to make your flush, there's $30 in the pot, and it's costing you $10 to call. It's a dilemma. If you know you can get one more bet on the river after making your flush, you'll get a 4:1 return on your investment. Who knows whether you can or not? Maybe you could get *two* bets on the river. Or maybe none at all. Call or fold?

Hey, it's your own fault for getting yourself into this dilemma. Suppose, by raising his $5 bet on the flop, you can buy a free card on the turn. (This means he calls your raise, but backs down and checks to you on the turn.) If you think this is a reasonably likely scenario, it may be worth a try. Here are the new odds: You are investing $10 now for the chance to win about $35. How did I arrive at this figure? I'm guessing that you'll get another bet and a half, on average, if you hit the flush. You're expecting one of two possibilities, if you win:

> 1) You hit the flush on the turn and extract both a turn bet and a river bet. Or at least one more bet.
>
> 2) You miss on the turn, but your raise on the flop bought you a free card, so no more bets are required to see a river card. Then, you hit your flush on the river. Because you showed weakness on the turn, your opponent might even bet into you on the river. You raise, and perhaps win *two* river bets.

$10 to win $35 is a 3.5:1 return, for 2:1 odds (you're about a 2:1 dog to make your flush by the river, with two cards to come). Thus, a little strategy (raising to buy a free card) has turned a questionable proposition into a no-brainer. It all depends upon how you read your opponent: Will your raise on the flop buy a free card or not?

Concept 7

Aggressive Play Can Create Outs

No discussion about outs would be complete without breaching the topic of creating outs.

Sometimes aggressive betting can create additional outs. Let me give you an example. You hold Q♦-J♦ and three other players see a flop with you of 2♦-8♣-9♥. This is a pretty good flop for you. It's a rainbow, so it offers nobody any flush draws. You have an inside straight draw to the nuts (four uncompromised outs) and two overcards (valued together at about three outs, because you have three opponents, and because jacks and queens are commonly held in other hands, with higher kickers than yours). You also have a backdoor flush draw for another out.

Player one bets the flop, and you're next. What do you do? Clearly, you belong in this pot, with eight outs. Do you call or raise?

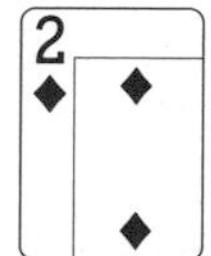

You should raise to buy additional outs

I hope you didn't give it a second thought. You raise! You want the two players who follow you to pay dearly to stay in this pot, if they're holding only overcards. If anyone is holding A-Q, A-J, K-Q, or K-J, you want them out of there.

What you've done by raising is effectively bought yourself two or three more modified outs! If a jack or queen comes on the turn or river, it's much more likely that you'll hold top pair. And if the two players after you fold, you've probably just bought a free card with your raise.

Concept 8

If Bet Odds Are Positive, Get As Much Money In The Pot As You Can

There are different reasons to bet or raise on the flop. Some say, in fact, that anytime you are considering calling, you should think twice about raising. *Controlled aggression finds its reward.* Here are a few well-known reasons for raising:

Reasons for raising

1) You might raise to gain information. Raising on the flop to learn now whether you are beat is a far sight better than meekly calling two double-sized bets on the turn and river, and *then* finding out you are beat.

2) If you don't bet, your opponents can't fold. Betting thins the field when you have a good hand, and gives your opponents a chance to make the mistake of folding when you have a worse hand.

3) There is something to be said for putting extra bets into the pot when you have a good drawing hand, merely because it marries your opponents to the pot when you *do* hit your hand. If the pot is already big, they'll keep putting more in there. This is usually something you think about pre-flop, however, with a hand like Q♣-J♣ against multi-way action.

4) You may bet or raise for value. Just because you're on a draw doesn't mean you shouldn't bet for value. A good drawing hand is often likely to have a better chance of winning a multi-way pot than anyone else out there. You put more money in the pot because the odds of winning justify it.

TIP: A good drawing hand is often likely to have a better than average chance of winning a multi-way pot.

Let's talk a little about #4. There is often so much discussion about pot odds, implied pot odds, reverse pot odds, and so on, that authors neglect the most simple odds of all: pure bet odds.

In other words, given the situation, do you want to put more money into the pot or not? If you had your druthers, would you rather nobody bet, or would you rather everyone just chipped in a few dozen bets?

Let me give you an example. You hold A♥-K♥ and the flop comes J♥-8♣-6♥. With three opponents, your hand is probably worth about 12 outs (nine flush outs, three overcard outs).

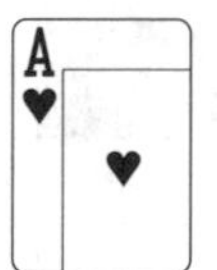

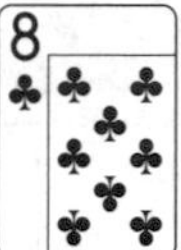

Against two or more opponents, you should raise for value

Ignoring, completely, how much money is in the pot, or how much money you can earn on future rounds if you make a good hand... the question becomes: Would you bet money *now* against your opponents that you will win the hand? Like a side bet?

You bet'cha! A 12-out hand on the flop is going to win the pot about 45% of the time! It hardly matters *what* those guys hold, if you can get more money in the pot, you want it in there! You would need only a 25% chance of winning to make it an even bet against three opponents.

Therefore, forget about what's in the pot. Forget pot odds and implied odds and all that jazz. None of that is relevant at the moment. You want to bet money *now*, as much as you possibly can. You'll keep raising as much as you can with this hand, unless it looks like you're going to chase away some people who would otherwise pay you off. Of course, it's your instincts that will tell you when to call and when to raise, because you want to pull in the other players in case you hit your flush...but some experts would tell you not to worry at all about chasing players from the pot because it creates even *more* outs for the ace and king (you might get an A♦-8♠ or A♣-6♣ to fold, I guess, or another A-K) but the bottom line is, you want as much money in this pot as you can possibly get there, and you want it there *now*.

With this in mind, it's possible to devise a chart that will tell you, based upon your number of outs, exactly when you have proper *bet odds* to bet or raise. The chart below tells you how many calling opponents you need on the flop and on the turn to have favourable *bet odds*. In other words, when it's appropriate to make a 'value bet'.

Number of Modified Outs	Opponents on the Flop	Opponents on the Turn
4	6	11
5	4	9
6	4	7
7	3	6
8	3	5
9	3	5
10	2	4
11	2	4
12	2	3
13	2	3
14	1	3
15	1	3
16	1	2

To use the chart, first calculate your modified outs. Then look at the *On the Flop* and *On the Turn* columns to see how many calling opponents you need for the correct bet odds. If the number of calling opponents equals or exceeds this number, you want to get as much money into the pot as you can.

Clearly, you need a lot of outs, or a lot of opponents, to make a value bet on the turn with a drawing hand. On the other hand, on the flop, lots of typical drawing hands should be bet for value! Looking at the above chart, we find:

- ♠ Any flush draw can be bet for value if you have three or more callers.
- ♠ A decent open-ended straight draw (seven or more outs) can be bet for value if you have three or more callers.
- ♠ A flush draw or good straight draw with overcards can be bet for value if you have only two or more callers.
- ♠ Amazingly, an inside straight draw (four outs) can be bet for value if there are six other callers!

If you were to play like a robot...that is, strictly by the numbers... then you would call with your drawing hands any time the implied pot odds indicate that the hand is worth playing (we'll discuss this in the next chapter), and you would raise anytime the bet odds in this chart indicate that you are a favourite to win more often than your share.

I don't want you to play like a robot. But I want you to know when you're chasing because of pot odds, and when you're actually favoured to win the hand. You want as much money in the pot as you can get, when the odds are in your favour.

Ace Speaks...

Two drawing hands

Hand No. 1

Middle pair plus nut flush draw – Now, what to do?

Recently, while waiting for my regular big pot-limit Omaha (PLO) game to start, I was playing in a $10-20 limit hold'em game. I got involved in a hand with someone else who was killing time waiting for our big game, an aggressive and creative player who doesn't like me much, but who respects and fears my play a lot. In the cutoff, I found the A♠-9♠. With three callers, I often would have decided to raise for value, but as the tight under the gun (UTG) player could have limped with a bigger ace than mine or some other premium hand, I did not want to escalate the pot at this point. I called, the button and small blind folded, and then my fellow PLO player in the big blind raised. Everyone called, as did I. Five players in the pot, total pot size $105.

Now, for this player to raise out of the big blind with the tight UTG player in and especially with me in (as I said, someone he respects and fears a lot), I knew he probably had a big hand: A-Q minimum, but more likely A-K or a big pair. So, when the flop came Q-9-4 with two spades and he bet into the field, I was pretty sure he had at least one big pair now – a hand that would certainly beat my current middle pair plus nut flush draw.

When all three players called the bet, it was up to me. What was my best course of action – call, because I am currently behind, or raise, because I have a premium draw and am getting great odds? Well, this was an easy decision, of course: I raised. Using the counting outs system described in this book, I probably had nine pure flush outs (unless of course the bettor had top set, but even though this was possible, it was not very likely), plus maybe an additional three or four outs for improving to two pair or better – all in all, say, about 12 outs total. (I was of course hoping that in this case the flop bettor had K-K instead of the slightly weaker A-Q he could also hold, as this would buy me some additional outs: any ace on the turn would now give me an almost certain winner, instead of costing me a whole lot of money.) I indeed raised, the flop bettor re-raised, two of the initial callers now called again, and I capped the betting at $40. Total pot size after the flop: $275.

To cut a long story short, I caught a third nine on the turn, got called in two places on both the turn and river, and indeed my three nines were good. When the dealer pushed me the pot, my fellow PLO player flashed his cards to his neighbour, saying: 'See how lucky this fella is. I read him perfectly for being on a flush draw, I make him pay the maximum for trying to draw out, and yet again he gets away with it. It's just not fair.'

What this player forgot was that even though indeed he had the current best hand when the money went in, I was actually a clear money favourite. I needed only 25% pot equity for my bets from that point on to have a positive expectation, and it should be clear that even in this four-way field I would probably have won the pot well over 40% of the time. So, this meant that even though I knew I was currently behind, I would have been willing to put in as many chips as possible into the pot—provided that both other players would stay in as well—because every bet would theoretically make me money! Now, while my opponent had probably made the right decision as well to re-raise on the flop (with a hand like A-Q or K-K he would probably have about 30 to 35% pot equity, and indeed he did need to charge the others for the privilege of drawing out), he forgot to acknowledge the fact that I also had the odds in my favour. As it happened, we were both making money in this hand – at the expense of the other two players.

Hand No. 2

The almost exact same situation. Should we play it the same?

It is interesting to note that just 30 minutes before this hand, I had played almost exactly the same hand in an entirely different manner. Again in the cut-off, this time with two weak callers in front of me, I had A♠-8♠ and decided to raise it up to $20 this time. The big blind called and four players saw the flop, total pot: $85.

The flop came J-6-4 with two spades, again giving me the nut flush draw. It was checked to the third player, a young man who was very inexperienced and quite easy to read. He had not made any bets up to that point and had been playing very passively, but now he could not wait to get his chips in. Acting very confused, he actually put no less than four $10 chips into the pot, when the betting limit was of course just one chip.

Now, often it would seem normal to go for the semi-bluff raise, being in position with my nut flush draw. After all, by playing my hand in this manner I could possibly give myself a free card on the turn. (And in addition to that, I could possibly gain myself two extra outs when the bettor has a pair of jacks, for instance, if by raising I could get someone to fold a bigger ace than mine – so that if an ace were to come on the turn or river I would now win the entire pot.) Still, in this case I just flat called. I was fairly certain that this young guy had just hit the whopper, and equally certain that by raising I would: a) make the other two players fold their hands; and b) give my opponent the chance to re-raise – a chance he would undoubtedly take. Because both these things would be bad for my expectation in this hand, I made a play that most 'good' players would consider weak-tight: just calling, hoping to get paid off only when I hit my hand.

The turn again went bet-call, and when I made the nuts on the river by catching a third spade, the young man again bet, I raised, he re-raised and I re-raised again, with him finally calling. I had gotten him to do what I had expected him to do: pay me off once I had improved over his obviously good hand, keeping the initial costs low, and taking advantage of the fact that he probably would not recognise the flush possibility on the board once the third spade had hit.

But in hand no. 1, I had done exactly the opposite. I had made as many raises as possible early in the hand, knowing I was currently behind, but fully aware that I would be getting a great return on my investment – not by waiting until I had found improvement, but quite the contrary: by putting in the chips before making my hand.

The point

So, you ask, what is the point of all this? Well, the point is that at all times you should look at more factors than just your number of outs. You should take into account what your opponents probably hold, and how they will respond to any action you may make – both now, as well as on the later streets. And from there you should then try to find the proper balance between minimising your investments and maximising your rewards, in order to make the play with the highest expected value.

This means that counting outs is not all there is to it. It is only in combination with situational analysis and hand-reading abilities that it will become truly beneficial to your overall results. Yes, all of this may be a bit beyond the scope of this book – but in order to be a great player, it is simply imperative to take all these things into account.

Concept 9

It Hurts To Lose

It hurts when you flop a nice draw, and then miss it on the turn. It hurts when you carefully recalculate your drawing odds, scrape up enough money to call again on the turn, and then miss on the river. But it hurts most of all, when you hit your draw on the river, throw lots of cash into the pot, and lose it all to some monster hand that actually had you beat the whole way.

Drawing hands naturally do best against multiple opponents. The more, the merrier. And they make their living off the turn and river, where the bets are doubled. Most of the time, you miss your draw, but the reason you keep playing them is because you salivate at the thought of perhaps check-raising three players on the river. It's all about implied odds.

You need good pot odds to play drawing hands. The theory of these hands is, you lose a little when you miss, and win a lot when you hit. That's why good draws are profitable. But there is a third result that sometimes throws a monkey wrench into the theory. If you hit, and *still* lose, you lose a *whole* lot.

This is simply a fact of poker. Most drawing hands lose a little, win a lot, or lose a *whole* lot. This third result can't be ignored, and because the pain is so great when things go terribly wrong, it skews the return on investment. Let's look at an example.

You've flopped a good open-ended straight draw, with eight outs, but there are two clubs on the board, and lots of opponents. Recall that we figured out in chapter two, if you're facing six opponents, there's about a 30% chance that one of them will be on a club flush draw, and you're going to lose the hand to a flush about one-eighth of the time you make a straight (remember that the third club doesn't have to be your straight card; you could, for example, hit the straight on the turn and then see another club on the river). Since you have eight outs, you may as well consider one of those outs to be a loser.

The problem comes on that 'eighth out'. You know, the one that makes your straight, but still loses the hand.

Let's say you're playing $10-$20, there's been a bet and a raise ahead of you on the flop, and the pot contains $70 when it comes your turn to act.[6] Let's say you anticipate that the pot will grow to $140, not counting any further contributions by you. In other words, you think the original bettor will call, and you think you can get about three more large bets from other players on the turn and river if you hit your draw. That adds up to $140.

So the pot is laying 7:1 to you, right? Implied odds, that is. Let's ignore the fact that you might be re-raised if you call. You're investing $20 to win about $140.

Since you have seven modified outs, and there are 47 unknown cards, your odds against winning the pot are 39:8 or about 5:1. An easy call if the pot is laying 7:1, right?

Oops! Here's where the monkey wrench comes in. It doesn't cost just $20 to call. Why not? Because one out (the eighth, 'no good', out) spells total disaster. If that card comes, you're going to wind up putting a lot more money in the pot—probably at least $60—just to find out that you're beaten! Maybe we should factor in a 'disaster adjustment!'

Out of every 47 tries, you'll miss your draw and lose a little 39 times, hit your draw and win a lot seven times, and hit your draw and lose an awful lot one time.

WARNING: When things go wrong, they can go *really* wrong. If you hit your draw and still lose the hand, it's going to be expensive. This 'chance of disaster' robs the average drawing hand of about half an out in value.

How much does it *really* cost, then, to call the flop raise? It costs $20... plus one chance in 47 of paying an additional $60. In other words, it's really costing about $21.28 on average! All things considered, the pot is only laying you about 6.5:1, not

---

[6]Yep, another one of those impossible scenarios, if you really have six opponents. Bear with me, again, for the sake of simplifying our example.

7:1. This translates into about half an out. The chance of disaster has therefore robbed you of half an out. In fact, this isn't a bad rule of thumb: If you count your modified outs by literally trying to figure out your chances of winning, you're overestimating the true value of your hand by about a half out, on average. This 'overestimation' is already taken into account in the counting methods I presented in chapter two. For example, your chance of being up against a club draw in the above example doesn't reach 50% until there are five opponents; however, my suggestion from chapter three is that you drop a full out from your count if you have only three opponents, not five.

So, if you're using my rules of thumb, you're already taking into account the 'disaster adjustment'. Carry on as usual.

Concept 10

Exposed Cards *do* Matter

This is so obvious, that it's embarrassing to have to mention it. If a card is accidentally exposed, and it's one of your outs, drop one from your out count. Why, oh, why, do so many players ignore the obvious? It's as if they have some rule in their head that says, 'an open-ended straight draw has eight outs', even when they know better.

Chapter Five

Table Action Charts

Pretty soon, we're going to start talking again about the types of drawing hands, such as flush and straight draws, and we'll decide how to play each type of hand. But in order to make a decision, you must be able to make a reasonable guess about how the action will continue if you decide to play the hand at all. How many players will remain in the hand on future rounds? How many bets can be expected?

How We Will Use The Table Action Charts

In a moment, I'm going to introduce you to an invention of mine, called the *table action chart.* The biggest reason I use table action charts to teach implied odds, is that it gets you into a habit of constantly thinking about the *future.*

A table action chart is like peeking into the future to see what will happen on the turn and river. It's every poker player's dream. We're using the chart to decide whether or not to play the flop and turn, but we're making that decision by looking ahead as if we somehow know how the betting is going to continue on the turn and on the river.

Or, think of it this way. We play the hand to its conclusion, and *then* we go back and calculate the *true* pot odds for the flop and/or the turn. It may seem a little counter-intuitive to do this, but it's the *only* pot odds that are entirely accurate. It's called implied pot odds, and it's the only pot odds that mean anything before the river.

We'll be doing this over and over throughout the rest of the book. Playing the hand to a logical conclusion through the river, and then drawing more conclusions about whether or not we made the right choice on the flop and/or the turn.

What's the point of all this? The point is, if you can make a reasonable assumption about how the hand will play out if you hit one of your outs, and you can figure out how many outs will actually *win* the hand, then you can make an educated decision about whether or not to continue with the hand.

Ultimately, I want you to begin playing most hands by instinct. You'll have studied enough table action charts to understand, intuitively, which hands are playable in which circumstances; and you'll develop a feel for the players at your table, helping you to know how the betting patterns are likely to go.

It means you have to know a little something about your opponents and the type of game you are in. Will these guys make crying calls on the river? Will they continue to push on the more expensive streets, with top pair, so that you can raise or check-raise? Will they always *call* your raise? Many players go on auto-pilot and unthinkingly call anytime their bet is raised, as if it's their pride playing the game instead of their head. Does this describe your opponents?

Please don't misunderstand me. I am not mandating that you memorise these betting charts. I don't want you drawing little charts in your head while you're playing poker. I'll say it again. *I want you to develop a feel* for when each drawing hand is profitable to continue. This takes time, but the feel *will* come, and when it does, you'll play as accurately as if you carried a calculator in your pocket and kept precise track of the odds.

I want you looking at the *players*, not the pot. You should be able to glance around the table, note how many people are still in the pot, and classify the remaining opponents and their likely hands to how you think they will play future betting rounds. All this can be done fairly quickly, with practice, and you can arrive at a logical *intuitive* decision for how to play the hand. This is possible because you'll be spending most of your time watching opponents, not memorising and calculating. You'll be playing poker the way it was meant to be played.

With a little practice, it'll become second nature for you to classify your opponents. If you can take all of the unnecessary counting out of your game (so that you are not constantly trying to remember how many bets are in the pot and constantly calculating pot odds), then you can concentrate more intently on your opponents.

Most hands can be played in this manner, after I give you some guidelines. Only with the borderline hands does it become necessary to watch the pot, and we'll get to that in a later chapter.

Without further ado, then....

Charting The Action

Take a look at the chart below. I'll be using charts like this throughout the remainder of the book, to present betting patterns.

Pre-Flop	⬭ ⬭ ⬭ +1½
Flop	⬭ ⬭
Turn	⬭
River	⬭
Flop: 17½ bets, 8.75:1 (4.8 outs) Turn: 19½ bets, 9.75:1 (4.3 outs)	

This is what I'm calling a table action chart. Here is how you read it:

Reading the table action chart

- The chart always indicates bets by other players, not by you. See the three little stacks of chips under *Pre-Flop*? Two chips in each stack? That means two small bets were made by three players *other than you,* before the flop. We always count hands *other than your own,* so there were originally four players, counting you.
- The '+' sign indicates additional dead-money bets (players who bet money but folded in the same round). It would be logical to guess that the 1½ bets of 'dead money' pre-flop were the big blind and the small blind, who folded immediately.
- On the flop, you lost a player. Two others now, besides you, and all three of you put in two flop bets.
- On the turn, another player dropped out of the action, leaving only one other person to make one large bet. Again, your own bet is not shown.
- On the river, again one large bet was made by one other player.
- All bets are tallied to give a total pot size at the bottom. What we are tallying up is how much money you can win, if you win the pot. This is measured in small bets (the size of the bet pre-flop and on the flop). In other words, if you're playing $20-$40, this is the number of $20 bets. This total *does not* include your assumed bets on the current or future betting rounds, but it *does* include bets you made before the current betting round.

To understand this concept better, let's take time to count the number of bets for your 'flop' decision, and for your 'turn' decision.

First, the flop odds. There were 7½ bets invested pre-flop, plus two of your own bets, for 9½. (Bets that you put in the pot pre-flop are no longer yours; they belong to the pot, remember!) Now, from the flop forward, *your* bets don't count. We're measuring how much you can *profit* by continuing, which is not quite the same as how big the pot will become. So, we have four bets from other players on the flop, plus one large bet (count it as two small bets) on both the turn and the river. Add it up: 9½ + 4 + 2 + 2 = 17½. Since it costs two bets to stay in on the flop, the expected return is 17.5:2, or 8.75:1

Now the turn odds. Why are they different than the flop odds? Because by the turn, *you* have put more money in the pot, too! Your flop bets. Money that is no longer yours. Money that you have to win back. The pot has two more small bets, so there are now 19½ bets that you can win by staying in on the turn. Since it costs one big bet to stay in on the turn (equal to two small bets), the expected return is 19.5:2, or 9.75:1.

- ♠ The return will always be displayed as x:1, where x is the total pot size divided by the number of bets required for you to continue on, in the round in question.
- ♠ Now let's calculate how many outs you need to make it worthwhile to pay your dues and continue on, both on the flop and on the river.

After the flop, five of the 52 cards are known (the three cards on the table and the two cards in your hand are the only cards you see); so 47 cards are left. The implied pot odds (counting all the money you expect to win through the river if you get lucky) is 8.75:1, which means you need to win one time out of every 9¾ attempts to break even (9¾ = 8¾ + 1). Does that make sense? If you lose 8¾ times, and win one time, you break even. So we divide 9¾ into 47, and we get 4.8. You need at least 4.8 outs. If exactly 4.8 of the 47 cards remaining in the deck would win for you, you'd break even, on average. Thus a five-out hand would offer good odds (better than 100% return), but to call two flop bets with only four outs would be a losing proposition.

On the turn, however, the odds are 9.75:1. You've seen one more card out of the deck (the turn card), so there are 46 cards remaining. Dividing 10¾ into 46 gives us 4.2. In other words, like the flop, if you have five outs to make a winning hand, you should stay and see the river; four outs or less, don't do it.

Why did your odds improve after the turn card? Because:

1) There is more money in the pot after the flop...*your own* flop bets now contribute to the possible winnings.

2) There are fewer cards remaining in the deck.

3) Remember, the flop cost you two small bets to continue, or it surely wouldn't be the case that the turn gives better odds to continue than the flop.

TIP: You *always* measure your expected return by counting how much is in the pot already, and then add to that the additional bets you can expect to win if you make your hand. You *always* measure your cost to play during any given betting round by guessing how much money you will have to pay to stay in the hand (you might get raised and have to put *more* money in). And you *always* measure your outs by estimating your chance of actually *winning* the hand; not just by whether you will hit your draw.

Remember, you are trying to decide whether or not it is appropriate to continue with the hand, given the expected winnings, *if you make your hand on the next card.* You don't know, of course, what is *really* going to happen after the flop or after the turn. You don't know how many more bets you will be able to scoop if you win the pot. It's a guess. It's always a guessing game. But the way it played out, according to the chart, was a reasonably likely result. One bet, from one opponent, on the turn and again on the river.

We could call this a moderately loose, moderately aggressive hand. Three of your nine opponents see the flop for two bets each; two stay in for two bets on the flop; one more drops out after the turn card so that it's just you and one opponent; and that same opponent stays for one bet on the river. A fairly typical hand, in a fairly typical middle-limit game, resulting in a fairly typical pot: 23½ small bets, counting yours.

It's very important to understand what a table action chart is telling you. If it hasn't sunk in yet, take the time to read this section again before continuing. We'll be using these charts a lot.

Now *you* try putting together a chart. There's no better way to learn. I've provided an empty table action chart for you to fill in.

Pre Flop	
Flop	
Turn	
River	
Flop: 12½ bets, ____:1 (6.5 outs) Turn: ____bets, 7.25:1 (5.6 outs)	

1) Let's say you're under the gun and call with a hand like Q♥-J♥. Four of you see the flop for a single bet, including the big blind. The small blind folds. Fill in the pre-flop action now.

2) There's a bet and a raise on the flop. You call. The big blind folds now. The original bettor calls, so you have two opponents. Fill in the flop box.

3) On the turn, both of you check to the raiser, and he bets. Both of you call his bet. Fill in the turn box.

4) On the river, you make a flush. You try for a check-raise, and it fails miserably when everybody checks. Fill in the river box.

5) Add up all of the bets for the FLOP statistics. If you do it right, you should sum to 12½ bets.

6) Add your own flop bets to 12½, and put this next to the TURN statistics.

7) Now calculate the flop return on investment. Divide the total bets by the number of bets you put in on the flop. You'll come up a return-on-investment specified in the format x:1.

8) Do the same with the turn. If you do it right, you'll come up with a 7.25:1 return on your turn bet.

9) Want to tackle calculating the number of outs needed to call on the flop and again on the turn? Give it a try. If you do it right, you'll come up with 6½ outs needed for the flop, and 5.6 outs needed for the turn.

Pre-Flop	+½
Flop	
Turn	
River	
Flop: 12½ bets, 6.25:1 (6.5 outs) Turn: 14½ bets, 7.25:1 (5.6 outs)	

Completed Table Action Exercise

Committing On The Flop

Before we continue, there's one common circumstance that plays havoc with table action charts, and the assumption that the two middle betting rounds (the flop and the turn) are independent. Let's look again at that first table action chart.

Pre-Flop	+1½
Flop	
Turn	
River	
Flop: 17½ bets, 8.75:1 (4.8 outs) Turn: 19½ bets, 9.75:1 (4.3 outs)	

If the flop odds are worse than the turn odds, then by calling on the flop, you're usually committing to call again on the turn. Let me say that again for emphasis. *Any time the flop odds are worse than the turn odds, you're usually going all the way to the river.*

It's true that a scare card can appear on the turn to change your mind. It's true that you can lose some of your outs on the turn, and decide not to go further. But in general, a call on the flop means you'll be calling again on the turn.

So, when does this happen? When do the turn odds become better than the flop odds?

Ignoring for now the possibility that your number of outs may increase (you may be drawing to a flush and flop a low pair, for example), this anomaly happens anytime you have to pay as much or more to stay in the hand on the flop as you do on the turn.

Recall concept number four: Flop odds change if you are committed to the hand. This is because they generally get *better* between the flop and the turn. Perhaps now you have a better understanding of why this is so: It's because additional money has gone into the pot out of *your* stack...money that counts towards the pot odds on the turn, but that you couldn't count towards the pot odds on the flop. This additional money makes a call on the turn a better bet than calling on the flop for the same cost.

Because of this, we need to change our presentation of the table action chart anytime the flop costs as much or more than the turn. Let's call it *committed* flop odds. What we should do is represent the flop odds as the cost to call on *both* the flop and turn...and of course, we must roughly double your outs, because you're now getting *two* cards. Basically, it's like averaging the pot odds between the flop and the turn.

Think of it like this: You're paying for the turn card and the river card all at once...agreeing to pay on both the flop and the turn.

Perhaps the easiest way to understand this is to consider that by paying to see the turn, you are paying also for the privilege to draw *again* after the turn card at a *lower* price. By committing to both streets up front, you receive two cards, and you pay in instalments, on the flop and again on the turn. Your average cost (per card) is the average of these two bets. And the average return on investment is also the average of the two streets!

Therefore, we could say that you should continue after the flop, in the above example, anytime your number of outs justifies pot odds of 9.25:1 (the average of the flop and the turn odds.)

Anytime the flop costs as much, or more, than the turn, we will represent the odds...and thus the number of outs needed to continue...with *committed flop odds,* like this:

Committed: 17½/19½ bets, 9.25:1 (4.6 outs)

The 17½/19½ line indicates that you are playing to win 17½ bets on the flop, and 19½ bets (counting two more of our own contribution) on the turn.

How did I calculate the odds and outs on a committed flop call? It's simply a matter of figuring the flop odds, and the turn odds, and taking the average of the two. This isn't quite accurate, but it's close enough.

In this example, you now need only 4.6 outs to continue on the flop, rather than the original 4.8 outs, because you are committed to calling on the turn.

Some Happy Endings

Let's continue our discussion by looking at some table action charts, to see if we can guess what happened in the hand.

Pre-Flop	
Flop	
Turn	
River	
Flop: 8 bets, 8:1 (5.2 outs) Turn: opponent folds	

What do you think happened here? It looks like a pretty loose, passive game, with four other pre-flop limpers, including the small blind. The big blind plays for free, making five opponents.

Then, probably, there was a bet on the flop, you raised from an early position, and all trailing players folded. The original bettor called your flop raise, and then folded to your bet on the turn.

Well, that was boring, wasn't it? And not exactly the type of hand this book is about. Let's try another.

Pre-Flop	+1½
Flop	
Turn	
River	
Flop: 12½ bets, 6.25:1 (6.5 outs) Turn: hand made	

Can we tell a story about what happened in this hand, as well? Perhaps you raised pre-flop from middle position with K♦-Q♦, and got only one caller. The flop brought A♠-10♦-7♦. You checked and called, hoping that by showing weakness, you would gain an extra bet on the turn if you hit pay dirt. It worked: When the turn came J♥, you check-raised your opponent, and then bet out on the river. He called both times, and you turned over your straight to take the pot.

Pre-Flop	+1½
Flop	
Turn	
River	
Flop: 20½ bets, 20.5:1 (2.2 outs) Turn: 21½ bets, 10.75:1 (3.9 outs)	

Care to make a conjecture about what happened this time? Here's a possible scenario: You raise in early position holding J♠-J♥, a middle position player calls, and the button re-raises, forcing out the blinds. You and the middle position player both call.

The flop brings 9♦-10♥-A♠. Two checks to the raiser, the button, who bets. You're probably beat by both hands, but because of the size of the pot, both you and the middle position player call. It's a reasonable call, because of your runner-runner straight possibility, and the remote chance that your jacks *are* the best hand.

The turn brings an 8♦. Suddenly, you have picked up an open-ended straight draw! You check to the button again, who instantly bets, and of course you call with all of the outs you have now. All three of you see the river.

That middle-position player is a bit of a Cally-Wally, isn't he? Who knows what he has. But it really doesn't matter; he's just along for the ride. It only takes one better hand to make your own hand so much toilet paper, and you figure you're beat by the button, at least. Forget the Cally-Wally.

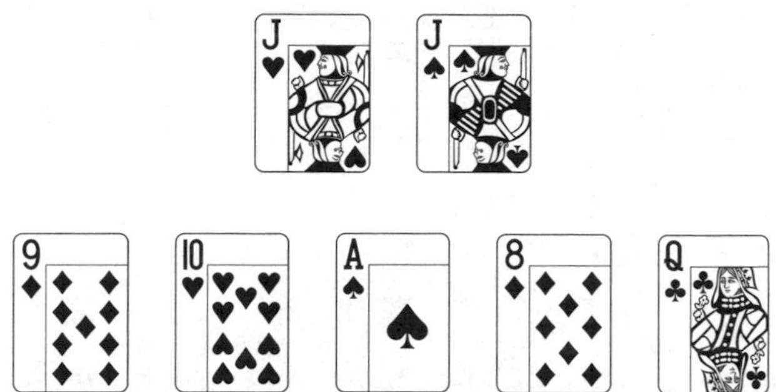

Should you bet out on the river, or try for a check-raise?

The river brings a Q♣. You've made your hand! By now, you've figured out that the button is probably playing A-K... and if he is, he's surely not going to bet out again! After all, what kind of hand is left that he can beat? Both of his opponents have hands that were worth raising or calling raises pre-flop. It's tough to find something he can beat now. No, he won't bet anymore. So if you're going to extract any more money on the river, it's not going to be by check-raising! You bet out, and get crying calls from both other players, who turn over A-K and A-Q. You bring home the pot with your straight.

Have you noticed that all of these charts have a happy ending? Of course they do! The point of drawing these charts is to project your probable winnings if you *make* the hand. If you *don't* make your hand, the betting will, of course, go differently. And those different results are not applicable to our study. We only care about what happens when you win.

OK, let's look at one more happy ending:

Let me give you a story that fits this table action chart: You're on the button, and several limpers entice you to limp in as well holding J♠-9♠. The small blind calls, and the flop brings a flush draw for you with A♠-Q♠-2♣.

Pre-Flop	
Flop	
Turn	
River	
Flop: 16 bets, 8:1 (2.6 outs) Turn: free card	

What a wonderful flop! You hold the second-nut flush draw, and the flop has enough high cards to hopefully keep a few of your opponents in the hand. An early player bets, several players call, and because there are at least three callers, you raise for value. Everyone calls your raise except for the small blind, who drops out. The turn brings a 7♥, and everyone checks to the bettor (you). It looks pretty unlikely that you can bluff everyone into folding, so you take the free card.

On the river, you make your flush with 6♠. Unfortunately, the third spade shuts down the betting, and no one leads into you. You bet, get one caller, and show your flush to take down the pot.

Charting the Free Card

Notice something very interesting about that last chart. The return on investment for the two flop bets is only 8:1 (you win 16 bets for an investment of two bets). So why is it that the chart shows that you need only 2.6 outs to make this play profitable? After all, 9 divided into 47 would seem to indicate that you need 5.2 outs to continue! Did I make a mistake on the chart?

Nope. You need only 2.6 outs because you bought a free card on the turn! That gives you two tries to make your flush. What would normally require 5.2 outs to be profitable now requires only half as many outs. Not that you need them; your hand is easily valued at all nine flush outs.

A Few Observations

Let's stop, now, and make some observations about these charts.

1) When you begin to observe how loose or tight a game or a particular player is, it's important to watch *all* betting rounds. Don't just count the number of hands each player plays. It's just as important to observe how *far* they typically go with these hands.

2) Classifying your game, and the individual players in the game, becomes as important a skill as counting outs. That guy in the cowboy hat on the button who bet the flop out with probably nothing but overcards...will he continue to bluff on the turn if you keep checking to him? Will you be able to check-raise him on the turn? If you can develop a talent for predicting betting patterns, and use this talent to decide what hands can be played profitably, you're well on your way to becoming an expert player.

3) Position is extremely important in helping you predict and even manipulate betting patterns. For example, you can't semi-bluff in early position to buy a free card...but neither can you check-raise from late position! Pay close attention to your position as you estimate what future bets you can extract.

4) Relative position is also very important. That is, your position relative to the raiser. Because of the tendency of players to check to the raiser, if you are sitting just to the right of the raiser in a hand, and he's the type that will continue betting his hand, it's like having the button. Perhaps even better than being on the button, because of the possibility of check-raising the entire table. Again, this drastically changes the range of hands with which you can continue playing, if you *know* how many bets are already

in the pot before you choose, and you pretty much *know* you can extract an extra bet on the turn or river when you hit your hand.

TIP: Most experts will tell you to sit on the maniac's left. I like to sit on his right, if he's the type that will keep ramming and jamming after the flop is dealt.

What kind of poker book would it be if I didn't at least make mention of the maniac at your table? Well, here's the token mention of him. Do you want to sit on his left or his right?

It depends entirely upon your playing style! Aggressive players often prefer to sit on the maniac's left, because when the maniac comes in raising, they can re-raise and try to isolate him, hopefully with the better hand.

I think most experts will tell you to sit on the maniac's left. But I also like to sit on his right, if he's the type that will keep ramming and jamming after the flop. This is because it is *so* valuable to have the person on your immediate left bet the pot for you. Having relative position opens up a lot more hands that you can profitably play on the flop and beyond.

If there is a maniac at the table, I'll try to find him and sit by him. One side or the other.

Ace Speaks...

The best seat versus a maniac

While for years it had been common wisdom to think of the seat on the immediate left of the maniac as being best by far, both Bob Ciaffone and I have shown that the seat on his immediate *right* can have a lot of merit too. In fact, I have even gone a bit further than that, by showing some of the downsides of sitting on a maniac's immediate left. For a detailed analysis, just go to www.cardplayer.com. In the archives there, you can find both relevant articles by me on this subject: 'The best seat versus a maniac', and the more recent 'The trouble with maniacs'.

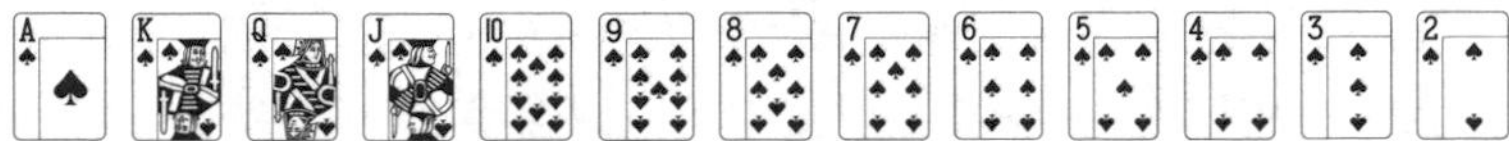

Homework and Good Playing Habits

Every time you sit down at a game, you should begin classifying the game and the players. Pay close attention to how many players see the flop, how many continue after the flop, and which players are willing to keep chasing with double-sized bets into the turn and river.

If you have trouble teaching yourself to do this, you might try this exercise: Simply keep track of the number of players on each street. Do it with a pencil and paper. Use a notation such as 4-4-2-1 to indicate how many players put money into the pot on each betting round. Don't count your own bets. Maybe circle the number of players when multiple bets were required. For example, 4-4-②-1 would mean four players limp in before the flop; all four call on the flop; two players pay two bets on the turn; one player bets the river but is not called.

Anybody that watches you taking notes will have no idea what you are doing. A bunch of meaningless numbers. Tell them you're doing your son's homework between hands. It's none of their business.

This exercise will accomplish several things:

1) It will start you on the path to watching your game and classifying hands similar to the table action charts presented here.

2) It will help you begin to recognise betting patterns and begin to read hands. Almost subconsciously, you will automatically begin trying to put players on hands, as you try to match betting patterns with probable hands and probable outcomes. This can't help but elevate your game.

3) It will condition you to keeping track of the number of bets going into the pot; you'll need this to play certain hands, as you'll learn in a later chapter.

4) It will provide you with data about your game, that you can take home for study, if you're really dedicated. You can then classify your game according to the categories I'll be presenting shortly.

5) It will keep you active in the game when you're not in a hand, watching and learning about the players. Poker really *is* more fun and profitable when you begin the play the players, not just the cards.

6) *By turning poker into a fun exercise and occupying your mind with learning about the players, it makes the game less results-oriented.* You have a reason to play other than to bring home money. This can't help but improve your game, decreasing the chance of you beginning to tilt or chase, those times when the cards aren't falling your way.

Soon, the pencil and paper will no longer be necessary. Three or four rounds around the table, and you'll have a handle on just about any game you sit down in.

Chapter Six

So, What Good Are All These Outs?

This chapter is your opportunity to lay a little groundwork for that 'intuitive side' I want you to develop. I'll be presenting several different 'out counts', from ten down to two, and providing table action charts which indicate profitable circumstances where you can play each count.

You may be surprised by what you read. In particular, you may decide not to criticise, quite so often, those guys that continually seem to suck out on you by calling with low-percentage hands. More often than you might believe, they're getting the proper odds to play the way they do.

Let me start out by giving you a chart showing the chance of success with each out-count. If you call through the river, this shows the percentage of time that you will win the hand.

A quick look at the chart will show that, against multiple players, it's not at all unlikely that a drawing hand has the highest chance of winning. Good drawing hands are powerful hands.

Number of Outs	On the Flop	On the Turn
2	8%	4%
3	12%	7%
4	16%	9%
5	20%	11%
6	24%	13%
7	28%	15%
8	31%	17%
9	35%	20%
10	38%	22%

Out For The Count

You've spent a lot of time learning how to count outs. A *lot* of time, without really seeing any of the benefits. You're about to see some now.

Playing With Ten Outs Or More

	1 bet	2 bets	3 bets	4 bets
Flop	3.7	7.4	11.1	14.8
Turn	7.2	14.4	21.6	28.8

I'll be presenting a chart like the above for each out-count level we discuss. This chart was prepared for ten outs. The chart tells you how many small bets you need to be able to win, by the end of the hand, in order to profitably call one or more bets on the flop and turn with any drawing hand.

For example, if it's two bets to you on the flop, in the above chart, you need to be able to win 7.4 small bets to call.

Those 7.4 bets include all money that has been put into the pot in prior rounds (including your money), plus the other players this round, plus implied profits on the turn and river if you make your draw. In other words, if you are playing $5-$10, so that it costs $10 to cold-call a raise on the flop, you need to expect to win $37 (not counting the money you, yourself, put into the pot from here on out) to make calling profitable. 7.4 × $5 = $37.

For the most part, you'll probably only skim these charts as you read over the material. That's fine. I'll pull it all together for you a bit later.

Examples of ten outs or more hands

A good example is flush or straight draw with overcards, e.g. A♥-K♥/2♠-3♥-6♥. Another is a hand that contains both a flush and a straight draw, such as 9♠-7♠/A♠-5♦-8♠

An 11-out hand: both a flush draw and an inside straight

Value Bet: (2/4) A value bet would be profitable once you get called in two places on the flop, or four places on the turn.

Table Action Charts: I'll present a bare-bones chart to show how unlikely it is that you'll ever not have proper odds to continue play with ten outs.

Pre-Flop	
Flop	
Turn	
River	
Flop: 7 bets, 7:1 (5.8 outs) Turn: 8 bets, 4:1 (9.2 outs)	

This chart is pretty stark, isn't it? One caller, no dead money, one bet each round. Pay close attention on these charts to the number of outs needed: In this case, 9.2 outs is sufficient to play on the turn. This chart is presented to show that even under the most unfavourable conditions, you'll be playing a ten-out hand against one player to the river.

It's important to know, also, that you can call multiple bets on the turn. If there are two or more players in the pot, it's possible that you will have to call two or more turn bets in order to stay in the running.

Pre-Flop	
Flop	
Turn	
River	
Turn: 16 bets, 4:1 (9.2 outs)	

Take a look at the example above. There were two players other than you putting in just one bet apiece until the turn, when suddenly one player comes out raising. On the river, the betting dies again, with just one caller of a single bet.

Is it worth paying such a high price on the turn to stay in the pot? Yep. You need just 9.2 outs. Even if you get re-raised, and the betting gets capped with four bets apiece on the turn, you're not too badly hurt: You need only 11½ outs for a 100% return on investment.

As this example shows, you should be ready to stay in the pot *regardless* of how much it costs on the turn, with ten or more outs. There are only a couple reasons for possibly folding on the turn:

- ♠ You might fold on the turn against a single opponent if there were no bets on the flop to build the pot. This will rarely happen, unless you have only just picked up your draw on the turn. If you had ten outs earlier than that, why on earth didn't you come out betting on the flop?
- ♠ You might fold against a single opponent if you think it's unlikely that you will get paid off on the river after you make your hand. You would need 15 outs for a profitable call on the turn if you expect to make nothing on the river. But you're most likely to get a crying call on the end from an opponent who has been betting into you all the way...unless he's on a total bluff, in which case your hand might win unimproved in a showdown anyway.

You may as well just plan on going to the river.

Discussion

If you have ten outs, you have a very strong draw. On the flop, you're almost always the favourite to win the hand in a multi-way pot. It's a premium hand, and you'll be along for the ride clear to the river.

In general, you want to put as much money into the pot on the flop as you can. Especially if you have overcards, don't be afraid to ram and jam on the flop. You'll either build the pot with bet odds that favour you, or you'll knock out some opponents, which buys additional outs for your overcards. Either way, bet hard and strong.

Playing With Nine Outs

	1 bet	2 bets	3 bets	4 bets
Flop	4.2	8.4	12.7	16.9
Turn	8.2	16.4	24.7	32.9

Example

The classic example of a nine-out hand is an uncompromised flush draw, such as K♦-9♦/2♣-J♦-A♦.

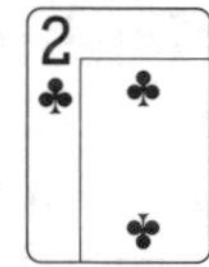

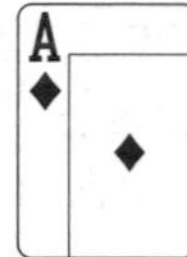

A nut flush draw is worth nine outs

Value Bet: (3/5) A value bet would be profitable once you get called in three places on the flop, or five places on the turn.

Table Action Charts: Again, a single chart should suffice in the discussion of nine-out hands.

Pre-Flop	
Flop	
Turn	
River	
Flop: 8 bets, 8:1 (5.2 outs) Turn: 9 bets, 4.5:1 (8.4 outs)	

Here you see that two other players before the flop, and then one caller to the end, is plenty of bets to make drawing to a high flush worthwhile, both on the turn and the river. It's just one bet more than the example given for ten-out hands.

Like the ten-out hands against a single opponent, you really need to be able to collect that single bet on the river, to make drawing worthwhile on the turn.

Discussion

A nine-out hand is definitely also a premium hand. It should be played pretty much like a ten-out hand. You want as much money in the pot on the flop as you can get, unless you're up against a single opponent...but even then, if you have position, you should usually raise on the flop as a semi-bluff.

You will *never* fold a nine-out hand on the flop (even for multiple bets), and very rarely will you fold it on the turn.

Playing With Eight Outs

	1 bet	2 bets	3 bets	4 bets
Flop	4.9	9.8	14.6	19.5
Turn	9.5	19.0	28.5	38.0

Example

The most common eight-out hand is a perfect (uncompromised) open-ended straight draw. 10♠-9♥/3♦-8♣-J♠. Note the rainbow flop. Another good example is a medium-sized flush draw, such as 8♣-7♣/2♣-9♣-A♠.

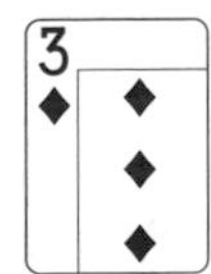

An uncompromised open-ended straight draw

Value Bet: (3/5) A value bet would be profitable once you get called in three places on the flop, or five places on the turn.

Table Action Charts: If we throw in one more bet, we again find that it's worth calling all the way to the river, this time with only an eight-out hand:

Pre-Flop	
Flop	
Turn	
River	
Flop: 9 bets, 9:1 (4.7 outs) Turn: 10 bets, 5:1 (7.6 outs)	

Have you detected a pattern? Eight bets in the pot by the end of the hand is enough to call on the turn with a ten-out hand; nine bets is enough for a nine-out hand; ten bets is enough for an eight-out hand.

We should probably start looking at whether or not we can still call multiple bets on the turn. The answer is...*probably,* if there has been any flop and pre-flop activity to speak of.

Pre-Flop	
Flop	
Turn	
River	
Turn: 19 bets, 4.75:1 (8 outs)	

In this example, there were no raises, but there were four pre-flop players and three flop players. It puts enough money in the pot to make calling a double bet on the turn a worthwhile proposition.

You're hoping, of course, that you don't get raised again. Calling three or four bets would be a loser.

Discussion

Eight outs is still a very good hand. It's a rare case when you shouldn't play eight outs all the way to the river.

Nevertheless, there is one rare situation when you should fold on the turn. Here it is:

- ♠ You can't get more than one player to play on the flop, or
- ♠ You might not get that one player to call again on the river if you make your hand, and
- ♠ There have been no raises.

TIP: If you have a good drawing hand, get your money into the pot on the flop!

If you have position against just one or two opponents, you had better be doing everything you can to get a free card on the turn. I'll say it one more time: With a good drawing hand (and eight outs is still a good drawing hand), get your money in on the flop!

Playing With Seven Outs

	1 bet	2 bets	3 bets	4 bets
Flop	5.7	11.4	17.1	22.9
Turn	11.1	22.3	33.4	44.6

Example

A compromised straight draw. 10♠-9♥/3♣-8♣-J♠ with at least three other players. Note the possible flush draw.

A compromised open-ended straight draw

Value Bet: (3/6) A value bet would be profitable once you get called in three places on the flop, or six places on the turn.

Table Action Charts: Let's add one more small bet and see what we get:

Pre-Flop	
Flop	
Turn	
River	
Flop: 10 bets, 10:1 (4.3 outs) Turn: 11 bets, 5.5:1 (7.1 outs)	

What do you know? The pattern continues! If you can gather 11 bets by the river, you can call on the turn with only seven outs. Well, 7.1 outs. Close enough.

This pattern continued all the way through what we will call our 'good' draws. That is, draws with seven or more outs. This is a logical cut-off point, since most open-ended straight and flush draws are worth at least seven outs.

With 'good' draws, the magic number is 18. If the bets you can win, plus your number of outs, is 18 or more, it's worth calling a single bet on the turn. Of course, if you think you can win two bets with a raise on the river, you should call that single turn bet.

NOTE: If the number of bets you can win, plus your number of outs, is 18 or more, it's worth calling a single bet on the turn with a good draw.

Discussion

It's time to stop and consider. Our major drawing hands...that is, flushes and open-ended straights...are usually worth at least seven outs. Most any flush draw is worth seven outs, unless you can tell by the betting that someone has already filled to a full house. And most legitimate straight draws that use both of your cards are worth seven outs.

Of these seven-out hands, we can draw a general conclusion: *You're usually in the game until you see the river card.* You never fold on the flop, of course, ever, with a drawing hand this strong...and you don't fold on the turn unless it's for multiple bets. If the betting has been scarce before the turn, then two opponents doesn't put quite enough money in the pot to call a double bet on the turn with only seven outs. Nor is it enough for even eight or nine outs, if it's highly likely that the betting will be raised again after you call.

Playing With Six Outs

	1 bet	2 bets	3 bets	4 bets
Flop	6.8	13.7	20.5	27.3
Turn	13.3	26.7	40.0	53.3

Example

The most likely example of a six-out hand is a severely compromised straight draw, such as 10♠-8♠/9♣-J♣-J♦ against multiple players. Note the presence of both a possible flush draw and a pair. Also note that you are not drawing to the nut straight with all of your outs.

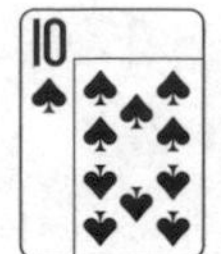    

A severely compromised open-ended straight draw is worth no more than six outs

Another reasonable example is an inside straight draw with overcards. Sometimes a hand like this is worth approximately six outs. For example, K♣-8♣/6♦-9♦-10♠ against a single opponent. A king may or may not win, and a seven might split the pot, so a reasonable valuation is six out of a possible seven outs. With only one opponent, you don't worry so much about the two diamonds on the flop.

Value Bet: (4/7) A value bet would be profitable once you get called in four places on the flop, or seven places on the turn.

TIP: If you have only six outs, you need to be able to win seven times the amount of your bet.

Table Action Charts: Here is where things get interesting. In general, you need to be able to win seven times what you are betting. In other words, you must win at least seven small bets to put in a single flop bet, or 14 small bets to put in a single turn bet. Let's look, then, at some table action charts that provide the proper odds to continue.

Pre-Flop	⬭
Flop	⬭
Turn	⬭
River	⬭
Flop: 7 bets, 7:1 (5.9 outs) Turn: 8 bets, 4:1 (9.2 outs)	

It's not hard to justify calling a single bet on the flop with six outs. In this example, you have a single opponent that you think will play through to the river even after you hit one of your outs. Of course, if you miss on the turn, it's time to give up the hand.

Pre-Flop	
Flop	
Turn	
River	
Flop: 14 bets, 7:1 (5.9 outs) Turn: 16 bets, 8:1 (5.1 outs)	

Here is another situation. There are three other players, and it's raised to you on the flop. If you can expect to win three bets on the turn and river after hitting your hand, do you call on the flop?

It's close, but yes, you do. And you call again on the turn for a single bet.

This is, of course, a very borderline call on the flop. Unless you can get those three double-sized bets on the turn and river, it's a bad investment.

Pre-Flop	
Flop	
Turn	
River	
Turn: 26 bets, 6.5:1 (6.1 outs)	

It's nearly impossible to justify a double bet on the turn. In this example, we see a pre-flop raise with four other players, and two callers on the river. It still isn't enough to warrant two double-sized bets on the turn.

Discussion

Six outs is a borderline drawing hand. We're reaching a crossroads. It's halfway between the good drawing hands (a decent straight draw) and the bad drawing hands (hands like inside straights and low pairs).

Most players seem to understand this difference. The difference between good and bad draws. Maybe their daddies told them never to draw to an inside straight. Whatever the reason, many players will intuitively hold on to a good, solid straight and flush draw until the river, and will quickly throw away the lousy draws like inside straights and low pairs.

Such players are usually right about the better draws, but play far too tight on the other draws. It's these middle-of-the-road draws that aren't so clear, where you have a seriously compromised open-ended straight or an inside straight with a couple of little perks like overcards and three-card flushes.

If you have six outs, you can play most flops. If there has been little betting and you are against a single opponent, or if you have to pay multiple bets, give it up on the turn.

Playing With Five Outs

	1 bet	2 bets	3 bets	4 bets
Flop	8.4	16.8	25.2	33.6
Turn	16.4	32.8	49.2	65.6

Example

A common five-out hand is a low pair, because the draw to a better hand is typically worth four outs, plus one more out on the chance that you already hold the best hand. Another typical five-out hand is two strong overcards against only one or two opponents, such as A♣-K♣/7♦-9♠-J♥. I would value your overcards here at about five outs, considering that you may actually hold the best hand.

Two strong overcards against few opponents can be played as five outs

Value Bet: (4/9) A value bet would be profitable once you get called in four places on the flop, or nine places on the turn.

Table Action Charts: It's a bit harder to find favourable circumstances for five-out hands on the turn, but still pretty easy to find charts where you can play the flop. Often, you'll call on the flop for a single bet, but then you wind up folding on the turn.

Pre-Flop	⬭ ⬭ ⬭
Flop	⬭ ⬭
Turn	⬭
River	
Flop: 8 bets, 8:1 (5.2 outs)	

If you have two other callers on the flop, you're pretty safe calling with five outs. In this example, you see three other pre-flop bettors and lose just one on the flop, then win just one turn bet when you make your hand. Eight small bets by the river turns out to be enough for a five-out hand.

Pre-Flop	◯ ◯ ◯ ◯
Flop	◯◯ ◯◯
Turn	◯ ◯
River	◯
Flop: 15 bets, 7.5:1 (5.5 outs) Turn: 17 bets, 8.5:1 (4.8 outs)	

In this example, you got trapped by a raise on the flop, and wound up paying two small bets. Even with all of that pre-flop dead money, and three large bets on the turn and river, it isn't worth a double bet on the flop. Had you known you would be raised, you wouldn't have called. Now that you're in, though, there's enough money in the pot to see the river.

Pre-Flop	◯ ◯ ◯ ◯ ◯
Flop	◯ ◯ ◯ ◯
Turn	◯ ◯
River	◯ ◯
Turn: 18 bets, 9:1 (4.6 outs)	

In extremely loose and passive games, you can sometimes get away with calling with a five-outer on the turn. This example is *almost* enough for a pure five-out hand. But, usually, you need multiple bets from multiple players pre-flop to see the river.

Here is a fairly typical example; two other callers besides you of a pre-flop raise, who all see the turn at a single bet on the flop. Then attrition slowly knocks them out on the turn and river. There are plenty of bets in the pot to make calling on the turn worthwhile.

Pre-Flop	◯ ◯ ◯ +½
Flop	◯ ◯ ◯
Turn	◯ ◯
River	◯
Turn: 17½ bets, 8.75:1 (4.7 outs)	

Discussion

The examples show it all. Even with only a couple other players, you can probably take one off on the flop. But then, unless there's a lot of money in the pot, get out if the turn misses you.

Playing With Four Outs

	1 bet	2 bets	3 bets	4 bets
Flop	10.8	21.5	32.3	43.0
Turn	21.0	42.0	63.0	84.0

Example

The most common four-out hand is an uncompromised inside straight. J♠-10♠/9♦-K♥-A♣. Another example is two pair, when you are certain you're already beaten. J♦-10♣/10♥-J♥-Q♥ against heavy betting from multiple players.

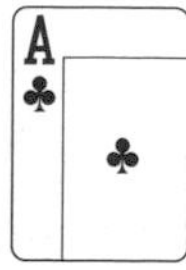

The most common four-out hand is an inside straight with no overcards

Value Bet: (6/11) You can bet for value if you're able to get six callers on the flop. Forget about the turn.

Table Action Charts: It's still very easy to find profitable opportunities for four-out hands on the flop. You just need a few more players.

Pre-Flop	
Flop	
Turn	
River	
Flop: 10 bets, 10:1 (4.3 outs) Turn: 11 bets, 5.5:1 (7.1 outs)	

This is a fairly typical passive betting sequence, but notice that you don't quite have enough outs to call on the flop, and it's not even close on the turn. Even when you can expect to win two big bets on the turn and river. But we don't need to add much to make it profitable.

Pre-Flop	
Flop	
Turn	
River	
Flop: 11 bets, 11:1 (3.9 outs)	

Three other callers on the flop, and you can assume you're fine to play any four-out hand for a single bet.

It's really pretty amazing. Even if your daddy *didn't* tell you to never draw to an inside straight, you may have read other books that say you need five or more opponents to make this play. It's just not true. In loose, passive games, you can almost always call a single bet on the flop with a four-outer.

Then, on the turn you give it up without a second thought.

Pre-Flop	 +1½
Flop	
Turn	
River	
Committed: 23½/25½ bets, 12.25:1 (3.8 outs)	

Pre-Flop	 +1½
Flop	
Turn	
River	
Turn: 23½ bets, 11.75:1 (3.6 outs)	

Here we see a couple of examples with a lot of action pre-flop, and a little dead money from the blinds. It's more than enough to call a double bet on the flop, or a single bet on the turn.

Pre-Flop	
Flop	
Turn	
River	
Committed: 22/24 bets, 11.5:1 (3.7 outs)	

In this example, four players see the flop for two bets. Should you call a raise on the flop with your four-outer? Yes, but it's close. If there's any chance you're stuck in the middle of a raising war and you'll have to put *more* bets in on the flop, you'd better ditch your hand.

Discussion

Four outs is a very common situation, and it's definitely worth learning when you can play this kind of hand. Generally, you need three other players to call a single flop bet. If the pot gets very big...several players for two or more pre-flop bets...then you can call a raise on the flop or play on the turn for a single bet.

Playing With Three Outs

	1 bet	2 bets	3 bets	4 bets
Flop	14.7	29.3	44.0	58.7
Turn	28.7	57.3	86.0	114.7

Example

A compromised inside straight, such as 8♣-5♥/7♦-9♦-9♣ against multiple players, is a typical three-out hand. You are against both a flush draw and a paired board. You're not even drawing to the nut straight. Another common example is a pair of overcards against about three opponents. Such a hand is often worth about three outs.

An inside straight that is highly compromised is worth only three outs

Value Bet: Just say no to this idea.

Table Action Charts: It's starting to get pretty scary. I'll present a couple charts to convince you that sometimes a call is appropriate, but most times you'll fold these hands immediately.

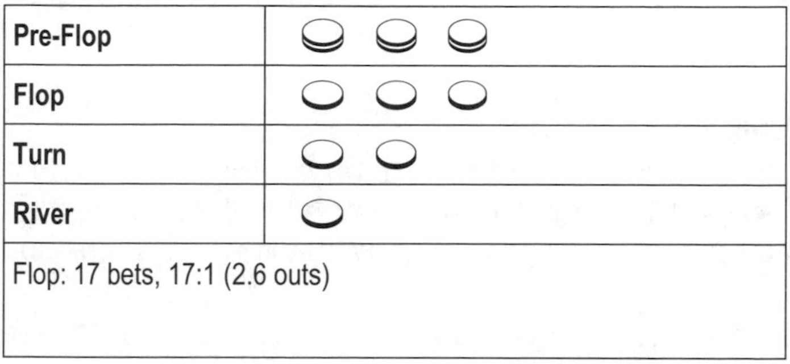

Pre-Flop	
Flop	
Turn	
River	
Flop: 17 bets, 17:1 (2.6 outs)	

If there are three or more callers of a pre-flop raise, then you're pretty safe calling a single flop bet with just three outs.

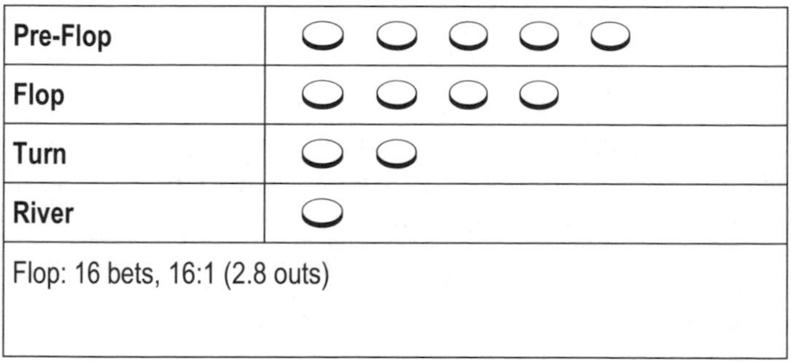

Pre-Flop	
Flop	
Turn	
River	
Flop: 16 bets, 16:1 (2.8 outs)	

If you can look around a loose-passive table and see four other callers on the flop, you're pretty safe calling with a three-out hand.

Discussion: Three outs sure doesn't sound like much, but against several players, it can be worth paying a single bet on the flop. Forget about calling a raise, or drawing again after the turn.

Playing With Two Outs

	1 bet	2 bets	3 bets	4 bets
Flop	22.5	45.0	67.5	90.0
Turn	44.0	88.0	132.0	176.0

Example 1

An underpair is the most common example. You hold 3♦-3♥/9♦-10♦-A♠. Note that you hold the 3♦, so that neither of your outs are compromised by the two diamonds on the flop.

An underpair has only two outs

Value Bet: Don't even think about it.

Table Action Charts: Profitable opportunities are pretty scarce, and simply don't exist for two or more bets on the flop, or for even a single bet on the turn. But at least it's *possible* to find playable two-out hands for a single flop bet.

Pre-Flop	○ ○ ○ ○ ○
Flop	○ ○ ○ ○
Turn	○ ○
River	○
Flop 26 bets, 26:1 (1.7 outs)	

Five pre-flop opponents each putting two bets into the pot? Six, counting you? It's almost absurd. But when there's that much money in the pot, you'll often see a lot of crying calls on the river.

In this example, you draw to a two-outer, feeling confident that if you hit your hand, you can check-raise on the turn. It works, you get the extra bets, and the call turns out to be worthwhile.

The bottom line is, you need at least 23 small bets in the pot by the river to make it worthwhile to call a single bet on the flop. And if you're calling with, say, an underpair, you'd better be pretty darn sure that you'll win if you make trips.

Pre-Flop	+1½
Flop	
Turn	
River	
Flop 31½ bets, 31.5:1 (1.4 outs) Turn: 32½ bets, 16.25:1 (2.7 outs)	

Here, let's pretend you have you have J♥-J♠ and four other players four-bet the flop with you. There's a little dead money from the blinds as well. The flop comes A♣-K♦-9♥; a disaster. You're beat for sure, and might even be up against trip aces or kings. But if by some miracle you can see the turn for a single flop bet, do you take one off if you can close the betting with your call?

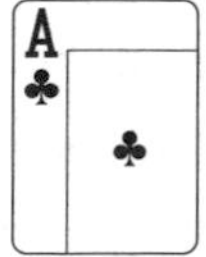

Is it time to give up?

Sure, go ahead, unless you can read your opponents well enough to know they wouldn't three-bet or cap the pot without K-K or A-A. I suppose that if there's only one bet on the flop and three callers ahead of you, it's less likely that anybody has one of these two hands.

But you sure don't call two bets on the flop, and you sure get out of there unless you improve by the turn. Note, by the way, that a queen or a ten is an improvement worth continuing to the river...you then would have about a four-out hand!

Discussion

Usually, you're trying too hard if you somehow manage to convince yourself that you should call with a two-outer. That's why, with a small pair, you either hit the flop or you fold. But if there's lots of money in the pot...and I mean *lots of money*...go ahead and take one more off, while you pray.

A Quick Review

It's very important to understand that most of the above charts present the *minimum* action you need in order to make a call on the flop and/or the turn profitable in the long run. I've presented some borderline cases for each out-count. What you really want are *better* odds. If you're going to play these borderline cases, do so discriminately. Do so coupled with good reads, and careful analysis.

Most of the examples provided assume a reasonable return on the turn and the river. *It's very important that you get a read on the players at your table. Will they continue playing on the turn, and then make a crying call again on the river? Knowing how your opponents play the double-bet rounds is crucial to knowing which hands you can draw to.* We'll come back to this concept.

Another consideration, of course, is anytime you make the decision to take off another card for a single bet on a long shot, you'd better be pretty certain that you aren't going to get raised. Position is *extremely* important when playing with only a few outs. If it's at all possible that you may get raised, it quickly turns a marginally good call into a horrible one.

Having said that, here's a quick summary of what you learned in this chapter:

Exceptional draws

'Exceptional' draws, that is, hands with ten or more outs, usually come in two flavours: Combined straight and flush draws, and straight or flush draws with over-cards. These hands are quite often the favourite to win on the flop against multiple opponents. Use whatever tactics you can to simply get as much money into the pot as possible, on the flop. If you have overcards, don't worry too much about chasing out opponents, since that often buys you even more outs. You're betting for value, and should play with confidence. You'll be seeing the river, even against a single opponent.

Good draws

'Good' draws, such as open-ended straights that aren't too badly compromised, and flush draws, you can pretty much count on playing all the way to the river except in very special circumstances. These are draws with between seven and nine outs. You might have to give up the hand against a single opponent on the turn with very scarce betting on the first two rounds, or against two opponents if the betting gets strong on the turn. Don't be afraid to build the pot on the flop against multiple opponents.

Complex draws

'Complex' draws are hands that have multiple ways to win, but without an open-ended straight or flush draw. These are hands usually worth about five or six outs. Most of these hands combine several little benefits, such as inside straight draws, low pairs, overcards, three-card flush draws, and three-card straight draws. Sometimes you can find so many of these little benefits, that they add up to a 'good' draw. On the other hand, sometimes an open-ended straight will be so heavily compromised it should be considered only worth about six outs, dropping it down to this category. These hands are almost always worth seeing one more card after the flop, if you can stay in cheaply, but often require that you give them up if you haven't made your hand by the turn. The decision whether or not to call two bets on the flop, or a single bet on the turn, often depends upon how well you can read your opponents...whether or not they will pay you off on the river if you get lucky.

'Long-shot' draws

'Long-shot' draws are all other hands that are behind on the flop. The decision, here, is whether or not to pay to see the turn. Four-out hands are often worth seeing the turn, if you can get by with only a single flop bet, but then require a lot of other players in the hand for you to go any further. Two- and three-out hands require a lot of opponents to be worth calling even a single flop bet. Also, be strongly cautioned about calling on a long shot if you're likely to get raised. That will quickly turn a marginal call into a horrible one. Nevertheless, there are a lot of circumstances when a flop call is correct, based purely on the odds, because of the pot size.

NOTE: It would be a gross oversimplification, of course, but perhaps we can sum up this entire book with one sentence: Excellent draws always take you to the river; good draws you usually also play to the river; complex draws are usually worth a single flop bet, but you must think carefully about paying two flop bets or one turn bet; long-shot draws are worth a single bet on the flop against many opponents or large pots, but you almost always have to give up them up on the turn.

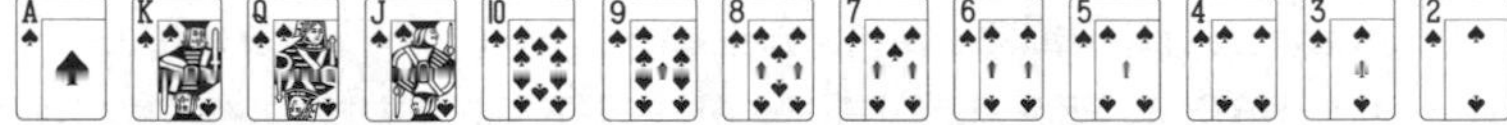

Ace Speaks...

The importance of position

On more than one occasion, we have read the words in this book 'You *could* call here, provided it will cost you only one bet' or, as in the last page, 'Be strongly cautioned about calling on a long shot if you're likely to get raised. That will quickly turn a marginal call into a horrible one.' Your position plays a key role here. There are two ways where your position can be helpful in finding profitable situations for borderline hands:

1) You are on or near the button, and face a bet from an early position player.

2) You are in bad (early or middle) position yourself, but the bettor is sitting on your immediate left, giving you last action.

What is important here is that your call will *close the betting*, or at the very least that there will be very few players behind you who are still to act. The absolute worst thing for borderline hands and/or fairly weak draws is having someone *bet through you.* If you are seated to the immediate left of the bettor, and there are a couple of players still to act who may or may not have received help from the board, then you cannot correctly analyse the strength that may be out there and/or the willingness of other players to play back at the raiser. Even if you know that the bettor often puts his money in on light values, you still have to fold many marginal to decent hands simply because of your bad position. In this situation, being sandwiched between the bettor and the other players, you will need a much better hand than usual to continue playing. Both complex draws as well as fairly weak made hands will often have to be abandoned, even though you *would* happily have called if you could have closed the betting for just a single bet.

Chapter Seven

Classifying Your Opponents

WARNING: This chapter contains lots of charts and numbers and other hard-to-read stuff. Don't bury yourself here! Just skim the chapter if you prefer, and save your brain for chapter eight. You'll need it there!

I've already touched on the importance of classifying your game, and the players in your game. Your goal in classifying games and players is to try to get a handle on how big the pot will swell, in order to decide whether you can play certain drawing hands.

In a typical 10-player game of middle-limit hold'em, you'll lose about 40% of the pre-flop callers on the flop. The other 60% will continue on to see the turn card. You'll lose another 18% between the turn and the river, and you'll lose 8% more on the river. That leaves 34% of the original bettors who will play all the way to the showdown.

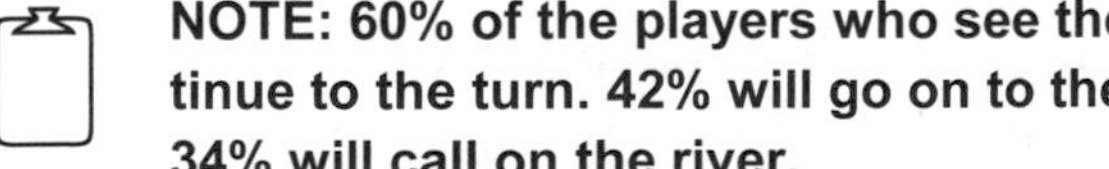

NOTE: 60% of the players who see the flop will continue to the turn. 42% will go on to the river. And 34% will call on the river.

Put another way, 60% of the players who see the flop will continue to the turn. 42% will go on to the river. And 34% will call on the river. On their own, these numbers mean very little. We can't really draw many conclusions about how much money will be in the pot by these numbers.

TIP: As the turn card is being dealt, look around the table. You can expect 1¼ more large bets from each remaining player.

What we *really* care about is the answer to the question of how big the pot is likely to get if you have, say, six pre-flop limpers, and four of them continue on to the turn. The statistics presented above show that about 70% of these four players will pay to see the river card, and 57% will pay to be a part of the showdown. That's good news! If you look around the table and see four survivors as the turn card as being dealt, you can expect to see about five more large bets (other than your own) go into the pot. That's a rough rule of thumb: Expect 1¼ more large bets per remaining player as the turn is being dealt.

Of course, each game is different, because each player is different. Let's look at some typical games, and what you can expect from each.

Loose vs. Tight

We'll be categorising games using two sliding scales: Loose vs. Tight, and Aggressive vs. Passive.

You'll have seen this kind of categorisation several times before, if you've read a few many poker books. A loose game refers to a game where many players see the flop, and continue to play after the flop with marginal holdings. Everyone likes to play in loose games, because, generally, they're more profitable.

Five or six pre-flop callers is a good standard for 'loose' games, and two or three pre-flop callers is a good standard for 'tight' games.

Oops. I did it myself. I defined the 'tightness' or 'looseness' of a game in terms of pre-flop activity.

Actually, we're interested in no such thing. We're interested in how loose the table continues to play *after* the flop. Because we're interested in projecting the *future*. Any idiot can look around the table and see how loose it was before the flop cards were spread.

Please don't misunderstand. It's *very* important to categorise pre-flop play as well, for two primary reasons:

1) Game selection

You want to play in loose games. They simply are more healthy for your bankroll.

2) Starting hand selection

You can play more drawing hands up front if you can expect to see several limpers after you. Loose, passive players open up the game for more types of hands.

But you've been over this time and time again with other authors. Let's move beyond starting hands and game selection and talk about what to do once you're already sitting down and pushing money into the pot.

From here on out, when I say the words 'loose' and 'tight', I'm referring to how likely a person is to chase to the turn and river with marginal holdings.

Aggressive vs. Passive

With this measurement, we want to get a handle on how many bets we can expect, on average, with each betting round. One bet on average? Even less? Or two? More? In other words, how commonly is the betting opened and raised?

Again, we are simply not interested in pre-flop activity. Many 'aggressive' players pre-flop are simply players who have been taught to thin the field with pairs or big cards...so they routinely raise with A-J and 8-8, with fear written all over their faces...and then grind to a halt after the flop, because in their heart of hearts, they're passive individuals.

We're really not even that interested in how aggressive the opponents are on the flop. What we really want to know is, will we continue to see multiple bets on the turn and river?

Many times, the 'aggression' on an aggressive table dies as soon as the turn card hits. This is because the players have figured out, through their aggression, where they stand, and they're now ready to just call down the hand or even fold. Unfortunately, that's the exact *opposite* of what we are trying to measure with our 'aggressive-passive' scale. Perhaps the label 'aggressive player' stirs up visions of a maniac capping the bet on the first two betting rounds, and then mysteriously folding on the turn. Drive that idea from your head, please. *An aggressive player, for the purpose of this book, is one who will continue to bet aggressively on the turn and river.*

Perhaps the most important playing quality to get a handle on is how often a player will bluff or bet for value on the river. If he only bets the nuts on the river, he's passive in my book, regardless of how strongly he begins the hand.

Setting The Standard

Let's define, then, in exact terms, what we mean by passive and aggressive, and by loose and tight. Let's say that in a passive game, the bet size averages one bet per betting round. In an aggressive game, the average size increases to two bets on the flop and 1½ bets on the turn and river.

But I don't want you to get hung up on my own criteria. 'Aggressive' and 'passive' are just meaningless labels. I chose these standards for the sake of simplicity. None of your games will match exactly this average, but by setting the standards very simply, it gives you an easy reference point for comparison.

You may have, in your mind, a different standard for these words, 'aggressive' and 'passive'. I'm not here to change your standard. I'm here to help you get a handle on how to play.

Likewise, let's talk about the 'loose-to-tight' scale. Recall how I started this chapter, by stating that, on average, 60% of pre-flop callers continue after the flop; 42% will continue on to the turn; and 34% will pay to see the showdown. That's a good place to start, then, to define an 'average' table. Let's round a little bit and come up with 60%/40%/30% as our standard. A table where 60% of the pre-flop players continue after the flop, 40% continue after the turn, and 30% see the showdown, we'll call 'average'.

Put another way, we lose 40% of our pre-flop players to the betting on the flop; we lose 33% of our flop players to the betting on the turn; and we lose 25% of our turn players to the betting on the end.[7]

What if we tighten this up, and take away another 10% each time, so that more people are folding? Let's define this as a *tight table*. Likewise, suppose we loosen the standard, and let 10% more continue in each betting round. We'll define this as a *loose table*. So, without further ado:

An Average/Passive Table

Let's look at a table action chart now, but rather than displaying precise bet sizes and number of players, let's generalise a little.

Do you see what I've done? At the *average* table, where the average bet size is exactly one bet per round, you can look around, count the pre-flop callers for a single bet, and count on seeing a pot size at the end of about three small bets per person. This does not count, of course, any money you yourself put into the pot.

---

[7]Do you see where these numbers come from? Suppose all ten players see the flop. We would drop down to six players for the turn, four players for the river, and three players for the showdown. Therefore, we've lost 40% of our players on the flop (from ten down to six); 33% of our flop players on the turn (six down to four); and 25% of our turn players on the river (four down to three).

Pre-Flop	One bet
Flop	60% will pay one bet
Turn	40% will pay one bet
River	30% will pay one bet
Pot size: 3 bets per pre-flop player	

TIP: On your average passive table, expect to see about three small bets by the end of the hand for each person that plays.

Four other players out there? One small bet on the flop? The implied odds on the flop are 4 × 3 + 1 (don't forget your own pre-flop bet) = 13:1, so a little calculation shows that you need 3.4 outs to play on the flop.

Life isn't quite this simple, of course. The more players at the table, the more likely you are to see more bets per player (there are more people out there who might want to raise).

Moreover, when deciding what to do on the flop, it doesn't really interest you too much to know that 60% of the pre-flop callers are likely to call again. Heck, you can look around the table and see how many callers there were before it's your turn to act. What interests you is only that 60% of the *remaining* players...those that haven't yet made a decision...will stay in the pot.

Likewise, on the turn, it is of no interest at *all* to you to know that 60% of all pre-flop callers will call on the flop. You already *know* exactly what these guys did.

Nevertheless, this is very useful information to begin to develop a feel for which hands are playable. I'm going to put you in the worst possible position for a drawing hand...that of second to act, and I'll assume that the first person to act bets into you. So you know you have at least one other player (the bettor) staying in the hand with you, but you have to assume that only 60% of the remaining players will call the bet. In fact, you may wind up paying two bets (I'll take it easy on you and assume that you never have to face three bets or more).

Take a look at the following chart:

Average/Passive: One Pre-flop Bet

Number of Players	1	2	3	4	5	6	7	8	9
Flop: 1 bet	7.4	5.0	3.8	3.1	2.6	2.2	1.9	1.7	1.5
Flop: 2 bets		6.9	5.4	4.5	3.8	3.3	3.0	2.7	2.4

Legend:

(dark shading)	Play Good Or Exceptional Draws (over 6 outs)
(medium shading)	May Play Complex Draws (4.1 to 6 outs)
(light shading)	May Play Long-Shot Draws (3 to 4 outs)
(no shading)	May Play Extreme Long Shots (less than 3 outs)

This chart presumes an average/passive table, with one pre-flop bet. To read the chart, first look around the table at how many players *other than you* are in the hand (one through nine, across the top). Then cross-reference this number of players with the number of bets (on the flop) that you have to pay to continue. The chart shows the number of outs you need in order to play. This is far from a scientific process, so we're ignoring dead money.

Hey, now we're really getting somewhere! You're sitting at your favourite average/passive table, holding a four-out inside straight, and you're bet into on the flop. You look around the table to count four players other than you holding cards. The handy-dandy 'pocket calling chart' you cut out of this book and slipped into your lap says you only need 3.1 outs to call a single flop bet, so you call. What could be simpler?

The truth is, it's *too* simple. I really don't want you to play that way. I want you to use all the information that is at your disposal when making your decision, such as:

1) How many players have already called the flop bet? (remember, in this chart, we're putting you in the worst possible position, that of acting second, directly after a bet...but you won't be in that unenviable position all the time!)

2) Of the remaining players, which do you think are likely to play? Again, the chart above was constructed under the assumption that 60% of the pre-flop callers will call on the flop; 40% on the turn; and 30% on the river. That's how we defined 'average/passive'. But hopefully, you know your opponents better than I do!

3) How likely is it that you will be raised or re-raised after you call?

So, while the information in this chart is useful to help build guidelines in your head, you'll want to adjust those guidelines to changing circumstances, and your ability to read your opponents, as you play.

Now let's look at play on the turn. Again, I'll assume you're second to act, and the first player bets into you.

Average/Passive Turn Play: One Pre-flop Bet

Number of Players	1	2	3	4	5	6
Turn: 1 bet (1 on flop)	9.0	6.1	4.6	3.7	3.2	2.8
Turn: 1 bet (2 on flop)	7.6	5.1	3.8	3.2	2.7	2.4
Turn: 2 bets (1 on flop)		9.0	6.9	5.5	4.8	4.2
Turn: 2 bets (2 on flop)		7.8	6.0	4.8	4.2	3.7

This time, of course, as you look around the table and count how many players are in the pot, you'll be looking at the number that called *on the flop,* rather than pre-flop. Some of those pre-flop bettors disappeared with the flop betting. I'll be using the attrition rate at your table (the percentage that usually drops out on the flop depending upon how loose or tight your game is) to make an assumption about how much money was put into the pot pre-flop. You must also know whether one bet or two bets per player went into the pot on the flop.

For example, the chart shows that if there are four other players, and there was a raise on the flop, then you need 3.2 outs to call a bet on the turn.

This is even less scientific than the process we used for the flop! There are so many assumptions going on here, you may think that the data is practically useless. *But it does give you a general idea of the sort of hands that are playable.*

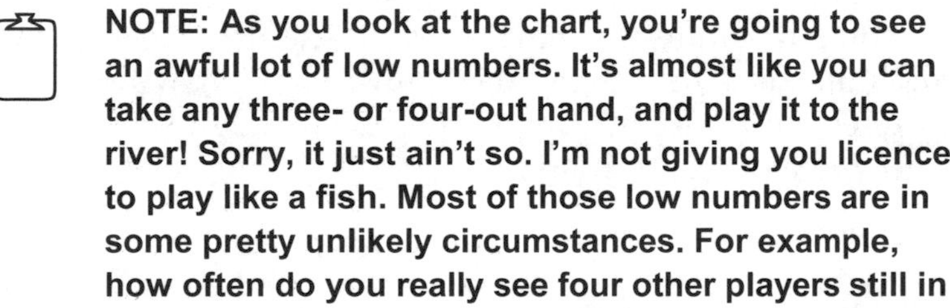

NOTE: As you look at the chart, you're going to see an awful lot of low numbers. It's almost like you can take any three- or four-out hand, and play it to the river! Sorry, it just ain't so. I'm not giving you licence to play like a fish. Most of those low numbers are in some pretty unlikely circumstances. For example, how often do you really see four other players still in the hand with you on the turn?

But it does happen, in those low-limit, no-fold-'em hold'em games! You can take an inside straight...a typical four-out hand...and play it to the river, fully justified by the odds to do so! Amazing, isn't it? Could it be...all those fish that have been laying bad beats on you, in those family pots...have been (ugh) out-playing you? This is almost too much to take!

It gets worse. Take a look at a chart, now, with two pre-flop bets instead of one. Look at all the white space on this chart! There are some pots, here, in these no-fold-'em games, that become literally monstrous. An abomination to the game of poker, if you ask me.

Average/Passive: Two Pre-flop Bets

Number of Players	1	2	3	4	5	6	7	8	9
Flop: 1 bet	5.6	3.8	2.9	2.3	1.9	1.7	1.5	1.3	1.2
Flop: 2 bets		5.6	4.4	3.6	3.1	2.7	2.4	2.1	1.9
Turn: 1 bet (1 on flop)	7.2	4.7	3.5	2.8	2.5	2.2			
Turn: 1 bet (2 on flop)	6.2	4.1	3.0	2.5	2.2	2.0			
Turn: 2 bets (1 on flop)		7.4	5.6	4.5	4.0	3.6			
Turn: 2 bets (2 on flop)		6.6	5.0	4.0	3.5	3.1			

You're bet into now, on the turn, and you look around the table and see four people with cards. Half of the table is in this pot, counting you. Three players yet to act. There were probably six pre-flop callers, seven counting you, paying two bets apiece, and only a couple of them folded on the flop. Lots of money piled up there in the middle. Think anybody will raise, if you call now on the turn? If not, you're actually justified in taking your *three-outer* to the river!

TIP: Sometimes you just have to play like the fish. Throw your money out there and cross your fingers.

Some decent players become so frustrated playing in these 'good' games, because they can't seem to win...*and, dammit, they're better than these fish and ought to be winning...* that eventually they give up in disgust. This chart shows why: In extremely loose games, you may be mathematically justified in calling to the river even if you catch only a marginal piece of the flop! Sometimes you just have to learn to play like the fish. Throw your money out there and cross your fingers. Helluva way to play, isn't it? I can't offer much advice with this kind of game, because I'm one of those guys who becomes frustrated.

Certainly, I'll play in these games if I can find one. The hourly rate is wonderful. But the swings are large, and the tilt factor is frightening.

When The Game Gets Aggressive

Let's look at what happens, now, if we make the game a little more aggressive. In other words, if we assume stronger betting on the turn and on the river. Remember that in an aggressive game, the average number of turn and river bets increases from one per player to 1½. These charts again show the number of outs you need to call one or two bets on the flop.

One Pre-flop Bet, One Flop Bet

Number of Players	1	2	3	4	5	6	7	8	9
Average Game	7.4	5.0	3.8	3.1	2.6	2.2	1.9	1.7	1.5
Aggressive Game	6.3	4.2	3.2	2.5	2.1	1.8	1.6	1.4	1.3

One Pre-Flop Bet, Two Flop Bets

Number of Players	1	2	3	4	5	6	7	8	9
Average Game		6.9	5.4	4.5	3.8	3.3	3.0	2.7	2.4
Aggressive Game		5.9	4.6	3.8	3.3	2.8	2.5	2.2	2.0

Notice how all of the numbers went down when the game turned aggressive. The 'playability' loosened, so that you can play more hands. This is to be expected, of course. More turn and river bets means bigger pots, which means better implied odds.

But *how much* difference do the extra double-sized bets make? A quick scan of the charts shows that the extra half-bet per player, on the turn and river, decreases the number of outs you need to play on the flop by about 15%. If you need seven outs to play a hand on the flop in a passive game, you need only six outs to play the same hand in an aggressive game. 'Passive' and 'aggressive', of course, being defined by how strongly you can expect the betting to continue into the turn and river.

I'll spare you the study of charts on the turn; suffice it to say that on the turn, when there is only one more of these double-sized rounds to come, the effect on playability is about half of what we see on the flop. The number of outs needed on the turn decreases by about 8%. If you require seven outs to continue with your hand in a passive game on the turn, then you need about 6½ outs to continue in an aggressive game.

Ma'am, Can We Get More Drinks Over Here?

Let's compare the other sliding scale now. We've studied the difference between passive and aggressive; how about the difference between loose and tight games? As you look over these charts, try to keep your focus on reality, looking at only the first few columns. Unless you plan to join in the gambling with that low-limit no-fold-'em game in the corner.

On these charts, we stick with an average of one turn and river bet, but increase the number of callers by 10% for a loose game, and decrease by 10% for a tight game. Again, we're looking at the number of outs you need to call on the flop.

One Pre-flop Bet, One Flop Bet

Number of Players	1	2	3	4	5	6	7	8	9
Tight Game	7.9	5.6	4.3	3.5	3.0	2.6	2.3	2.0	1.8
Average Game	7.4	5.0	3.8	3.1	2.6	2.2	1.9	1.7	1.5
Loose Game	7.2	4.7	3.5	2.8	2.3	2.0	1.7	1.5	1.4

One Pre-flop Bet, Two Flop Bets

Number of Players	1	2	3	4	5	6	7	8	9
Tight Game		7.3	5.9	5.0	4.3	3.8	3.4	3.1	2.8
Average Game		6.9	5.4	4.5	3.8	3.3	3.0	2.7	2.4
Loose Game		6.7	5.2	4.2	3.6	3.1	2.7	2.4	2.2

Modifying Your Out-Count By Classifying Your Opponents

Does a quick study of these charts reveal anything? It shows that you need fewer outs to play in a loose game than in a tight game. That should be no surprise. But how *much* fewer?

On the flop, the required out-count drops 20% or more between tight and loose games![8] The more players in the pot, the more it drops.

Of course, I don't need to explain that you will be seeing a lot more multi-way pots in a loose game than in a tight game. With more players, you're going to be playing more drawing hands on the flop and turn, because the pot odds justify it. What perhaps is seldom remembered is that, if you look around the table and count four players with cards tucked under their chips, it makes a big difference whether *those four players* are loose or tight, passive or aggressive, as the hand rolls into the turn and river.

Here are two useful rules of thumb for adjusting your out-count to the type of game:

> 1) If your opponents are particularly aggressive, meaning they will play aggressively on the turn and river, bump up your out-count by about 15% on the flop. For example, a seven-out hand plays as an eight-out hand on the flop.
>
> 2) Modify your out-count further by plus or minus 10% on the flop, depending upon how loose or tight your opponents are. Add outs for loose games, and subtract outs for tight games. Do this only against two or more players.

---

[8]On the turn, the required out-count drops about half that much, as it did with the passive/aggressive scale: Somewhere around a 10% drop in required outs.

TIP: On the flop, bump up your out-count by about 15% if your opponents are particularly aggressive over the turn and river. Then add or subtract about 10% more, depending upon how loose or tight your opponents are.

Let me give you an example. You hold a hand worth six outs against three players in a loose, aggressive game. You should add one more out for the aggressive nature of your opponents, and a half-out or more for their loose playing style. A six-out hand can be played on the flop as if it were a 7½-out hand!

Now you hold the same hand in a tight, passive game. This type of player won't see the river without a great hand, and won't bet into you without the nuts. Leave the passive-to-aggressive scale alone, since in this book we're making conservative assumptions already, but drop your count about one-half out down to 5½ for the flop.

Believe me, there's a *tremendous* difference between 7½ and 5½ outs. With the former, you're going confidently to the river, almost as a given. With the latter, you'd better think hard about that turn bet.

The Advantage Of Relative Position

Can you see why it's a tremendous advantage to have position with your drawing hands? Position does more than just give you a chance to raise with a semi-bluff. Position also makes a great number of drawing hands more playable. Especially *relative position;* that is, position relative to the expected bettor.

Let's refer back to the chart titled **Average/Passive: One Preflop Bet.** Suppose you've flopped a good inside straight draw, nothing more. How many players do you need in the hand to continue on the flop with a four-out hand? Suppose you look around the table and see three other players. You don't know these guys, so you can't really adjust your out-count for their style of play. You've got four outs to work with, period.

The guy on your right bets into you. Do you call?

No! You toss that hand into the muck faster than a hare on a hotplate. Yes, I know, you have four outs and the chart says you need only 3.8 to call a single bet. But what if you are raised after you call? Then it isn't even close! You need 5.4 outs to call two bets! *What if you're re-raised?*

But what if you have relative position? This means you're sitting on the *right* of the aggressive player at your table. Now, when he bets, the action goes all the way around the table before it comes back to you. You can call or fold with confidence, because you'll be closing the betting (you can't be raised), and because you know exactly how many players are still in the hand.

Recall that the way to use these charts is to look around the table *before* all of the players have acted, and count how many are in the hand. If you count four other players on the flop, you only know what one of them did. He started the betting. The other three are a mystery. I put you in the worst possible relative position, that of being directly after the bettor.

Let's see what happens if I give you better position. Suppose you're last to act, and can make a decision after everyone else has decided what to do. This time, as you look around the table and count players, you're counting the players who are *still in the hand* after the betting round. Column four on the chart means four players have already called one or two bets, and you're closing the action by calling or folding.

One Pre-flop Bet, One Flop Bet

Number of Players	1	2	3	4	5	6	7	8	9
Horrible Position	7.4	5.0	3.8	3.1	2.6	2.2	1.9	1.7	1.5
Excellent Position	6.7	3.9	2.8	2.1	1.8	1.6	1.4	1.3	1.1

One Pre-Flop Bet, Two Flop Bets

Number of Players	1	2	3	4	5	6	7	8	9
Horrible Position		6.9	5.4	4.5	3.8	3.3	3.0	2.7	2.4
Excellent Position		6.3	4.5	3.5	3.0	2.6	2.3	2.0	1.8

Can you see the difference? Just a glance ought to convince you. Lots more white space. How much more pleasant it is to know exactly how many players are in the pot with you, and exactly how much it costs you to stay! Position is a wonderful thing

How much is position worth? Particularly, relative position? It depends upon how many players are in the hand, of course...the more, the better...but good position is worth an entire out or more! A five-out hand on the flop acting out of position can be played like a six-out hand with good position. Why?

1) When the turn comes, if you have position, you will be better able to decide if there is enough money in the pot for you to continue. Having position helps you make better choices down the road.

2) With position, of course, you are better able to cash in on a good hand by raising the entire table. If you can get just one or two more large bets by having position, after you hit your draw, then your hand is worth at least one more out!

Feel free to add a 'position adjustment' on the flop of about ½ out to your count, if you feel really good about your relative position. Then subtract about ½ out from your count if you have horrible position. Or, just use your position to help make any marginal decisions that come your way. If the number of outs you need is about the same as what your hand is worth, then play the hand if you have good position, and muck it if you have bad position.

Another way to factor in the benefits of position will be discussed in chapter eight.

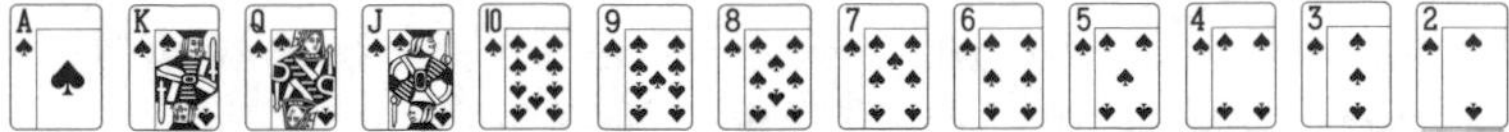

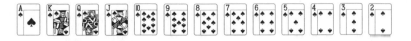

Ace Speaks...

Some more on position

While some poker writers think that position in limit hold'em is of paramount importance, and that on or near the button almost any hand is playable, I am a bit more conservative, and lean towards playing with fairly solid values at all times – also in late position. A lot of good players – myself included – are actually pretty good at playing in bad position, i.e. being first or one of the first to speak. Because of the possibility of using the check-raise and even the check-call to my advantage, I am usually not that worried about having what seems to be a bad position.

What I *am* worried about is when, despite a seemingly better position in the betting, I am in danger of being put in the middle – being sandwiched, that is. As we have just seen, many decent draws will have to be abandoned once someone bets into a large field and it is you who is sitting immediately behind this bettor. Now, few things upset me more than being forced to lay down my hand, because of action behind me, after having called one bet. That is, having contributed money on the flop without actually reaching the turn. And just as bad is when you fold a decent draw because of the distinct possibility that someone behind you will raise the pot, yet in the end no one does – meaning you could have made a cheap and potentially profitable call. In both situations, you will have given up expected value because of your bad position relative to the bettor, and because of the problems you sometimes encounter when you lack information regarding your opponents' possible actions.

Now, while it is sometimes quite easy to predict some players' future actions once you have seen their initial flop decision to either check or bet, it will be much harder to do this when they have not made any action yet. So, upgrading and downgrading your calling requirements not just because of your position relative to the button, but more importantly because of your position relative to the bettor is not just recommended – it is *imperative* in order for you to make the (mathematically) correct decisions.

But What About The Turn?

You'll notice that I've pretty much ignored the turn and focused on the flop in this chapter. There are two reasons for this emphasis:

1) The impact of position and playing styles upon the turn betting is only half as large, because there is only one betting round remaining.

2) Generalities and rules of thumb are much more useful on the flop than on the turn. This is because, by the turn, you have a much better idea of what your opponents actually hold, and what sort of opponents will be going to the river with you.

Before the turn, the players are all still flopping around, paying cheap bets, drawing to poor odds, and generally trying to get a feel for their hands. Deceptive play is much more common on the flop than on the turn. Nobody wants to tip his hand yet. But when the bets double on the turn, the game gets serious. Admit it: You never really know very much about what's going on in the hand until the turn.

It is my recommendation that you use the guidelines given in this chapter only on the flop, while you're still struggling to figure out where you stand. By the time the turn arrives, your knowledge of the players who remain and your position at the table can be used to formulate a much more accurate estimation of how many more bets will go into the pot.

We'll talk about this more in chapter eight. For now, it's better to adjust your out-count for position and playing styles only on the flop; not on the turn.

What Good Are All These Charts, Really?

I have a confession to make, now that we're nearing the end of the chapter: These charts are not here to tell you how to play. You can't just carry your handy-dandy pocket calling chart into a game, and expect it to be the Holy Grail. So why have I wasted your time?

- The charts are intended to give a rough idea of the playable hands, given the number of players in the hand.
- They are intended to give you a feel for how much circumstances differ between loose and tight games, and between aggressive and passive games. Play more hands in loose, aggressive games, where the reward is greater.
- They are intended to help you understand how much difference it makes when there is a pre-flop raise. Extra money in the pot means more hands that you can play.
- They are intended to help you understand how much it costs you if you call a bet with a reasonable drawing hand, but then get raised. Look back at the charts if you haven't already, at the difference between one bet and two bets. Generally, you need one or two more outs to call a raise on the flop; two or three more outs to call a raise on the

turn. The more players in the pot, the fewer extra outs you need to call a raise.

- They are intended to hint at the value of position. Especially relative position.

TIP: You need one or two more outs to call a raise than a single bet on the flop. You need two or three more outs to call a raise on the turn.

All this, the charts can do. But they *cannot* give you precise instructions. They cannot, because there is a critical piece of information missing in the charts: There is no consideration for the exact number of bettors on prior betting rounds. The charts assume you are looking around the table now, it being your turn to act, and counting players. But how many players were there before this round? How many folded? These charts all make the assumption that there were more players in prior rounds, and you lost some due to the attrition rate.[9] In other words, the charts aren't working with precise pot odds. They are great for developing a feel for what kind of hands can be played, based on the number of remaining players, but this information, with its lack of precision, can only take you so far.

We need a more exact method of determining which hands are playable. Are you ready? Turn the page.

---

[9]This process of 'projecting backward' to estimate the number of pre-flop or flop bets is not as straightforward as it sounds. It would be, if the number of players at the table were not bounded. For example, if you have six callers on the turn, how many pre-flop callers were there? Remember that on average, only 40% of the pre-flop callers make it to the river. Would you then have 2½ times as many pre-flop callers as turn callers? Fifteen of them? Of course not. Should we say ten pre-flop callers? No...it's hard to imagine that the *average* number of callers would be a full table. The answer is quite involved, and requires making a further assumption about variability. If you are interested in learning more about these calculations, please contact the author.

Chapter Eight

How Big is the Pot?

'People who think math isn't important in poker don't know the right math.'

Chris Ferguson

Frankly, we don't care. How big the pot is, I mean. We care about how big it will get.

NOTE: It makes no difference how big the pot is. It only matters how big it will become.

Maybe you've gotten the idea from prior chapters that I never count the number of bets going into the pot. That I recommend making each decision by glancing around the table and counting *players* instead of *money*. Nothing could be further from the truth!

I *do* count how much money is going into the pot. You should, too. Sometimes. You need to know what's in the pot, to know how to play certain hands. Actually, you need to know how much is *going into* the pot. I'm going to give you a simple and elegant way of projecting the final pot size. But, as simple and elegant as it is, it will take some getting used to. *You will need to read this chapter twice.* If chapter two is the most important chapter in the book, then this chapter is the second most important.

Look. If you're serious about poker, sometimes you have to keep track of the pot. Do me a favour: Just try it. You'll find out it isn't as hard as you think. Your next poker session, just concentrate on this one thing: Counting the pot and estimating the final pot size.

That's what matters: The final pot size. That's where implied odds come from.

TIP: Always measure the pot size by the number of *small bets.* This means the turn and river bets count as two bets.

As soon as bets start going into the pot, start counting them. You want to know how many players are in the hand, anyway. Count your bet, too, before the flop. By the time the flop is dealt, there is absolutely no excuse for not knowing exactly how big the pot is.

Don't worry about counting the small blind if he folds. Especially in low-limit games, where the house rake is going to take that much away anyway. His half-bet is inconsequential, and if anything, ignoring it will cause you to err on the side of caution.

Maybe you have a dealer that announces how many people are in the pot as he deals the flop. Hey, that's cool! Takes all the work out of it for you.

Pot Size On The Flop

They say the flop is the defining moment in a hold'em hand, and I agree. When the flop comes, you pretty much know whether it hits you or not. If there's the slightest chance that you might want to continue with this hand, *now* is the time you perk up and starting paying serious attention. (Figuratively, of course; watch those tells!)

You're watching each player closely, now, trying to get a read on what he has. How well the flop hit him. And as you're watching players, you're calculating pot size.

Romomber how I said that each player who calls on the flop will continue to put, on average, 1¼ more large bets into the pot on the turn and/or river? 70% of them play the turn, and 57% continue to call to the showdown. If the average bet size is one bet per street, that's about 1¼ big bets per player. Two and a half small bets.

However, 2½ is an odd number to work with. It would be easier to round down to two bets, or up to three bets. Which way should we go?

We should round *up* to three small bets. Why? Because if you hit your hand, you're going to do everything you can to extract extra bets on either the turn or the river.

TIP: As you count the bets going into the pot on the flop, count an extra three bets for each opponent. This will give you a projected final pot size.

So, here's what you do as you're counting bets on the flop. *Count four bets each time somebody bets or calls!* You're counting not only how much is going into the put, but also how much you think will go in on the turn and river. Four small bets per player.

Anybody can count by fours. 4, 8, 12, 16, 20...easy, right?

Of course, if a player raises or calls a raise, that's five bets for him. Counting by fives is even easier than counting by fours!

Got it? Everybody that stays in on the flop gets three extra bets to their credit.

You might find it easier to add the flop bets after the round is done. 'Three flop callers for two bets each? That's 3 × 5 = 15 bets I should add.' But I prefer to add them as I go, because then it's easier for me to make my own decision when my turn comes, having the estimated final pot size already in my head. We'll talk shortly about what to do when your turn comes and others have yet to act.

Most of the time, you don't care what's in the pot. Most of the time, the flop either hits you hard, or not at all. Don't bother keeping track anymore of the pot size unless it matters, or you have one of those hands that might matter by the turn.

Let's practice with an example. Suppose you have five callers other than you for two bets before the flop. Now on the flop, two of them fold, leaving three besides you to put in one more bet apiece. What's the estimated pot size by the end of the hand?

6 × 2 = 12 bets before the flop; 3 × 4 = 12 more for the remaining three streets. Total estimated pot size: 24. Your own money gets included before the flop, but of course your flop bet doesn't count while you are trying to make your flop decision.

Pot Size On The Turn

Now the turn card has been played, and perhaps you again find yourself in a position of needing to know the estimated final pot size. Remember that you've already counted this final pot size, so all you do now is a little tweaking with any new information. There are four things you need to know:

1) What was your estimated pot size before the turn? We'll start with that. In the prior example, this was 24.

2) How many bets did you put in on the flop? Those count, now, since that money is part of the pot; it can't be retrieved. You're up to 25 bets.

3) How many bets are going into the pot, per player, on the turn? Let's assume one, for now. One bet is all it costs you to play the turn. Note that we're only concerned if *one or more* bets are required; if you don't have to pay to play, you don't have to calculate the odds. If it's passed around, there's nothing to calculate, and no reason to count the pot.

4) You are hoping to get another bet and a half, on average, over the last two betting rounds, from each player still in the pot. Can you get this much?

This last question is the hard one. Figuring out whether you can get another bet and a half from everybody.

Here is how I want you to do it:

Count on getting one more bet, on the river, from anybody that calls on the turn. Then, assume that ¾ of the players will call on the turn. These two assumptions add up to exactly 1½ bets per player. Exactly what you predicted on the flop. If ¾ of the players pay two bets apiece, and ¼ pay nothing at all, that averages 1½ bets per player.

Now, here comes the elegant part. *Anytime you see somebody call on the turn, just add one more small bet to your count. If somebody folds, drop three small bets from your count.* Do you see why this works? Because ¾ of them are supposed to call!

NOTE: If somebody bets or calls a single bet on the turn, add one more small bet to your projection. If somebody folds, drop three small bets.

What about the people who haven't acted yet? Ignore them. What about the people who checked when it was their turn, instead of betting? Ignore them. You only modify your count when somebody folds or puts money in the pot.

Here are the rules, then, for 'tweaking' your projected pot size on the turn:

1) Be sure to add in your own flop bet(s). It's easiest to do it at the time you put your money into the pot.

2) Anytime someone calls on the turn, add one more bet.

3) Anytime someone folds on the turn, subtract three bets. If multiple bets are required on the turn, then add an extra large bet (two small bets) for each player who stays in.

Take heart; this really is easier to do than it is to explain. I'll give an example shortly.

What If You Don't *Know* What Your Opponents Will Do?

Let's reiterate. Most of the time, you don't care about pot size. When the flop comes, you usually know, intuitively, whether you belong in the pot or not. If the flop hits you hard, you play; if it misses you, you fold.

But sometimes it's a questionable call. This usually happens when you have a long- shot draw. Or maybe you have a complex draw, where it's obvious that you should call on the flop, but it's likely that you're going to have a tough decision to make on the turn. So, you begin calculating the estimated final pot size. Each player who pays to play on the flop adds four or more bets to the final count (more than four if he puts in more than one bet on the flop).

TIP: To help you make your flop decision, you should add a couple bets to your projection for every player who has yet to act.

The tricky part comes when it's your turn to act on the flop, and you look around the table at three more players, wondering what they will do. Suppose you need to know *now,* in order to make a decision on the flop.

The simplest answer is, expect half of them to fold, and half of them to call. We're still talking about the flop, not the turn. The actual number is 60% should call on the flop, but 50% is close enough for what we're doing.

It's not as hard as you think: As you look around the table at the players yet to act on the flop, give them each *two* bets instead of *four,* because only half will call. Even if the betting has been raised, so that the undecided folks will have to chip in multiple bets, stick with just counting two bets per undecided player. They're more likely to fold if the betting has been raised.

Your job, now, as a poker player (after all, you *are* a poker player) is to read your opponents as best you can. That's what poker is all about. Glance left to see who's fingering their chips for a call, and who's totally lost interest. Modify that estimate as best you can, to come up with a guess at how many will call or fold. Then tentatively calculate your final pot size from there, by adding in bets for them, too. If a person is going to call, they're worth four bets instead of two; more than four, if the betting is raised. But if they're going to fold, don't give them any credit at all!

Are you always right with your guesses about whether a player will call or fold? No? Then maybe you should give a person just three out of four bets if you think he will call, and maybe one bet instead of zero if you think he will fold.

Do not at this time factor in the possibility of a raise after you call. It just isn't worth it. Calculate your pot size based upon how much the bet is to you *now*. To do more during the heat of the battle is expecting too much. If, after calculating the final pot size, you find that you have a borderline hand (right near the edge of whether you should call or fold), you should probably fold, unless you're pretty sure there will be no raise behind you.

Keeping track of the pot size sounds cumbersome, but really it's not. Practice, practice. Do it *every hand* the next time you play until it becomes second nature. When the process starts to sink in, then you can back off and begin to keep track only when you need to.

Summarising The Rules For Counting The Pot

Let me review the rules for you in a chart:

General Concepts	Always count by the number of small bets. Therefore, extra turn and river bets count double.
	The final pot size is projected during the flop betting, and then adjusted during the turn betting.
Pre-flop	Count every bet that goes into the pot; your own bets count, too.
	Ignore dead money from the small blind if he folds.
On The Flop	Count every bet that goes into the pot, as it occurs; your own bets count, too, once you've made the decision to play.
	For each opponent who decides to play the flop, add three more bets to your count.* Don't do this for your own bet.
	If you need a projected pot size when your turn comes, in order to make a decision about whether to play on the flop, then add two bets for each person that has not yet decided. Then, drop these extra bets and go back to your original count after you have decided to play, so that you'll be ready for the turn.
On The Turn	Add one bet each time someone calls or bets.*
	Subtract three bets anytime someone folds.*
	If the pot has been raised, remember to add two more small bets for each additional double-sized bet.
	Ignore all players who have not yet acted, as well as those players who so far have only checked on the turn. They're already accounted for.
	You are hoping to get one river bet (two small bets) for each person that remains on the river...these two bets are already factored into the equation...but if you are able to supplement your final count with good reads on your opponents, by all means do so!
* If you have poor position, you may want to add only two bets on the flop for each calling player, and then add/subtract two bets on the turn for calling/folding. We'll discuss this more shortly.	

An Example Of Counting The Pot

Let's work through an example, now, to help it sink in. Follow along slowly, so that you understand each step.

Let's put the blinds in positions one and two. You're in position five. One player calls before it's your turn, and you call as well. Then two more call after you, one of them being the button. The small blind calls, and the big blind checks, to give a total of six players.

How big is the pot? *Six bets.*

The flop is now dealt. It brings you an inside straight, nothing more. Four outs.

Back in chapter six was a chart for *Playing With Four Outs:*

	1 bet	2 bets	3 bets	4 bets
Flop	10.8	21.5	32.3	43.0
Turn	21.0	42.0	63.0	84.0

Remember that? You need a projected pot size of 10.8 small bets to continue, if it only costs you one bet to stay in.

There are three players to act before you. The small blind checks, the big blind bets, and the third player folds.

You have to make a decision. How big will the pot get? Add four bets for the one player already committed. That's *ten bets.* How about the players left to act? There are two after you, plus the small blind, who hasn't yet made a decision. Count two bets per player. You're now projecting *16 bets.*

So far, you think the pot size will grow to 16 bets, not counting money you haven't yet put in the pot. It's enough; you only need 10.8. Even if you get raised, you figure you're looking OK. The pot would probably grow to the needed 21½ to make it worthwhile for you to call a raise. You decide to play on.

Your decision having been made, you can forget about the projected 16 bets, and go back to reality. When you left off, you were up to *ten bets.*

Your call can now be added into the pot. It's money that can't be retrieved. That's *11 bets.* As the betting continues around the table it goes call (4 more), the button raises (five more), fold (nothing more) call (just one more; this guy has already put in one bet so we've already counted his turn and river impact). *21 bets.*

Now you call again *(22)* and the last player calls *(23).* The projected pot size is 23 small bets. Four other players are left in the pot: Two before you and two after.

The turn card is dealt. Everyone checks to the button, who bets *(24 bets).* One of the players before you calls *(25)* but one folds, so you subtract three *(22).*

What about the final player after you that hasn't acted? You ignore him. He's already factored in to the equation; you expect him to call ¾ of the time and fold ¼ of the time. You're pretty sure he won't raise, so *22 small bets is your final projection.* It's enough; all you need is 21 bets.

The river card makes your straight, and you praise Dew Mason for telling you it was OK to play your inside straight with this much money in the pot. Don't you just love happy endings?

The Advantage Of Position On The Flop

What I've introduced to you in this chapter is a fairly accurate method of projecting the final pot size. It's based on the general idea that you'll get 1½ large bets, on average, from the turn and the river, for each person that stays in on the flop.

It assumes that ¾ of your opponents will call on the turn, and those remaining on the river will average one more large bet.

Does this sound overly optimistic? Well, it is, a little. Remember that the average we *should expect* is only about 1¼ large bets per player, and we rounded up to 1½, because it's an easier number to work with, and because you will try to extract additional bets by raising either on the turn or the river if you hit your hand.

The opportunity to raise, of course, depends on your position.

Likewise, the opportunity to check-raise depends upon your relative position to the probable bettor. And, of course, if you have horrible position...maybe acting first with no real expectation of somebody else betting the pot for you...then when you do make your hand and bet out from early position, it will give away the strength of your hand. You'll get fewer callers. Back in chapter seven, we determined that position makes a big difference in the value of your hand, even for drawing hands.

The bottom line is that 1½ large bets *really is* a bit optimistic if you don't like your position. I'd like to give you an alternative method of counting the pot when you don't care for where you're sitting at the table.

Suppose we take that 1¼ large bets that you can expect from each player over the turn and river, and round it *down* instead of up! Suppose we round it down to one bet instead of up to one and a half bets. Thus, you expect to win, on average, *one* more large bet (two small bets) from each player who sees the turn card with you.

WARNING: If you have poor position on a hand, perhaps you should add only two extra bets per player on the flop. Then, add two bets (instead of one) when an opponent calls on the turn, and subtract two bets (instead of three) when an opponent folds.

This is a legitimate policy. Here is how you do it. It's simple.

- Remember how you added an extra three bets for anybody that called on the flop? Those three bets were supposed to anticipate their turn and river bets. Three small bets is 1½ large bets. *Instead, you should add only two extra bets if you don't like your position in the hand!*
- Remember how you added one bet each time somebody called on the turn, and then subtracted three bets when somebody folded? *Instead, you should add two bets, and subtract two bets.* The net result is the same: By the time the river card is dealt, you have added in each player's turn bet, you have

> you have removed their projected bets (though the river) for the players who fold, and you are still projecting one extra large bet (on the river) from each person that is still in the hand.

At the end of chapter seven, I suggested that good position...especially good *relative* position...is worth approximately one out. I suggested that you might want to take this into account when playing on the flop. I suggested adding or subtracting about half an out based upon your position. If you are using that method to factor in the benefits of position, then you shouldn't duplicate that benefit with the method in this chapter. Use one method or the other.

The Advantage Of Position On The Turn

The pot-counting method I have introduced you to assumes that you'll average one large bet per player remaining on the river. Do you think you can get more than this? Do you have an advantageous position, so that you might be able to extract more?

On the turn, you can often adjust your estimated final pot size by paying close attention to the river-playing styles of your opponents. Will they always call on the river? Will they always continue to bet if they have been leading the betting all the way through the hand? Will they call a check-raise?

Or, instead, will they never bet the river, and possibly fold if you come out betting?

If you think you have your opponents figured out, you must use this knowledge! Since my counting method assumes each player will contribute, on average, one more bet on the river, you should adjust this expectation if you know better.

Remember that each river bet is worth two small bets. If you *know* he'll bet, and you can raise him, and he'll call your raise, you can add a couple more bets to the final pot size (two small bets is one river-sized bet). If you're not quite so sure, but you *think* you can get away with a raise, maybe just add a single small bet to your count.

I recommend you make these sort of adjustments only on the turn. It's harder to read players on the flop, and too many things can happen between the flop and river. But if it's your turn to act on the turn, and you have a tough decision to make with your calling hand, what you've noticed about the other players can be invaluable.

A Chart You Can Finally Use

Now that you have a way of estimating the final pot size, let's go back and revisit chapter six, where I gave instructions for how to play each out-count. At the top of each section was a little chart showing how big the pot has to get before each out-count is mathematically correct to play.

Let me pull that all together for you now. It looks like this:

Number of Outs	2	3	4	5	6	7	8	9	10
Final Pot Size Needed to call One Flop Bet	22.5	14.7	10.8	8.4	6.8	5.7	4.9	4.2	3.7

This chart shows, for each out count across the top of the chart, exactly how big the pot needs to get by the river for it to be correct for you to call a single bet on the flop. Naturally, to call two bets on the flop, you need twice as big a pot. Three bets? Three times this size.

Finally, a chart you can use! If you get the scissors out now, I won't complain. But I believe the chart is worth committing to memory. Too many digits to remember? Try cutting your teeth on a simplified version:

Number of Outs	2	3	4	5	6	7	8	9	10
Final Pot Size Needed to call One Flop Bet	23	15	11	9	7	6	5	4	4

Or, if you're good with numbers, memorise this formula:

$$\text{Needed Pot Size} = (47 \div \text{Outs}) - 1$$

On the turn, you need twice as much to call one large bet, of course. Actually, marginally less, because there are only 46 cards remaining in the deck rather than 47. That's about 2% less. In other words, if you need a final pot size of 10 to call on the flop, you only need 9.8 to call on the turn. I wouldn't worry about such fine details unless you're calculating the needed pot size on the fly with the above formula; then, you might as well plug in the number 46 instead of 47, because there are only 46 unknown cards remaining in the deck after the turn.

If The Pot Is Raised

Suppose you are playing on the flop, and there is a bet and a raise before the action comes to you. You added four bets to your projection for the original bettor, and five bets for the raiser. Now it's your turn, and you need to project a final pot size in order to make a decision whether or not to call this raise.

As per the instructions I've given you, you first glance around the table and take note of how many players have yet to act, and add two small bets for each undecided player. But what do you do about the fellow that placed the original bet, and then got raised? Shouldn't you add another small bet to the pot on the assumption that he will call?

I wouldn't bother. Here are several reasons why:

1) One bet is not going to make a big difference. It may be best to err on the side of caution, by ignoring it.

2) You don't *know* that he's going to call. It's rather presumptuous to add a full bet on the assumption that he will call.

3) The original bettor hasn't really shown much strength, yet. The raiser has said, with his raise, 'I have a better hand than you do; you'd be wise to step

> back and let me have this pot.' Therefore, the original bettor is more likely than usual to give up the pot on the turn. Perhaps you have already given him too much credit, projecting three more small bets over the turn and river for him!

It's best, and simplest, to forget for now that the original bettor owes more money to the pot. You've got enough to worry about. Don't assume any more money from him, or from anybody else that called a single bet before the betting was raised. Just go about your business as if there is nothing to consider.

Of course, when the action comes back around to the original bettor, you definitely want to count how much more he puts into the pot!

Now, what if the pot is *re-raised?* Same thing. Don't automatically expect the original bettors to call. Go about your business of counting bets as they go into the pot.

On the turn, you should do the same thing. As you 'tweak' your projected pot size, adding and subtracting to your count for bets and folds, don't try to take into account the bettors that are raised by assuming that they will put more money in the pot. Remember, though, that on the turn, any extra bets that go into the pot count double, because the bets are twice as large. Thus, for example, you may have a bet (add one), a raise (add three...one for the decision to play, and two more for the raise), a call (add three more) and a fold (subtract three) before it's your turn to act.

One thing we haven't discussed much is what to do if you think you may be raised after you call. My suggestion, earlier, was that you should ignore this possibility when projecting the size of the pot, but that you should make sure you have extra outs in case you are raised. In other words, if there are several players to act behind you, it's not wise to go ahead and call with a borderline hand. A raise will easily turn a borderline call into a bad one.

Just how many 'extra outs' should you have, in order to call a bet out of position? Well, it depends! If you have enough outs to bet for value, then it's not an issue at all, right? You don't care how much money goes into the pot; you're golden, because you have enough outs to cover any number of raises! It just doesn't matter how much your opponents want to raise if you have enough outs.

But if you *don't* have enough outs to value-bet, it begins to matter. So let's make up a scenario. Let's suppose you are in a situation where you need four outs to call a single bet. Suppose you have five outs. Suppose further that if you had eight outs, you would have enough to bet for value. In other words, if you had exactly eight outs, you wouldn't care whether the pot is raised or not. It just wouldn't matter.

Should you call? It all depends upon how likely it is that you will be raised after you call. You clearly don't have enough outs to call two bets. Logic dictates that if you need four outs to call one bet, you need eight outs to call two bets. But if the pot is raised after you call, doesn't that mean that the projected pot size will grow even more?

Yes, it does! So how many outs *do* you need to call? Clearly, you need somewhere between four and eight outs. Four outs is enough if you know you won't be raised. Eight outs is enough to call any number of raises. Five outs is 25% of the way from four to eight, so it makes sense to think you should call only if there is a 25% chance, or less, that you'll be raised.

It's not quite that simple, because a raise means a bigger pot, which means you need fewer outs. Recall, however, our decision, when projecting the pot size, to not factor in money owed to the pot by any original bettors that are raised. For the same reasons, it's best to ignore these complications when deciding whether or not to call, given the chance of being raised. Besides, the pot may be *re-raised!* For this reason alone, it's best to err on the side of caution.

WARNING: If you think you may be raised after you call, then you need more outs! This number will be somewhere between the number you need to call a single bet, and the number you would need to bet for value.

Thus, if you fear a raise after you call, here is how you should decide whether or not you have sufficient outs to cover the chance of being raised:

- You need to know how many outs you need to call a single bet, and you need to know how many outs are needed to raise for value. These two charts...the one just presented to you, and the *bet odds* chart from Concept 8, really need to be memorised.
- How many outs do you actually have, and how close is it to the number of outs needed to raise for value? In the example we used, five outs was 25% of the way between four and eight outs.
- What is your estimation of the chance of being raised? If it exceeds this percentage, it's a risky call.

How To Play Marginal Decisions

Sometimes you follow all the rules, do all the counting, and finally come to the conclusion that it's a very close call. That's not uncommon. Poker is a game of marginal decisions, and the best players win by making the most of these marginal decisions.

One important issue, as you've learned, is your position at the table. Especially your position relative to the probable bettor. This consideration alone should greatly help you decide between folding and calling with a marginal hand, especially on the turn. Poor position means you may be raised after you call. Good position means you can often swindle extra bets from your opponents after you make your hand.

Ace Speaks...

A final thought on position

People always talk about the button being the best position – which in itself of course is true. But if you are on the button and call a pre-flop raise by the cut-off, then your position is suddenly not so great anymore. After the flop, it is quite likely you will be put in the middle. After all, if everybody checks to the raiser and he bets, you will have many players behind you who are still to act: players who may well have been bagging their hands, waiting for the pre-flop raiser to bet so that they can check-raise – and thereby bagging you as well.

As we have seen in this book, you will often win more and lose less with your draws when you have good position relative to the (probable) bettor, an conversely you will often be in unprofitable situations or tough decisions when your relative position is bad. You should already take this potential problem into consideration in your initial starting hand selection, to avoid problematic and potentially costly situations after the flop. This means that if you are facing a situation where the cut-off raises, then you should often re-raise or fold on the button with all your decent and/or playable holdings – depending of course on the exact situation, your read on the other players and your own table image.

Here are some additional things to think about, if you're still undecided. Maybe one or more of these can help tilt the scales one way or the other for you.

Reasons To Call:

- If you decide to play on the flop, you *might* get a free card on the turn. Especially against fewer players. You never know. If you do get a free ride, it's like doubling your outs.
- I could never fault you for playing *all* your close decisions, if it helps loosen up the game, or if putting a beat on someone may put him on tilt.

Reasons To Fold:

- The house rake and dealer tokes (tips) definitely add up, especially in lower limits, where you can be giving away over 10% of your winnings. It can definitely turn a good call into a bad one.
- Surprises can go both ways...you can misread your opponent, and find out he was bluffing with a worse draw than your own. Or, he could have made a straight on the river that you didn't even see coming. But one thing is for sure: The 'negative' surprises cost you a lot more when you're wrong than the 'positive' surprises win for you!

Online Play

Online games are a little different than brick and mortar games. The pace is quicker. The pot size is calculated for you. The expressions on your opponents' faces are hidden from you, and you can't see the chips in their hands to tell if they're about to call or not.

Consequently, the instructions I've given you for estimating the final pot size may be more cumbersome than they are worth, when playing online.

To counteract this, I've developed a simple computer program that you can run in the corner of your screen that serves as a quick outs calculator. At any time, you can simply type in the size of the pot, and click a couple buttons: One to tell the calculator how many players have already called before it's your turn to act, and another to tell the calculator how many players have yet to act. The program will tell you exactly how many outs you need in order to call up to four bets, by using the formulas presented in this book.

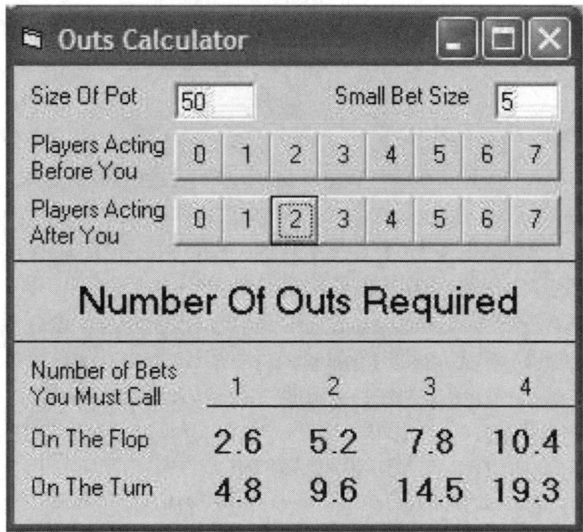

If you do play online regularly, I guarantee you'll find this helpful. You might only use the calculator one time out of 20 hands, but when you do need the information, it's just seconds away.

If you'd like to use this program, please contact Dew Mason at dataforc@eoni.com.

Chapter Nine

Playing For Keeps

If you've made it this far, and understood the material, you've earned your degree from U of C... the University of Chasing. It's time, now, to begin your graduate studies. Here's the basic idea: Sometimes, you should chase from out in front! That is, sometimes you take a passive situation and play it aggressively instead.

NOTE: Limit hold'em is a game of racing and chasing. If the action is checked all the way around the table before the river, someone has made a mistake.

When playing the flop and turn, there are two possibilities to consider: Either you think you have the best hand, or you think you don't. The approach you take to playing the hand differs radically, depending upon your assumption of whether or not you are winning the hand.

Limit hold'em is a game of racing and chasing. The racers want to make the table pay to outdraw them, and the chasers typically want to follow along as cheaply as possible, trying to get lucky. Because of this delicate balance, we can usually say that if the action is checked around the table before the river, someone has made a mistake. Someone should have bet.

If you think you may have the best hand, then when it comes

your turn to bet, you must choose between three options: Push, pull or pray.

Suppose you hold A♦-J♥ under the gun, and decide to limp in. Some experts would criticise this play, saying that A♦-J♥ is a borderline hand under the gun. They may be right in tough games, but I don't agree in low-limit or most middle-limit games. A♦-J♥ is a respectable hand, which will often be called by hands like K♥-J♠, Q♥-J♠, J♠-10♣ or A♠-10♣. Against any of these holdings, you could make a nice profit.

Other experts say that if you decide to play A♦-J♥ in this position, you should raise, representing a better hand. You want K-Q or maybe A-Q to fold. There is something to this strategy, except that the only hands that will play with you, then, are hands that can beat you. Why chase away the late limpers that you may have dominated?

Poker is a complex game, and each player tends to develop their own style and preferences, which may, in fact, be correct for their game.

But I digress. You have A♦-J♥ under the gun for one bet, and the flop comes 2♣-4-♠J♦. What do you do? You push. Like Hell. You give strong notice to anyone holding a king or queen that this pot belongs to you, and they'll have to pay through the nose to try to outdraw you.

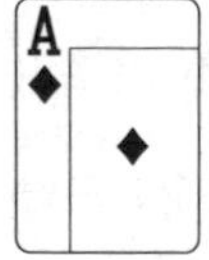

You're probably best, and should push to preserve your lead

Suppose the flop comes 2♣-4♠-A♥, instead. You pair the ace, instead of the jack. Now what? You probably still have the best hand, but who knows? So you pray. You glance around the table wondering if anybody really *would* play A♠-10♣ against an early bettor, or if anyone would just limp in holding A♠-K♣ or A♠-Q♣. You should bet out, but if called or raised, you slow down, and call the rest of the way, hoping the raiser is playing a small suited ace and just testing the waters. If you have a good read on your opponent, you might even fold.

What if your hand is A♦-K♥ when the flop comes 2♣-4♠-A♥? Now, instead of pushing or praying, you play confidently, pulling other players into the pot. There are no reasonable hands that can beat you, unless there are enough callers pre-flop for someone to think it profitable to sneak in with a hand like 4♥-4♦ or A♣-4♣. So you try to figure out a way to keep as many of those A-x hands in the pot as you can, maybe even checking the flop and hoping someone else will lead for you, setting up a check-raise on the turn or river.

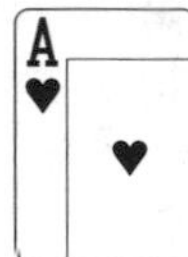

You're probably best, but you can pull

The difference between flopping top pair with A♦-K♥ and flopping top pair (another jack) with A♦-J♥ is that you no longer have to worry about overcards. You *welcome* someone playing K♣-Q♥ and hope they get a piece of the turn so they'll stay in the hand. You can safely pull instead of push.

So, there you have 500 words or less on how to play the flop and turn if you think you have the best hand. Push, pull, or pray. That's all you're going to read here on this topic, since there are a half-dozen or more good books out there about poker strategy.

Our focus in this book, of course, is what to do if you *don't* think you have the best hand on the flop or turn. Again, you have three choices, this time somewhat different: You fold, call or bluff.

WARNING: When the flop misses you, fold. Your ego might survive the ridicule if you're a constant chaser, but your bankroll won't survive.

Most of the time, you fold. Your ego might survive the ridicule if you're a constant chaser, but your bankroll won't survive. Chasing depletes a bankroll like nothing else. Everybody likes players who will keep paying and hoping for that miracle card all the way to the river. Occasionally, you get outdrawn by a chaser—well, more than occasionally, it'll happen once every night at least, if you're in a good game—but then, who is to say how much the chasers have already contributed to your pocketbook with ill-advised calls before they finally hit? You'll never know, because most times, you never see their losing hands. But surely you're way ahead of the game against the chasers.

My favourite saying is, 'No River, No Fish'. It becomes my mantra when I've taken a bad beat or two. The fish are the reason poker is good to me... and the possibility of getting lucky is the reason lesser players continue to play. Once in a while, they book a winning session. That's good. If they lost all the time, poker would die a quick death. The calling station is our Friend, with a capital F. No River, No Fish.

Yes, most of the time, you fold, if you think you have the worst hand. You're not a chaser. But first, you look carefully at the board, count your outs, and decide whether or not the pot is laying you proper odds to stay in the hand.

Once the decision to continue on is made, do you call or bluff? Let's be totally honest: A raise at this point, when you think you have the worst of it, is usually a bluff. Sugar-coat it by calling it a semi-bluff if you want. That's fine. Yes, I know, if you have a really great draw (such as a flush draw on the flop, with position, and several opponents already buying into the pot) then it becomes a raise for value. We've talked about semi-bluffs and raises for value, and how profitable these plays are, and we'll talk more about them soon, but this fact remains: You are putting extra money into the pot knowing you probably currently have the worst hand. What you really want is for everybody to fold. *And there's nothing wrong with that!* Controlled aggression finds its reward.

What I want to do, now, is revisit the most common drawing hands and discuss how each should be played. Fold, call, or bluff? But remember, there is seldom a single correct answer. We have spent a lot of time laying the foundation for profitable decision-making by discussing, primarily, when it's time to give up on a hand. This is not to say that you shouldn't mix up your play for the purpose of deception, or that you shouldn't override logic with a good read on an opponent, or even that you shouldn't occasionally play bad-odds hands to loosen up the game. But by now, you should *know* how much it costs you when you deviate from the 'correct' strategy. You need to be able to use that knowledge to make decisions about when you can afford to add some aggression or misdirection. A good bluff contains both.

A Word About Bluffing On The River

OK, maybe several words. It's an important topic.

Most of the focus of this book has been on deciding whether or not you belong in a hand. Clearly, bluffing is the complete antithesis of this focus. When you bluff on the river, you're putting money into the pot *knowing* it's a 'bad bet'. Nevertheless, I'd like to bring this topic up now, before we revisit the types of drawing hands, because it emphasises a point that I hope hasn't slipped by the wayside: You *must* be aware of how your playing style appears to your opponents. A predictable, unimaginative style frightens no one, and fails miserably against observant opponents. And nothing is more predictable and unimaginative than the way some players handle drawing hands, calling along meekly until they either hit or miss. I love to play against such players.

So here we go. The topic is bluffing. Sometimes your draws don't get there. Really. Believe it or not, sometimes you get to the river, and you don't have squat. In fact, more often than not, you *do* get there with nothing to show.

Should you bluff on the river? If the pot odds are laying you, say, 5:1, then you should bluff if there's a better than one in six chance of winning. The question is, will your opponents all fold more often then one time out of six?

A busted draw is, of course, the quintessential bluffing hand. You don't bluff when you have a mediocre hand and might win anyway. That's a check-and-call situation. You bluff when you know you mostly likely can't win *without* bluffing. Like when you have a busted draw.

Let me throw a completely meaningless statistic at you. In a recent study, about one in five of the players who played to the river then folded on the river. That would surely seem to entice you to bluff a lot! Lots of pots offer better than 4:1 odds to try a bluff on the river. But as I say, it's a meaningless statistic. People call on the river when they think they have a chance to win, and fold when they are pretty certain they're beat. I bring this statistic up for one reason only:

If bluffing into one opponent will work only 20% of the time, then bluffing into two opponents will work only 4% of the time.[10] Three opponents? Forget it. The pot odds aren't going to be there. Well, then, does that mean you should *never bluff?*

No. What could possibly be more predictable than a player who never bluffs?

Obviously, bluffing is more than an art form. It's also a science.

So, how often should you bluff? Clearly, if you bluff at every opportunity, your smarter opponents will begin calling or raising you every time. But if you don't bluff often enough, you're giving away money. A lot more money than you think!

You don't like to bluff, you say? It's like throwing money away? Let me ask you this. How would you like your opponents to play? Do you want them to play predictably, betting good hands and checking bad hands? Yep. Of course you do. It's comforting to know exactly what they have. Now, how do they want *you* to play?

You got it. They absolutely *hate* that you are able to bluff. That, alone, ought to be reason enough to do it.

---

[10]This is not quite true in practice, of course. The more players who remain on the river, the more easily each individual player can be bluffed.

Optimal Bluffing Strategy

Let's talk about how often you should bluff when you're heads-up against just one opponent on the river.

TIP: Game theory suggests that you should bluff at such a frequency that the pot odds your opponent is receiving by calling are identical to the odds against you being on a bluff.

Mathematically, your optimal bluffing strategy is to bluff in such a way that the pot odds your opponent is receiving by calling are identical to the odds against you bluffing. That's what a study of game theory will tell you. In other words, if the pot is four times the size of your bluff bet, then it is laying your opponent 5:1 odds to make a call after you have put in your bet, and thus, you should bluff one time out of six.

If you bluff more often than that, your opponent comes out ahead by always calling on the river. If you bluff less often, he wins by always folding when it looks to him like he's beat.

This may be a little confusing. Does this mean you should bluff only once out of every six reasonable bluffing situations, to keep your opponent on his toes? No! You should bluff far more often than that! It means that one out of your six river bets, in hands that look like reasonable bluffing opportunities with a pot this size, should be bluffs.

Let me give you a little quiz. Let's say the board has carried two spades since the flop. Therefore, it's reasonable that you could be on a draw, and it's reasonable that if you bet on the end, you could be bluffing. The river card has just been played (it wasn't a third spade), and you are first to act against one opponent. Let's also say the pot contains about four large bets (four times the amount of a river bet).

In similar circumstances, let's assume:

- ♠ You should win your share: Half the time. So let's say five times out of ten, you have the probable winning hand and bet for value.

- Three times out of ten, you check and call, or check and fold, with a reasonable hand.
- The other two times out of ten, you wind up with a busted draw at the river, and nothing to show for it.

Let's say this is one of those times you get there with nothing. What percentage of the time should you bluff?

Optimal bluffing strategy says you want one out of six of those river bets to be bluffs. So for every five times you bet with a winning hand, you should bluff one time with a losing hand. One of those two busted draws should turn into a bluff. In other words, half of your bluffing opportunities. Half of the *reasonable* bluffing opportunities.

That's a lot of bluffing! A *lot* of bluffing, for those of us that quiver in fear at the thought getting caught with our hand in the cookie jar. But do you see the fallacy here? The fallacy is, *how do you know when a reasonable bluffing opportunity has come along?* This is by no means an easy question to answer. It requires a certain amount of hand-reading skill and deception on your part. For example, if you're bluffing into the nuts, you have absolutely *zero* chance of success. Likewise, if you have given away the weakness of your hand by the way you played, and then you try to make up for it with an ill-prepared bluff on the river, you have about the same chance of success. And if you have a reasonable chance of having the best hand, such that you're likely to call if your opponent bets into you, then bluffing is silly; you might as well let *him* waste a bet trying to bluff *you*. But among reasonable bluffing opportunities...where you have represented strength and your opponent must truly make a decision about whether or not he is beaten...the 'optimal bluffing strategy' presented here is correct.

By the way, a little corollary to this statement is that you should be *calling* bets on the river that have a reasonable chance of being a bluff, with your mediocre hands, at exactly the opposite rate...in this example, five times out of six for a pot laying 5:1 odds. Did it sound like a lot, when I suggested earlier, that half the time you get to the river with the board showing a bluffing situation, you'll have a hand good enough to bet for value? Five times out of ten? You're only going to *have* the better hand about half the time! And I'm here telling you that you should bet *all* your probable winners for value? *Am I insane? Have I never heard of getting raised?*

TIP: If the board shows a reasonable chance that you are on a bluff, you should be much more inclined to bet for value with your good hands.

Remember that if the board shows a 'reasonable chance that you are on a bluff', and you have shown that you are capable of bluffing, your opponent is correct in nearly always calling your bets with mediocre hands. You should be much more inclined to bet for value if the board displays a reasonable bluffing opportunity. Besides, the more often you bet for value, the more often you can get away with bluff attempts.

Getting back to the topic, in order to bluff with the correct frequency you must be able to determine when a reasonable bluffing opportunity exists, meaning your opponent must have you beaten, but not so badly that the hand you are representing by bluffing is also beaten. Then you must bluff a reasonable percentage of the time in only those situations. No wonder bluffing is so difficult to master! No wonder some players come to the conclusion that you cannot bluff in limit poker!

But don't lose heart. The art of bluffing goes much further than simply using game theory to come up with a reasonable bluffing percentage. Bluffing is about deception. What you *really* want is to make your bluffs believable enough that your opponent will fold more often than he should. If the pot is laying you 5:1 odds, and you think you have played the hand in such a way that you think a bet will now cause your opponent to fold a better hand more often than one time in six, *then you should bluff without a second thought!* Of course, if you think he will call you more often than five times out of six, then you shouldn't bluff at all!

Remember that there are only two ways for a drawing hand to win:

1) You can make your draw and show down the best hand, or

2) You can bluff the better hands out of the pot.

Since you're going to miss your draw more often than you fill it, doesn't it make sense that you should play the hand in a manner that increases your odds of winning by method two? Doesn't it make sense that you should give yourself every opportunity to bluff?

Guilty until proven innocent

Let me give you a little advice. When you have a good drawing hand, something that will carry you to the river, *plan on missing your draw.* From the moment you find yourself on a draw, look around the table and decide whether or not the players in the hand are 'bluffable'. Then begin projecting yourself into your opponents' heads, thinking about how your hand appears to them. If it's reasonable, play the hand in such a manner that you can represent something other than a draw. Play the entire hand as if you are setting up a bluff on the river.

This doesn't mean you should carry my advice to extremes, throwing good money after bad. It means you are watching very carefully for signs of weakness on the part of your opponents, and it means a carefully placed semi-bluff, if the bet odds are not too bad, can pay dividends. You want to show strength *before* you get to the river, so that your river bluff will carry some clout.

One way to do this is to make up a different hand in your mind, and try to play consistently (according to the way *you* would likely play that imaginary hand) throughout the flop and turn. Deception is what poker is all about. But do so only when the cost isn't too great, according to the odds you are receiving. In other words, don't raise with a four-outer on the turn, simply to throw your opponents off track.

TIP: Unfortunately, draws usually don't materialise. The real goal of a drawing hand is to decide whether a bluff will work, and then to set up a bluff on the river.

Make hitting your draw your secondary goal. It's wonderful when it happens, but *anybody* can win the pot by showing down the best hand. The challenge of a drawing hand is to win when you're *not* best. *Consider the real goal of a drawing hand to be that of deciding whether a bluff will work, and then setting up your bluff on the river.* Or, at least, as you are playing the hand, pay close attention to whether or not the way you *have* played the hand could possibly represent strength. Don't simply throw money away on the river when you miss your draw; know before you get there whether or not it's possible that your hand even looks like a winner to the other players.

By the time you get to the river, then, you should then have a good idea of whether or not a bluff might work:

Conditions for a successful river bluff

- ♠ Are only the 'bluffable' players still in the hand?
- ♠ Have you played your hand in a manner that you might appear to have something other than a busted draw?
- ♠ Have your opponents given any hint of weakness?
- ♠ Do the pot odds exceed your estimated chance of success?

There is a lot that can be written about the art of setting up a bluff, and a lot that can be written about bluffing opportunities that just surface as the community cards are being dealt. I won't go into that here. Frankly, it's a worthy book topic on its own. Suffice it to say that you should think of a good drawing hand as a bluffing opportunity until proven otherwise... hopefully, by getting lucky and hitting one of your outs. Guilty until proven innocent.

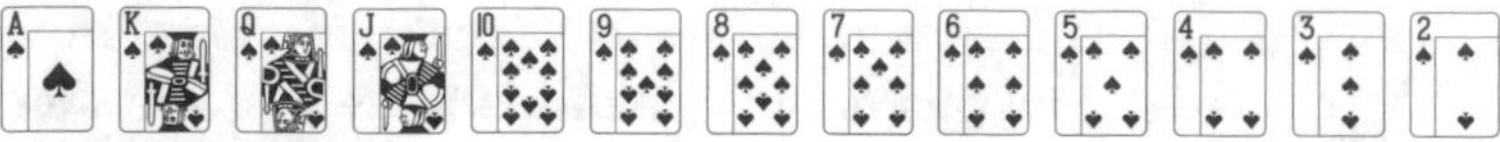

Ace Speaks...

Catching someone with a busted hand on the river

When I had not been playing poker for very long, possibly a bit less than three years or so, the following hand came up. I had K♦-2♦ on the button and with three callers in front of me, I made a very loose call. When the flop came T-9-3 with two diamonds and everybody checked to me, I bet – most of all to maybe get a free card on the turn in case I did not improve. Despite the many players in the hand and the fairly coordinated board, with two cards in the playing zone, I got just one caller. When an offsuit four came on the turn and this player checked, I skipped my original intention of taking the free card. I decided to bet, hoping to win the pot there and then on a semi-bluff, and also to pave the way for a credible river bluff if I was called. I had a fairly tight image back then (I still do), and I hoped that by betting I could get my opponent to fold a hand like A-3, J-9 or something similar. But my opponent called, and when another four came on the river for a final board T-9-3-4-4, he surprised me by suddenly betting – truly a bet out of nowhere. After all, what could this player have that he was suddenly so proud of?

It needs to be said that in the two or three years I had played with this person, I had *never* seen him bluff on the river – not once, not ever. Yet, in this case I knew for a fact that he had a busted draw. With him being in early position and having called my bets on both the flop and the turn, I was almost 100% certain he had specifically queen-jack. So, I called him instantly, confident that my king-high would be good enough for the pot. He said: 'You got me. I am bluffing,' and I prided myself for making this good and courageous call – courageous because, as I said, I had *never* seen this player make a river bluff before. He again said: 'I have nothing,' and then instead of folding his hand, opened his cards to show what he had: a king-jack offsuit, for a king with a better kicker. 'That is good,' I said, and then quietly folded my hand.

I guess I have never felt as silly in my life, calling on the river with a mere king high against someone who never bluffs – and then losing to my kicker! But at least I *had* been correct in reading him for a bluff. A good player would never have played his hand the way this person did, just check-calling all the way, to then suddenly spring to life on the river when the board did not seem to have changed much. A good player would probably have taken the initiative at some stage in the hand, in order to *pave the way* for a bluff on the end. But hey, a good player would also have raised on the river with my king-deuce rather than called if indeed he had labelled his opponent for being on a bluff, just to be certain that he would not get beat by a 'better nothing' – as happened to me.

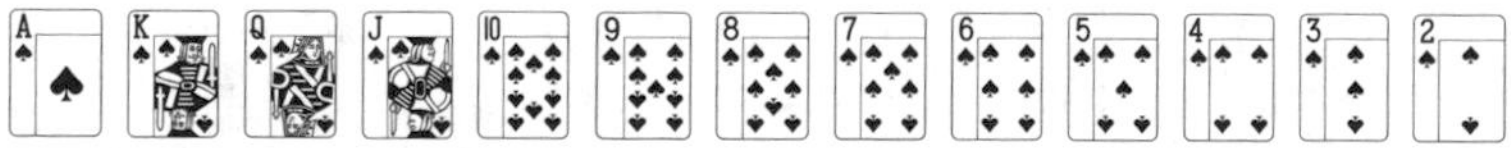

TIP: Some players can be bluffed, and some cannot. It's as simple as that. You *must* learn which players are bluffable.

I would like to reiterate one important comment on this topic. It is *extremely* important to watch every hand, trying to learn how your opponents play on the river. Some can be bluffed and some cannot; it's as simple as that. Bluffing doesn't work well in most low-limit games, so why bother with deception throughout the hand, only to look around when you get to the river and realise that carrying out the bluff isn't worth it? There are a lot of players, especially in those no-fold-'em games, that will simply never lay it down on the river. *Never*. Find them, and save yourself some money. Others can only be bluffed if there's a third player in the pot. They'll call automatically without a second thought, if you're heads-up. Like it's a matter of duty.

Finally, don't be easily discouraged when your carefully prepared bluff gets called. Typically, your river bluffs only need to work one time out of six, or so, to show a profit. One successful bluff per night is enough to make it worthwhile. But you don't even *need* to show a profit on your bluffs to make them worthwhile! All it takes is one bluff to sow a little doubt, making sure that the next time you *do* have a hand, you get called. It only takes one of these 'extra' calls, and your bluff attempt is paid for. Now, let's revisit some of those drawing hands.

Exceptional Draws

Remember, an 'exceptional draw' is a good straight or flush draw, with added benefits. Or perhaps a hand that includes *both* a flush and a straight draw. These are hands with ten or more outs. Such hands can be played with confidence, because even though you haven't got a bird in the hand, you *know* you're going to win more than your share of these pots.

A ten-out hand on the flop will win 38% of the time, assuming you are taking it to the river. It's enough to say that you are a favourite against just two opponents. An 11-out hand wins 42% of the time. Twelve outs, 45%. When you get up to 14 or more outs, like an open-ended straight flush draw, you're a favourite against even a single opponent!

These hands are winners, pure and simple. There is no way *possible* anyone can raise you off one of these hands, unless the betting indicates that it's time for you to re-evaluate the strength of your hand: Maybe you don't have as many outs as you thought you had. But unless you decide you have fewer outs than it appears, you can't be raised off your hand.

The one rule to remember about exceptional draws is this: *You never fold!*

Do you see why? Let's say you have two opponents. Here, the *bet odds* mean you're going to be betting and raising all you can on the flop. You want to build that pot all you can, because you're going to win more often than one time out of three. The bet odds favour you against two opponents.

Then, by the time the turn comes around, there is always enough money in the pot to make calling worthwhile.

Here, I'll prove it to you. I dare you to find a worse table action chart than the one below.

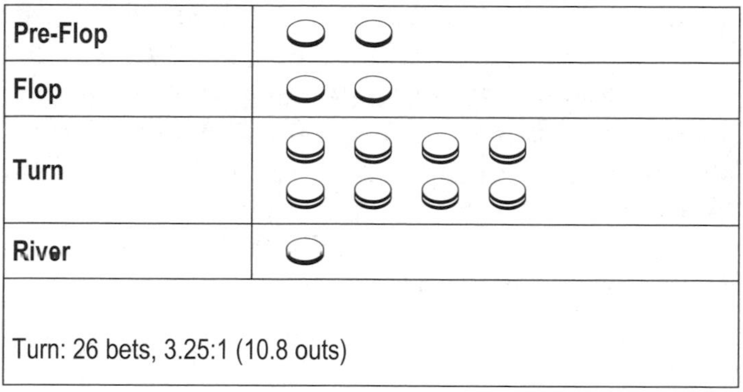

Pre-Flop	
Flop	
Turn	
River	
Turn: 26 bets, 3.25:1 (10.8 outs)	

You have two pre-flop opponents, you flop some sort of exceptional draw, and get one bet from each opponent on the flop. Then on the turn, the betting goes crazy, and you have to pay four large bets. On the river, you hit one of your outs and get just one caller. What could have possibly gone worse? But it's *still* playable for 10.8 outs on the turn. Even if you *knew* you were getting taken for a ride and would have to put four bets in on the turn before it was all over, you'd probably continue with a 10-outer, hoping for more reward on the river.

Playing exceptional draws means one thing: Get as much money into the pot as you can, by whatever means, on the flop. Then stay and pray.

The only real question about how to play these draws is, do you want to push or do you want to pull? Do you want to push players out, increasing your chances of winning the pot, or do you want to pull players in by slowplaying, so that when you hit one of your myriad of outs, you'll win more money?

Generally, you want to play it aggressively on the flop. If this means pushing, so be it. Here's why:

Reasons to play aggressively on the flop

- Hey, the absolute *worst* thing you can do is check around on the flop. You've got a wonderful hand, and the bet odds justify putting money in the pot. Put it in there.
- Should you just call along then, if somebody bets the pot for you? Well, remember, if you don't raise, you can't get re-raised. And you *want* to be re-raised, unless you're against just a single opponent.
- On the turn, if there are just a couple opponents, the bet odds imply that it's time to slow down (unless you're running a bluff). It takes 16 outs to bet for value against two opponents on the turn, and 12 outs to bet for value against three opponents. Therefore, aggressive play on the flop may buy a needed free card on the turn.
- Finally, pushing some opponents out might be a good thing. It depends upon what your 'added benefits' are. If you can push people off your overcards, that's a good thing!

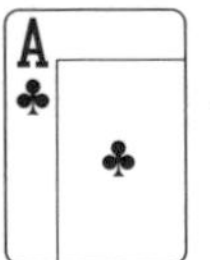

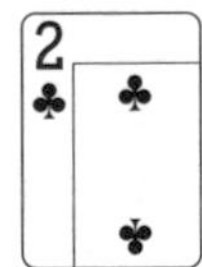

Pull: your overcards are great

Let me ask you this. If you have A♣-K♣ and flop 2♣-4♣-8♠, do you want to push or pull? You may want to pull. You probably have 15 outs here, since this is an unlikely hand for somebody to show down anything better than you, if you turn an ace or a king. What would they have to have to dominate you? A-8? 8-8? You worry too much. If there are *lots* of players in the pot, you might want to push, because you don't want somebody sucking out with a runner-runner two-pair, or something like that. But for the most part, you *want* the guys with A-J and K-Q to stay in there, because if you hit your ace or king, it'll probably make you even *more* money. With this hand, a legitimate case can be made for either calling to entice additional bets, or for raising for value. Consider a variation play, calling along some of the time, and raising for value some of the time, depending upon the circumstances and your position.

But what if you have Q♣-J♣ and flop 2♣-4♣-8♠? Then, by golly, you're pushing for all you're worth. Get those A-J and K-Q hands out of there, to give you some more outs.

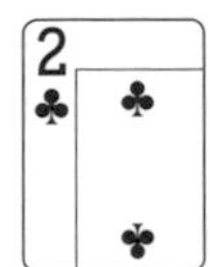
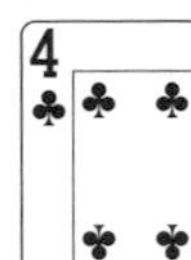

Push: try to buy outs for your overcards

I'll tell you a little secret. The very people you push out of the pot are the ones who wouldn't have called a bet from you on the turn, anyway, after you make your flush. Wanna know why? *Because you can't make a flush with a queen or a jack, the very two cards you are trying to protect.* So the chance of somebody with a hand like A-J or K-Q making his hand at the same time you make a flush is not very likely. And if they don't make their hands, they're not going to hang around on the turn, if they're not willing to pay two bets on the flop. Go ahead and chase 'em out now.

TIP: Sometimes you must play exceptional draws by closing your eyes and pretending you hold the nuts.

Perhaps the most exciting thing about playing exceptional draws is that you're almost always getting proper bet odds to put as much money in the pot as you can on the flop; then, on the turn, the odds are still so good that it costs very little to keep jamming the pot. This sets up a logical bluff on the river.

Seriously. Sometimes the best way to play these hands is to close your eyes and pretend you're holding the nuts. Just know when it's time to back down; you can't carry anything to extremes at the poker table.

Drawing To A Full House

I saw something atrocious in my poker game a couple of weeks ago. I saw someone fold on the turn, after he had flopped a set.

He was clearly beat by a flush. So he folded.

The board was something like A♥-J♥-6♥-5♥, four hearts, he held a pair of jacks in his hand, and he was facing two opponents. There was a bet and a raise, and he folded.

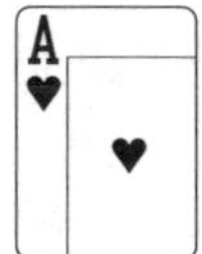

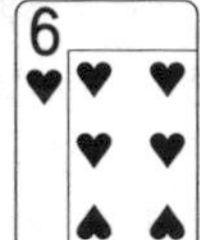

Is it time to fold?

The atrocious part is that he showed me the jacks and congratulated himself for saving his money. Sigh.

Just for the record, a set has ten outs to improve to a full house or quads. That makes it an *exceptional* draw, by our standards. And what does that mean? *You never fold.* There is no way anyone should be able to push you off a ten-out hand; not if it's truly worth ten outs. The odds are there to call all the way. The only way this fellow should have folded his hand is if he knew someone was playing pocket rockets...two aces.

Good Draws

We classified all unenhanced flush draws, and open-ended straight draws that are not too heavily compromised, as 'good draws'. Such draws have between seven and nine outs, and almost always warrant playing to the river.

Once in a while, a complex draw will have enough benefits to add up to seven or more outs. If so, it belongs in the category of 'good draws' as well.

Let's now go over some of the fine details of these draws, and how they should be played.

Flush Draws Revisited

A flush draw is usually a very strong hand. If you flop a flush draw, you are a 2:1 dog to make your flush by the river (that means, you'll miss two times for every time you make it). If you miss on the turn, you're still only a 4:1 dog to make the flush.

Because of these favourable odds, you rarely have to bother counting outs when you're on a flush draw. You're usually in for the ride, all the way to the river.

There is, however, one unique aspect to playing flush draws. In contrast to, say, a made straight, a made flush just isn't very well concealed. When that third flush card hits the table...filling your hand...the betting is likely to skid to a halt[11]. If the players at your table are particularly passive, they'll check and call the rest of the way, at best.

Therefore, the time to make money on a flush is on the flop...*before* you make your hand! 2:1 odds means, of course, that if you have three or more opponents, you want to get as much money into the pot as you can on the flop. With two players and 2:1 odds, you'll win exactly your fair share, so it's a discretionary call; you basically play the hand in whatever manner you think will best disguise your draw without losing

[11]I have seen games where the exact opposite is true: When the third flush card appears on the table, some players panic and begin throwing everything but the kitchen sink in to the pot, trying to scare out anyone holding a card of that suit. Of course, it never works. Anybody with a high card in that suit just throws the raises back at them in a semi-bluff. If your opponents are of this disposition, clearly it doesn't *matter* that flushes aren't well concealed. It even works to your benefit.

any callers. If you're in late position, you usually try to buy a free card with a semi-bluff. And against one player, you usually check and call, or, if you have position and you are fairly certain it will work, you try a semi-bluff.

Nevertheless, there are a couple occasions when it's correct to give up on a flush draw. Let's take a look at a table action chart where a flush draw becomes a bad bet.

Pre-Flop	
Flop	
Turn	
River	
Committed: 13/16 bets, 5.33:1 (7.3 outs)	

In this example, you limp in with 10♠-9♠ in middle position, and only the small blind calls. The big blind gets a free play. Now, the flop comes 6♠-6♣-Q♠. You have flopped a flush draw, but it's compromised, because your draw is small (fourth-nut draw) and because the board is paired with strong betting on the flop. No overcards in your hand. Thus your flush draw is worth about seven outs. The small blind bets out, and the big blind raises. You call, and the small blind re-raises. Everyone calls three bets.

Recall that, when the flop costs as much or more than the turn to play, we don't show flop and turn odds separately, and instead display committed odds.

What do these fellows have? A reasonable read would be to put the small blind on a six, if he is the type to mix up his play by occasionally betting strongly with trips, or the type to never slowplay a two-suited flop, and to put the big blind on the queen with a reasonable kicker...assuming that his flop raise was intended to chase you out if you hold an ace or king.

The turn now brings the 3♥. The small blind bets, the big blind folds, perhaps afraid he'll be trapped in the middle of a betting war, and you call. On the river, your flush appears with the 2♠. The small blind bets out, you raise, and he folds.

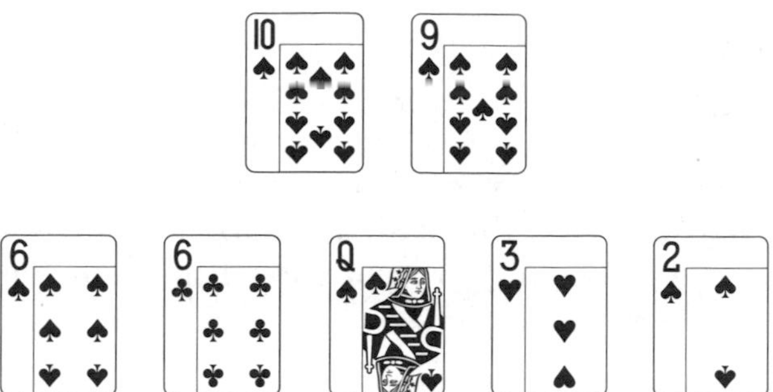

It's a happy ending chart, assuming you won, but the end result didn't justify the call; you needed 7.3 outs to play on the flop, but had only seven.

Did you make a mistake? Heck, no! You had a seriously compromised flush draw, everything possible went wrong when you played it, and you *still* had almost enough outs:

- The re-raise on the flop cost you three bets instead of just two.
- The big blind folded on the turn, leaving you with just one opponent.
- When you raised on the river, the small blind folded as well.

If anything at all had gone *right* with this hand, it would have justified your call. Here's what it looks like if there is no flop re-raise:

Pre-Flop	◯ ◯
Flop	◯ ◯
Turn	◯
River	◯
Committed: 11/13 bets, 6:1 (6.5 outs)	

With just two bets on the flop, you need only 6.6 outs to call, and it's an easy decision because your hand is worth about seven outs.

If there are two opponents, it's pretty tough to find a circumstance when you shouldn't call on the flop. Let's look at what happens if you have only one opponent. Here's a common enough scenario.

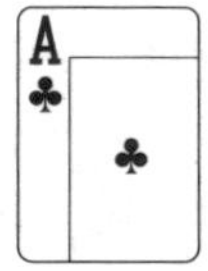

Should you call a bet against a single opponent?

You limp in from the cut-off position with J♥-9♥. The small blind folds, and the big blind checks. Now the flop comes A♣-K♥-7♥. He bets out, sensing weakness, and you call. When the turn brings a 3♠, and he bets out again. What do you do?

Here's a reasonable table action chart for this scenario. It assumes that if you hit your flush card on the river, and he paid you off when you bet...or folded when you raised.

Pre-Flop	+½
Flop	
Turn	
River	
Flop: 7.5 bets, 7.5:1 (5.5 outs) Turn: 8.5 bets, 4.25:1 (8.8 outs)	

You need 8.8 outs to call on the turn, and you have a nine-out hand. Calling that turn bet is damn close to being a mistake, but you have barely enough. So it turns out you should always call against a single opponent, both on the flop and again on the turn, unless you have some reason to think your flush won't be enough even if you hit it...or some reason to think that another flush card on the table will scare your opponent away on the river.

Frankly, I think you blew it. There was no reason to make calling on the turn such a scary proposition. If you raise pre-flop, trying to steal the blinds, you might take the pot immediately without a fight. And if you *don't* take the pot, at least you now have a little better pot odds to play to the river. The additional money in the pot from the pre-flop action makes calling on the turn correct.

But that's water under the bridge. So you screwed up pre-flop. Big deal. Maybe your mistake is reversible. Is there another way you could have continued on the flop, to give you better odds? Let's consider the infamous semi-bluff raise as a possible ploy to gain a free river card. You try raising on the flop. Suppose it works to perfection, so that your raise gets called and you don't have to put in a bet on the turn. We still assume you'll win one final bet after making our flush...either on the turn or on the river. Now your table action chart looks like this:

Pre-Flop	+½
Flop	
Turn	
River	
Flop: 6.5 bets, 3.25:1 (5.5 outs) Turn: free card	

Yes! Yes! You have nine outs and need less than six! You've found a way to stay in the hand until the river, giving yourself twice the chances to win! The semi-bluff raise is the Play of the Gods! The question is, will it really work? Will the big blind passively call your raise and then check to you on the turn?

A *failed* semi-bluff raise means he re-raises on the flop, and then bets out on the turn. You wind up paying two more flop bets than if you meekly called along. Of course, you're going to win about one third of those encounters; that's how often your flush will fill with two cards to come. Do the math: A failed semi-bluff costs you .33 bets.

Well, how much does the semi-bluff gain for you if it succeeds?

Ways in which a semi-bluff raise can succeed

1) Your opponent might fold immediately. The raise wins 2½ bets.

2) You might hit your flush card on the turn, so that you can bet again instead of taking a free card. This wins an extra small bet and occurs 19% of the time you opponent doesn't fold.

3) If you miss on both the turn and the river (a 65% chance), you have saved one small bet by paying two flop bets instead of one flop and one turn bet.

4) Of course, if you hit your flush on the river, you didn't save a small bet... you lost it. This occurs 16% of the time.

Add them up. Shall we say there is a 10% chance that your opponent will fold to your raise? If so, then a little mathematics shows that the semi-bluff raise wins 0.86 bets.

TIP: A semi-bluff raise has so many ways to win, that it's almost sure to be the correct play!

A failed semi-bluff costs 0.33 of a bet, and a successful semi-bluff wins 0.86 bets. This means that if your semi-bluff works more than one quarter of the time, it's profitable. I guarantee it'll work more often than that!

Another point is that aggressive play may put your opponent in the frame of mind that will bring rewards later, on other hands. For one thing, it'll serve notice that you're not about to be bluffed. Well-timed aggression brings success, either immediately or down the road. *Controlled aggression finds its reward.*

What have we learned by this example? We've learned that, even against a single opponent, unless everything possible goes wrong, it's worth continuing on the flop and turn with your flush draw.

Let's talk now about the turn. Will the turn ever be too expensive to continue?

Not likely. You'd have to be trapped for multiple raises. It's certainly OK to pay two turn bets with a flush draw, as can be seen in the following chart:

Pre-Flop	
Flop	
Turn	
River	
Turn: 16 bets, 4:1 (9.2 outs)	

If the turn costs two bets, you can surely expect to win at least one more bet on the river if you make your hand. You need 9.2 outs. If you can win *two* river bets, you need only 7.7 outs. But most flush draws on the turn are worth a full nine outs. You should be fine playing any flush on the turn, unless it looks like you're about to be trapped for multiple raises.

Summarising Flush Draws

There is seldom a time when you should lay down a flush draw. There are only two circumstances when you might even consider it, and both times it's on the turn, not the flop:

1) When you have a flush draw against only one opponent, and you do not have position, you *might* want to give it up on the turn. If there were no raises, and no bets on the flop, or if you think you won't get a call on the river if the third flush card comes, it's not giving the proper odds.

2) If there was very little betting before the turn, and now it looks like you might be stuck in the middle of a raising war.

Other than these two situations, you'll pretty much always play your flush draw through to the river. If the board gets *really* scary, such as K♠-K♦-8♠-8♥ or A♠-A♦-7♠-A♥, then you're done, of course. Time to move on. But usually, you're in it all the way.

With three or more callers, you'll want to get as much money into the pot as you can on the flop. But the bottom line is, if you have a draw as good as a flush draw, you should be playing it aggressively on the flop almost *regardless* of the circumstances or the number of opponents. Don't be afraid to bet and raise. It's mathematically sound, and aggression is usually rewarded.

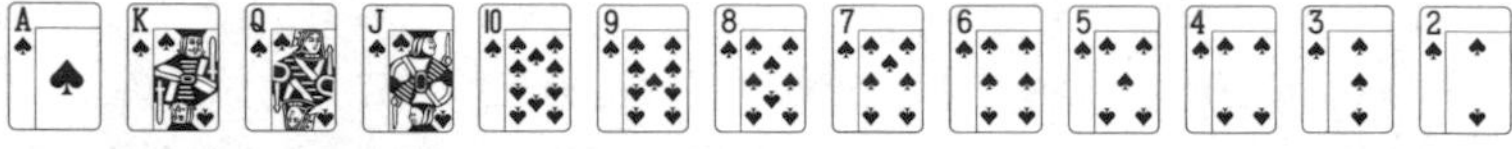

Ace Speaks...

One word of caution

While flush draws are almost always very strong holdings, it *is* important to keep an open eye for potential trouble. Let's say that you hold 5♥-4♥ and then the flop comes Q-7-2 with two hearts. Now, if many players seem interested in this hand, it may be time to think: What could they possibly hold?

With no possible draws whatsoever except for a flush draw, this is a situation where raising for value is probably *not* recommended – for the simple reason that there's the distinct possibility that your hand does not have any value. Of course, this does not mean you should *thus* fold any small flush draw when there is just the possibility of someone holding a higher one. What it does mean is that in multi-way pots you should not *automatically* start raising for value with your flush draw, but rather take into account the possibility that you could be drawing to a hand that will lose even if you make it. Even though the chances of flush over flush are small, you should be able to recognise those times when your draw may not have as much value as would seem at first glance – and you should be able to adjust your decisions accordingly.

Straight Draws Revisited

Some pros say they prefer straight draws to flush draws. Personally, I think anyone who does is a no-limit player. But straight draws *do* have one important advantage over flush draws.

It's true that a flush draw usually has more outs. It's true that a straight is more easily beaten. It's true that a straight can be counterfeited, so that you share a pot you should have won.

But the one advantage that a straight has going for it, is that it's often well-concealed. At least, more so than a flush. This means that you can usually extract more bets from your opponents after you make your straight. Most people will not believe that you made the straight until you turn it over and rake in the pot.

This deception has more serious ramifications than is first apparent. An extra double-sized bet, from a check-raise or an extra caller on the river, can quite easily turn an otherwise ill-advised play into a profitable one.

Let me give you an example. You hold 10♣-8♣ and limp in from middle position (probably a mistake; that's not the point). The player on your left raises, and the button calls. The blinds fold, you call, and the flop comes 6♥-9♦-A♠. Two other players. The player on your left bets, and the button calls again. You have an inside straight draw, and you're getting the right odds to call on the flop. Now, the turn brings a K♣. The player on your left bets, and the button calls.

What do you do? You have four outs... four sevens... all of them to the nuts. Did I hear you say call? With only two opponents? On the *turn?* Didn't your daddy ever tell you not to draw to an inside straight?

Here's the question: If you draw a seven on the river to make your straight, can you check-raise? If you can, and you're 100% certain that you will be called in both places (which, of course, you never are), then you're actually correct to take off another card!

Pre-Flop	⊖ ⊖ +½
Flop	○ ○
Turn	○ ○
River	⊖ ⊖
Flop: 21.5 bets, 21.5:1 (2.2 outs) Turn: 22.5 bets, 11.25:1 (3.8 outs)	

Unbelievable, isn't it? Two players, four outs, and you're calling on the turn... and getting correct odds to do so! You only need 3.8 outs.

Have you ever taken a bad beat? Of course you have. Some players seem to take a bad beat every other hand. Why is this? It's because they don't realise how many times they're beaten by a hand that didn't really have such bad implied odds to call! They think that every time they're outdrawn, they've taken a beat. How many times have you criticised another player, or at least inwardly seethed, when he won the pot by calling to an inside straight, or some other such 'obviously' bad play? You might be surprised how often these 'amateur' players are getting the proper odds for their action! The next time you suffer a bad beat, take a closer look. You may have just been outplayed.

NOTE: Some players seem to take a bad beat every other hand. Why is this? It's because they don't understand implied odds; what looks like a bad beat may be a carefully calculated risk.

Note: The above really was probably an ill-advised call on the turn. You need to be pretty sure you'll be paid four river bets if you hit your card. If you get only three bets on the river, you're not getting proper odds to call (you'd need 4.1 outs). But this does illustrate my point. No one would ever believe you should call with an inside straight draw on the turn and only two other players, but it's a lot closer decision that you might think...all because straight draws are often so well concealed that you can usually extract extra bets when you do get there.

Let's talk about two-way straights now: Hands that can be valued at seven or more outs.

The problem with straight draws, as I've already alluded, is that they are not all created equal. You must carefully analyse your draw to see if it has some hidden problems...some cards that help you, but might also help someone else.

Such hands play similar to a flush draw, because they have so many outs. But there is one thing I want to caution you about. Straight draws, by their very nature, can drop drastically in value between the flop and the turn. That fourth table card can open up *so* many possibilities for your straight to be beaten. Let me give you some examples.

Example 1

You hold 10♦-9♦ and the flop comes 8♥-J♣-A♥.

    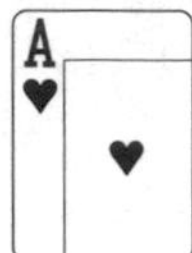

This is a decent hand, worth six outs against three opponents. Six, no more, because there are two hearts on the board and because you are not drawing to the nut straight (K-10 is a common playing hand, which casts a shadow on the value of your 10-9). Now the 2♥ appears on the turn. Even if nobody has a flush yet, you're not happy. Anybody holding a high heart is going to be there to the river, and you can quickly drop another out from your count, because the 7♥ or Q♥ is likely to give the pot to someone else. Even if it doesn't lose the pot, it'll probably freeze up the betting on the river so that you won't make any more money.

Example 2

You hold 10♦-9♦ again, with the same the same flop: 8♥-J♣-A♥. Now the 10♠ makes an appearance. Hey, you made a pair! Are you happy? Not a chance. All it did was counterfeit your own straight. If a seven comes, you split the pot with anybody that holds a nine. If a queen comes, you lose to anybody holding a king.

TIP: A flush draw can improve; a straight draw can't. Pairing up on the turn with a flush draw is cool; pairing up with a straight draw just counterfeits one of your cards.

Example 3

How about a king on the turn? Nope. Now a queen loses to any ten. Maybe another eight, jack or ace? Gag. A two through six? Half of them are ok; we don't want any hearts or clubs.

Here's the thing. Unless you hold overcards, *the turn card will probably either straighten you up or make you worse.* We're talking here about an open-ended straight, which already uses both of your cards. It isn't going to get any rosier unless you make your straight.

When you're drawing to a flush, pairing up on the turn is cool; it gives you more outs. When you're drawing to a straight, pairing up usually just counterfeits one of your cards. If you then hit the *other* hole card on the river, you're staring at two pair that is worth little more than the deed in your pocket to that beachfront property in New Mexico.

It isn't hard to see why. If you hold 10-9, and the board comes 8-J-A-10-9, you suddenly lose to any seven or queen.

Not so with a flush draw. It can improve by pairing; a straight draw can't. Not easily, anyway.

And another thing: Because straight draws generally mean the board is more coordinated, it's more likely that someone already has two pair. People like to play connected cards. That means more of a chance of a full house if the board pairs.

Do you still like straight draws better than flush draws?

TIP: Because even the best straights can be easily counterfeited and out-drawn, you should try to raise the four-out hands out of the pot on the flop.

Therefore... you should play your straight draws a little differently than flush draws. Bet them out on the flop, and raise into a field of three or more opponents, if you can. Make those four-outers fold, or they're going to jump up and bite you, on the river, by making a better straight than you do, or by taking away half of your pot when you get counterfeited.

Let's go back to our example again. You hold 10♦-9♦, and the flop comes 8♥-J♣-A♥. You don't want anybody with a nine, ten, queen, or king to stick around. Hey, isn't that well over half the decent starting hands in the deck? You *especially* don't want a hand like K♥-10♣ hanging around; what a nightmare that would be for you! *But if you don't raise the pot, these guys are all getting proper odds to stick around and try to ruin your draw.*

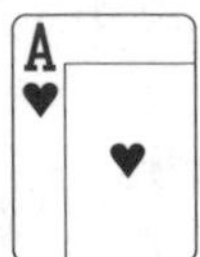

A raise may drive away other four-out straights

I realise that it's counterintuitive to raise with a straight draw on the flop. You don't want to pay very much for your chance to draw, and you want to pull more people in for the times when you do get lucky. But a straight draw is precarious; there are too many things that can go wrong on the turn and river if you don't chase away the four-out hands.

Take comfort in this: With a hand worth around seven or eight outs, you are getting proper odds to bet for value against three opponents. Three callers of your raise, and you're golden. If you get only *two* callers, the additional bet only cost you a small margin of that bet[12], and *probably,* your raise just bought you a free card on the turn.

This chase-'em-away strategy isn't a universal rule, but more often than not, it's the proper way to play. I encourage you to look closely at your straight draws, and decide for yourself whether the four-outers should be chased away or not.

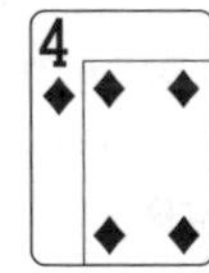

Will a raise accomplish anything?

Take a look at this hand: You have 5♥-4♦ in the big blind, and the flop comes 2♣-3♦-10♠ Chase 'em away? Of course not! The

[12]A seven-out hand is a 2.6:1 dog to win when you value bet; against two opponents, a value bet takes home two bets when it wins, so it has an expectation of -.6 for every 3.6 hands; Therefore, it costs you 17% of each bet you put into the pot (.6 ÷ 3.6).

only four-out hands than can hurt you are 6-4 and 6-5, and it should be clear that these are not the most probable starting hands for people to play. Maybe somebody has A-4s or A-5s, so that they can steal half of your pot if you're counterfeited, but it isn't likely. And don't you *dare* chase away anybody that is playing overcards! If an ace comes, you're going to get good action from anybody holding something like A-Q.

What's different in this example, then? The difference is, you're drawing on the top end of the straight, the board isn't coordinated (except on your end of the spectrum), and your cards are light years away from the type of cards most players hold. It's a very atypical situation.

Complex Draws

These are fun hands to play. There's just something very satisfying about searching hard for additional outs, finding enough to continue play, and then hitting one of those obscure possibilities to rake in the pot. Your opponent berates you for chasing with a sub-standard hand, often verbally throwing meaningless and incorrect pot odds at you, but you smile smugly at the knowledge that you outplayed him; that you were, indeed, mathematically justified in making the call. He misinterprets your smug smile to mean, 'Ha, ha, sucker, look at all these chips I'm stackin' up over here,' and goes on tilt, chasing your good hands the rest of the night.

Remember that a complex draw has five or six outs. In general, you can usually play a complex draw on the flop for a single bet, but you must consider carefully whether the pot is large enough to pay a double bet on the flop or whether you can continue past the turn. There is, however, a big difference between a five-out hand and a six-out hand. A five-out hand needs 8.4 small bets in projected winnings to call a single flop bet; a six-out hand needs 6.8 small bets. Double that, of course, if calling a raise on the flop or a single turn bet.

This leads us to the following basic guidelines for playing complex draws:

- Generally, you can play against two or more opponents on the flop for a single bet, and three or four opponents for a double bet.
- On the turn, you typically need three opponents to continue for a single bet and four or five to continue for a double bet.
- If the betting was raised on a prior round, you need one fewer player. Calling on the flop becomes automatic for a single bet, and requires only two or three players to call a raise. On the turn, you need only two opponents to call a single bet if there was a raise on a prior round, and three or four opponents to call a double bet.

Let me put this in a table for you:

To call one bet on the flop:	2 opponents
To call a raise on the flop:	3 or 4 opponents
To call one bet on the turn:	3 opponents
To call a raise on the turn:	4 or 5 opponents
If a prior betting round has been raised:	1 fewer opponent

Let me remind you that these are *very general guidelines* for *borderline decisions*. You really should be carefully projecting a final pot size before making any decision that comes close to these guidelines, and you must carefully consider the chance of being raised after you make your call. In other words, *please* don't think I am giving you licence to always call with a five-out hand on the turn if there are three other people in the pot. I'm telling you that it *might* be a reasonable call if you have carefully counted the pot and you are pretty sure you won't be raised.

The magic numbers, again, are 8.4 and 6.8. A five-out hand needs to win 8.4 times as much as you invest to be profitable; a six-out hand only needs to win 6.8 times as much as you invest.

Let's look now in detail at one of the most common situations that arise in hold'em.

Overcards Revisited

Everybody knows you're supposed to play big cards in hold'em. Hands like A-K and A-Q are premium hands. On average, they win a lot of money.

Take a look at the following chart, which shows the average winnings for each hand in $10-$20 hold'em. These averages were derived using Wilson Turbo Hold'em.

Hand	Unsuited	Suited
A-K	$24.26	$34.08
A-Q	$11.94	$22.76
A-J	$5.10	$14.90
A-10	$0.50	$9.14
K-Q	$1.20	$10.42

These are the only unsuited, unpaired hands that show an average profit (several more show a profit if suited: K-J, K-10, Q-J, Q-10 and J-10 are all profitable)[13]. Now, obviously, I'm not trying to tell you to play only these hands, nor am I trying to tell you to always play these hands. Each situation is different, especially in regards to table position, but the conclusion is inescapable: Just like basketball is a big man's game, so hold'em is a big card's game. The rebounds in basketball fall into the hands of the big men. The close pots in hold'em fall into the hands with big cards. And the bigger, the better.

[13]If you're curious, the same study shows that playing pairs down to 77 shows an overall profit. But please take this with a grain of salt; *there is no such thing as a starting hands chart that gives correct play in all circumstances.* Especially one that does not take table position into consideration! Hold'em is simply too complex a game for such precise rules.

Size does matter. Big cards make the money.

What is so frustrating in hold'em is that even when you hold great cards, the flop usually misses you. 80% of your starting hands will be big, unpaired cards, and 63% of the time you play these hands the flop will completely miss you.[14]

What do you do? Fold and wait patiently for the next opportunity? Drive the pot in frustration, hoping the flop missed everyone else as well?

TIP: The most important rule for playing overcards is not to play too predictably.

Neither one. *The most important rule I can give you for playing overcards is not to play predictably.* Most of the time, if you have multiple opponents and there was no pre-flop raise, you should quietly fold. Most of the time, if there *was* a pre-flop raise, you should call or even raise on the flop. But not all of the time! You *must* mix up your play, even if you lose a little money playing your overcards, knowing that the odds are slightly against you.

You should, of course, pick your spots to play. Remember that you have up to six outs, but generally, against multiple players, two overcards should be valued at between two and four *modified* outs. That means playing overcards is like playing a long-shot draw. This is no coincidence. It *is* a long-shot draw! You *must* look carefully for added value when playing overcards. I am consciously including this topic in the section on Complex Draws because I want you to look hard for added benefits, hopefully bringing your out-count up to five, before playing overcards. In particular, give consideration to the following items:

---

[14]You may have heard it said that 2/3 of the time when you play a hold'em hand, the flop misses you. That is not quite true. Any unpaired hand will pair up about 1/3 of the time, but there certainly other ways to hit the flop. AKo is one of the hardest hands to hit, but it will flop a straight, an inside straight draw, a flush draw (with three of the same suit on the board), or a pair 37% of the time. All of these flops are certainly worth playing.

1) How likely is it that you have the best hand? Remember, the flop misses the other players 63% of the time as well. That means that it misses two opponents 40% of the time; three opponents 25% of the time; four opponents 16% of the time. *You may have the best hand!* You almost always want to add in that extra one out for the possibility of holding the best hand, if you are playing strong overcards such as A-K or A-Q.

2) Is the board paired? *Generally, a low pair on the board favours your overcards!* Not only does a pair on the board make it more likely that the flop missed all of the other players too, but it also means that you can beat most two-pair hands by pairing one of your big cards. Your two pair will be bigger than their two pair. Suppose you're playing A♣-K♠ against Q♦-J♦, and the flop comes 7♠-7♦-J♥. You decide to take a chance and call with your overcards. Now you spike an ace or a king on the turn. Even if your opponent hits a queen on the river, you still win with a bigger two pair.

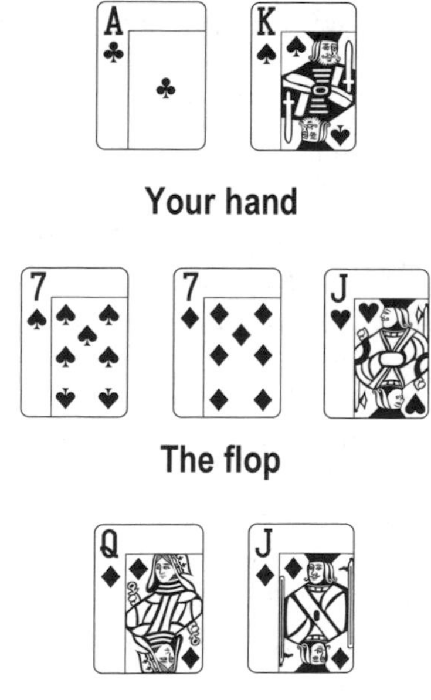

Your hand

The flop

Your opponent's hand

3) Is the board two-suited? And if so, do you have a card of that suit? A double-suited flop is to your disadvantage *unless you hold a card of that suit;* then, it may actually be to your advantage! For one thing, you gain an extra out for the runner-runner flush possibility if you hold an ace or a king in that suit. But also, you *encourage* the flush draws to stay in the pot if half of your outs are safe, and the pot is small. In other words, if you hold A♦-K♠ and the flop comes 2♦-4♣-7♦, it is generally good for you if someone is holding two diamonds; only one of your six outs helps him (the K♦), so if you hit any other ace or king on the turn, the extra bet that you can extract from him on the turn is usually worth more than the chance of being outdrawn on the river!

TIP: A low pair on the board favours your overcards. Surprisingly, a two-suited or coordinated board may also favour your overcards!

Remember, if you hold one of his diamonds, he has only eight outs instead of nine; he is thus a 4.5:1 dog to make his flush on the river, he has paid both a flop and a turn bet for the chance to draw on the river, and if he *does* hit a diamond on the river and comes out betting, you can probably quietly fold your pair.

4) Is the board coordinated? If there are straight draws out there, it may again be to your benefit if it's clear that the cards you hold in your hand won't help somebody's straight. If you hold A♣-K♠ and the flop comes 6♥-9♣-10♠, then by the same logic as #3, it may be to your benefit to encourage the straight draws to continue...*especially* the inside straights...since an ace or a king does not help them. An open-ended straight draw is the same 4.5:1 dog to hit on the river if you're holding two cards that do not help him; so, again, because he'll have to pay both a flop and a turn bet for the river draw, then it is to

your benefit to keep him around unless the pot is large (by 'large', I mean at least $3 \times 4\frac{1}{2} = 13\frac{1}{2}$ small bets, since he is a 4.5:1 dog and he has had to pay three small bets over the flop and turn for the chance to draw on the river).

5) Just as a flush draw lives in fear of a full house, and a straight draw lives in fear of a flush, so a draw to overcards lives in fear of...well, just about everything! In particular, you now have to worry about two pair. This is in contradiction to the point I just made, because the boards that most likely support two pair are coordinated boards. A flop of 6-9-10 is more likely to be a problem than a flop of 2-7-10, because 10-9 is a much more common hand than 10-7. So, does a straight draw on the board help or hurt you? There is no way to know except by learning to read your opponents.

6) How commonly do your opponents play A-x hands? Something like A-6? If the flop comes all small cards, and several loose players are in the game, then it may be better call with overcards like K-Q than A-K. The reason is that it is less likely that hitting one of your overcards will make two pair for another player.

So, pick your spots, look closely to see if your outs are compromised, and then close your eyes and take a chance now and then with nothing but overcards on the flop.

Playing Ace-King Before The Flop: One More Author's Opinion

Before I leave the topic of overcards, I'd like to discuss, briefly, whether or not you should raise pre-flop with Ace-King. A-K is, after all, a drawing hand. You usually have to improve to win. I used to see everyone raise with this hand without giving it a second thought; but lately, it has become much more fashionable to limp in for a single bet. There are several valid arguments for limping:

Arguments for limping pre-flop with A-K

- When you raise pre-flop, many of your opponents will automatically put you on A-K. It's the natural thing to think. Whether or not this is a good assumption or not on their part, you've been tagged, and you won't be fooling anybody with your hand.
- One reason for raising in early position is to limit the playing field by chasing out the players after you. A raise in late position does not accomplish this; everyone that limped in ahead of you is likely to put in one more bet. Why not save yourself a bet if it doesn't thin the field anyway?
- Of course, do you really want to chase away hands like A-Q, A-J and K-Q? You have them dominated. If you do hit your ace or king, you definitely want these guys to play with you. Therefore, some experts say just the opposite: If you are going to raise with A-K, do it only from *late* position after you've already trapped the lesser hands.
- You're going to miss on the flop 63% of the time. Why invest the extra money, which has the effect of tying you to the pot? Isn't it better to pay just one bet pre-flop so that you can quietly fold when the flop misses you?
- Is your hand suited? A-Ks is definitely a moneymaker; maybe you shouldn't chase away players who might otherwise pay off your flush?

These are logical reasons. Some are better than others. But on the other side of the coin, there is one powerful, inescapable reason for raising:

- You probably have the best hand. The best hand is most likely to win. Get your money in the pot *now,* and lots of it. A-K doesn't come along often enough to waste it winning just a few pennies.

It's my opinion that this single reason for raising outweighs all of the reasons for limping. I believe in 'bet odds'; if you have the best hand, you should raise for value. I also believe, of course, that you cannot play predictably; sometimes you should raise, and sometimes you should call. But the majority of the time, raising is correct.

Let's look at the general gist behind the idea of limping. The idea is, if you miss on the flop...and most of the time you'll miss on the flop...you've only wasted one bet. But if you raise, and *then* miss, you're probably going to be tempted to pay at least one more bet on the flop to try to make good, and you're A-K has cost you at least *three* bets with nothing to show for it.

Is there something to this logic?

No. It's faulty logic from the very beginning. Recall concept three: *Each Betting Round Generally Stands On Its Own.* Before the flop, if you are favoured to win, you should get lots of money in the pot, pure and simple. After the flop, you have now information and a brand-new decision to make, and what you did pre-flop is irrelevant. After the flop, you must decide whether you might be holding the best hand, you must count the outs and figure the implied odds, and you must make a logical choice based on the *new* circumstances.

Yes, it *does* often cost you three bets to play A-K if you raise pre-flop. This is because, with a pre-flop raise, there is generally enough money in the pot to see one more card on the turn. Is this somehow a bad thing that your pre-flop raise has given you the correct implied odds to continue play on the flop? Of course not.

Yes, it *does* tend to give away your hand when you raise pre-flop and the meekly call when no aces or kings come on the flop. Frankly, it's your job to play deceptively enough that your opponents can't come to such conclusions that easily.

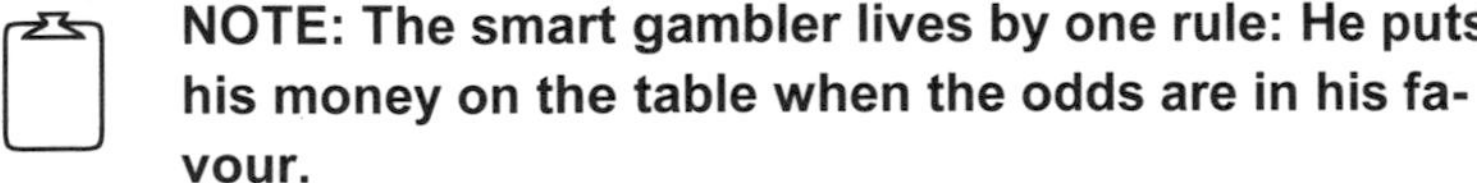

NOTE: The smart gambler lives by one rule: He puts his money on the table when the odds are in his favour.

Yes, it *does* hurt when you lose several bets with a great hand like A-K. So here is my token mention of avoiding tilt in this book: *If you can't play the game professionally, get out of the cardroom.* That may sound harsh, but damn it, if you're serious about poker, you sure as heck better be able to handle a few disappointments. It *is* a gambling game, regardless of what anyone says...and the smart gambler lives by one rule: He puts his money on the table when the odds are in his favour.

My recommendation is, from any position on the table, whether suited or not, raise about 2/3 of the time you hold A-K. Maybe a little more, depending upon how aggressively you play other starting hands.

Long-Shot Draws

Remember that we defined a long-shot draw as any draw that has four or fewer modified outs.

Playing a pair in your hand, when the flop comes with overcards, is a long shot to improve. A *really* long shot. Playing with nothing but overcards is also usually a long shot. Actually, it's almost *always* a long shot, if you're pretty sure you're chasing. Playing with an inside straight is perhaps the most clear-cut long-shot draw of all: Most times you have exactly four outs, which is right on the cusp of what we are defining as 'long shot'.

It's a little harder to give instructions for playing a long shot than it is for a complex draw. This is because a two-out hand is *far* worse than a four-out hand, but both are 'long shots'. Let me start the conversation by again providing a general guideline for how many players you need to have around you, and then let's revisit two common long shots: The underpair and the inside straight.

Again, these are very general guidelines, providing borderline circumstances.

As you have already learned, it's quite common for you to be correct in calling a single flop bet with a long shot. It's even possible that calling a raise, or a single turn bet, is correct.

Situation	You have 2 outs	You have 3 outs	You have 4 outs
To call one bet on the flop:	7 opponents	5 opponents	3 opponents
To call a raise on the flop:	(not profitable)	7 opponents	5 opponents
To call one bet on the turn:	(not profitable)	6 opponents	4 opponents
To call a raise on the turn:	(not profitable)	(not profitable)	(not profitable)
If a prior round has been raised:	2 fewer opponents	2 fewer opponents	1 fewer opponent

I must caution you, however, that it's very hard to provide an accurate chart like the one above. There are simply too many things to consider: chief among these things is how many players have dropped out of the action leaving behind dead money, and how many bets you think you can extract from the type of players who remain. I must recommend that you *always* count the pot and try to project how big it will get when you are on a long-shot draw.

Here are your magic numbers for long-shot draws: A two-out hand needs to be able to win 22½ bets to call a single flop bet; a three-out hand needs to be able to win 14.7 bets; and a four-out hand needs to be able to win 10.8 bets.

Have you memorised that little chart, yet, at the end of chapter eight? The one that tells you how many bets you need in the projected pot size to play each out count? You really should.

Enough preaching; let's move on.

Underpairs Revisited

A small pair in your hand that doesn't hit on the flop is the classic example of a two-out hand. Pocket pairs can be both the strongest and the weakest hands in poker. If you hit a set on the flop, you have a well-concealed hand, and you can make a lot of money. If you miss...well, it's pretty hard to improve your hand. Usually, the only thing you can look forward to is getting really lucky and hitting another card of the same rank for three-of-a-kind.

It's definitely a long shot! Nevertheless, sometimes it's worth it, if you can see the turn for a single bet on the flop.

The reason is because if you *do* make a set on the turn, you can sometimes extract a lot of money on the turn or river. This is because nobody expects you to turn over a set. It's well hidden.

Let's look at an example. You're in the cut-off seat (next to the button) and you limp in with 7♥-7♦ after four other callers. The small blind calls, the big blind checks, and the flop comes 9♠-9♣-10♣. You look around and see six other players. How many outs do you have? Really only two; against this many players, it's unlikely that you have the best hand. Maybe the action on the flop comes check, bet, call, fold, call, call, and it's your turn. This is a great flop to take a chance on the turn! Why? Because the board is coordinated enough to keep several players in the game, and you're in a position to make a *lot* of money if you hit another seven on the turn.

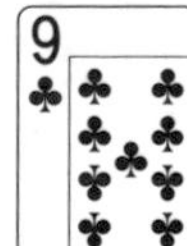

Your dream card, of course, is the seven of clubs. You want somebody to make a flush, so they'll pay you off. But the 7♠ isn't bad, either; it puts straight possibilities on the board, it gives backdoor flush chances, and it doesn't scare away anybody holding overcards. All of the old flush and straight draws are still there, keeping hands like Q♦-J♠ and A♣-8♣ in the game. Limit poker is about calculated risk. It's the very nature of the coordinated board, here, that is appealing: A seven will help lots of other hands at the same time it helps you...but hopefully, it helps you more than them!

Let's say you called, and the small blind folded. That's too bad that he folded; that hurts your pot odds. But let's say you now hit either of your outs (the 7♠ or the 7♣) on the turn. Both cards look innocuous enough. Nobody will think you just made a full house. The betting is likely to continue something like bet, call, fold, call, and back to you. You can now raise because of your position, and probably get two bets on the turn! Maybe you lose one of the two remaining players on the river, but here is what the table action chart looks like:

Pre-Flop	
Flop	
Turn	
River	
Flop: 21 bets, 21:1 (2.1 outs)	

To summarise, you held an extremely long-shot draw, and took a chance. When the small blind folded, you were disappointed, but you still received almost even-up odds for your long shot, because of your position on the hand. Because you were able to raise after you hit your magic card on the turn.

Note that there was no raise pre-flop, no aggressive river-betting, *and still there was enough money in the pot to tempt you!* If there's a raise pre-flop, you can usually take off a card if only three other players stay with you on the flop...assuming you have the position to raise or check-raise on the turn or river.

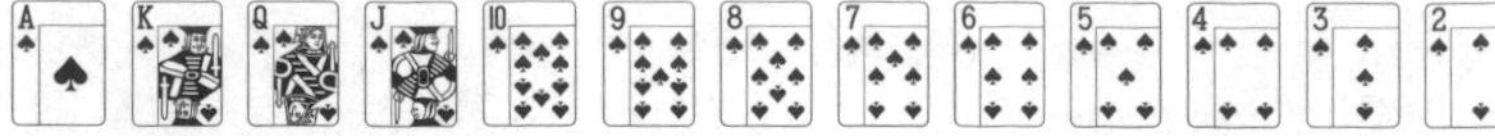

Ace Speaks...

One play – Two views

It is obvious that the play that Dew has recommended here (calling on the flop with the pocket sevens in what seemed to be a rather obvious fold), is profitable only in a situation with good implied odds – because with just 10 or 11 small bets in the pot, the current pot odds are obviously not good enough for calling with a mere two-outer. But having all the action in front of you, the big blind being the possible bettor, and lots of possible callers or even raisers in the middle, it will be entirely possible to scoop a big pot if you snatch that seven on the turn, thereby overcoming the short odds you have been taking on the flop. For instance, if a seven falls and someone has J-8 or 8-6 for a straight, or even better if the seven of clubs falls and one or two players have made big flushes, then you may actually be able to win a *very* big pot. This is in addition to someone who may have been slowplaying with a third nine, and who will obviously give you lots of action with his unimproved three nines if you make your small full on the turn.

Having said that, I still think that this is a fold. Even though you can close the betting on the flop with a call for just one small bet, I think one important factor is missing in Dew's analysis, and it is this one: Your implied odds are nowhere as good as they seem to be. Yes, if you hit your seven on the turn and indeed your full house turns out to the best hand, then you will of course win a big or even a very big pot. But this is not all there is to it. It is equally important to note that if you hit your seven and your sevens full is *not* good, that you will almost certainly lose a pot that is not merely big, but that may well be *huge*. If you make your full when one of the players has a bigger one, then you will almost certainly lose *at least* four big bets – provided that you play your hand in the correct, aggressive manner. And in my view, it is not just *remotely* possible that someone may have or make a bigger hand than you – with so many players in the hand, it is actually quite probable. When there is a bet and three callers on a flop like this, alarm bells should go ringing in your head. Why? Well, because lots of players will see a flop like this as an excellent slowplaying opportunity when they have flopped a monster. They want people to be drawing dead to flushes, straights and small pairs, so that once their opponents have hit their hands, they cannot get away from them anymore – despite the fact that they are dead in the water.

And with a flop like 9♠-9♣-10♣, there are lots of dangers for your two red sevens. After all, no less than six players have seen the flop for one bet, and it is clear that not all of these six players are in there with big cards. In fact, it is very likely that people are in there with hands like 9-7 suited, or 10-9, either suited or not. And against both these likely holdings you are drawing completely dead! Other possibilities that are a bit more remote are 10-10 and 9-9, remote because people might have raised with them – even though lots of players *will* limp with them, especially at the lower limits. And finally, it is important to note that one of the sevens that would give you a full, the seven of clubs, creates no less than two straight flush possibilities, and both of them are hands that most players in this game would judge as playable – the J-8 and 8-6 suited in clubs.

So, am I saying that you are probably up against a full house or better, and that thus you should fold? No, that's not what I am saying at all. What I am saying is that if you hit your seven and you win, that you will win a pot of probably around 30 small bets. And if you are lucky enough to have someone make a straight or flush in the process, or if someone with a third nine has made the mistake to go for the slowplay on the flop, well then the final pot may well be around 40 small bets. But if you are up against either a higher full, quads or a straight flush, then the pot will probably grow to about 50 small bets and maybe even more – and you won't get any of that!

In my view, calling on the flop with the sevens would probably have been correct with about 16 or 17 small bets in the pot already, not with the 10 or 11 bets right now. In Dew's example hand, you would knowingly be taking much the worst of it because of these perceived implied odds. Yet it is entirely possible that a) one of your opponents may have been trapping, and b) that you are drawing to a hand that may not win even if you make it. This relatively small chance to lose a massive pot takes away too much edge away from the (yes, much bigger) chance that you will probably win the pot if you hit your seven. This means that there are not just (positive) implied odds here for you – there is also the danger of *losing* a whole bunch of bets if you make the hand that you are drawing to. Now, because of all this, I would say that calling this one bet on the flop with 10 or 11 small bets in the pot is probably wrong even if you would be 85% certain that when you hit the seven on the turn it would give you the winning hand at the showdown. And the way I see it, there are just too many – for your opponents – playable hands that could have hit gold with this flop. Now if you add to this the possibility that even if no one is full yet, at least someone must have the third nine (that could easily redraw against you on the river), then I don't think the winning chances would be anywhere near this good – meaning that in my view a fold would be in order.

Anyway, this being about the only situation in the book where Dew and I actually disagreed rather ferociously, we judged it best to share both our views on this specific situation, rather than change the details of the hand in such a way that the proper play would be more clear-cut. By looking at this example from two opposite viewpoints, you can then analyse both our arguments on its respective merits to decide for yourself whether or not continuing with the hand would be profitable.

Inside Straights Revisited

There isn't a whole lot more I can teach you about playing inside straights. We've already talked about how they can sometimes bring extra dividends because they are often well-hidden. We've also talked about how you shouldn't be too overly concerned about two-suited flops or paired boards. If the flop comes with only two suits *and* the board pairs, then it's time to drop one of your four outs. Nor do you worry as much about being counterfeited (assuming you are using both of your cards in the straight) or about not drawing to the nut straight.

This is because you simply don't have enough outs in the first place to consider them too compromised.

Yes, there are lots of little things that can add up on the wrong side of the ledger with an inside straight draw. But in general, it's a better hand than you think! A straight is a good hand, when you hit the draw. If you have four opponents on the flop, or if the betting was raised pre-flop, you should usually go for it! Especially if you have position and cannot be raised. But if you *are* raised, it's not a disaster with this many players in the pot. Simply call the raise; you haven't been hurt too badly.

If you have three opponents on the flop, you should be watching the pot, and figuring out how big it will likely get. Can you get to that magic number you need: 11 bets? Or, if you're raised, 22 bets? It's not that hard. *Most multi-way pots are big enough for an inside straight draw to continue on the flop!*

Then, of course, you most likely give it up on the turn. But if there are several other players, don't give it up without counting the pot! You might be able to call on the turn as well!

It's my opinion that most players either give up too easily on the flop, or else they play far too many hands on the flop. There is a correct balance, and the inside straight draw is the perfect example of this. If you routinely throw away your inside straights, you're giving away money.

The Most Powerful Play In Poker

Can you guess what it is?

Several times in this book, I've made reference to semi-bluffing, and what a powerful play it is. It truly is *The Most Powerful Play In Poker*.

A semi-bluff is a bluff backed up by a good draw. If the bluff fails, and you are called, you still have a reasonable chance of winning the hand by hitting your draw.

A semi-bluff is not a raise for value. Some drawing hands are so strong that they are actually favoured to win, and when this is the case, you want to put your money in the pot because you hope to win *more* money. That's not a semi-bluff.

There are two primary reasons and circumstances for employing a semi-bluff:

> 1) In late position, a semi-bluff raise is a ploy to get a free card. You have a good draw, and you know you're going to play the hand anyhow, so instead of calling meekly in late position, you raise. You aren't expecting anyone to fold, really, since they've already shown strength by betting and calling. You're hoping instead that they will call along, and then do the natural thing on the turn: Check to the raiser. You. If you make your draw on the turn, you'll bet again, quite happy with yourself for getting extra money in the pot on the flop; if you don't make your draw, you will de-

cide at that time whether to continue the bluff or to take a free card.

2) In early or middle position, you may wish to be the first player to bet the pot, hoping that all the other hands will fold. You're rooting to win the pot right then and there. But even if they don't fold, then your bluff has helped to disguise your hand, so it has purpose. If you have a hand that is probably good enough to call a bet, or even *almost* good enough to call a bet, you should think about putting your money in first, and taking the initiative.

TIP: If you have a hand that is good enough to call a bet, or even *almost* good enough, you should think about putting your money in *first.*

It's been stated by many experts that you need a better hand to call a bet than to open the betting. That is certainly true.

Suppose that you have a hand worth around five outs, in the big blind, against two opponents. A very good example of this is a low pair with a runner-runner flush possibility. Something like 8♠-6♠/6♦-9♠-A♣. But as you start counting the pot size, you figure the amount you can win is only about seven bets. Five outs isn't quite enough if you're playing for only seven bets. You really need about six outs.

Too bad. Toss your hand in the muck? Of course not! You bet! You must take control of the hand! Neither opponent has shown strength, you very possibly are ahead, and you must represent an ace in your hand by betting out.

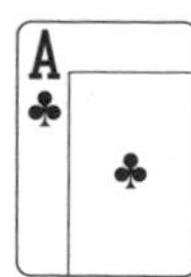

This hand is not good enough to check-and-call against two opponents: you should bet out

This is such a common scenario that it may as well be memorised. If you are in the big blind and get a free play against two other opponents, the projected pot size is seven bets; there are three bets already in the pot, and you can add two more for each opponent since they haven't yet acted on the flop. If you flop a pair and can find some added value...anything to give yourself another out or even a partial out...you should consider semi-bluffing. It's not a true bluff, since you have a pair, but you must represent an even better holding, so that you don't get blown out of the hand. And you do so knowing it's mathematically sound. Here's why: You have a hand that will win *almost* often enough, if you are second best. But almost is not good enough. If you're bet into, you have to fold. *If you give control over to someone having position on you, and* they *bet, you again have to fold.*

But you have five of the six outs you need! That means you're losing only 1/6 of a bet by playing the hand!

How much is in the pot right now? Three bets? Remember that against two opponents, the flop will hit neither of them about 36% of the time. What if you can get your opponents to fold, say, one time out of five? Then your semi-bluff wins three bets.

What happens if you're raised? Shall we assume this will happen about one time out of three? Maybe the second player raises and the third player folds. Then you're projecting the same seven bets in the final pot size, and you still have only five outs, so most of the time you can quietly fold to his raise.

A very rough assumption might be:

- 20% of the time the opponents fold; you win three bets.
- 30% of the time an opponent raises, and you lose one bet when you fold (if the third player calls instead of folding, then you have the proper odds to call as well).
- 30% of the time one opponent calls and the other folds. You lose 1/6 of a bet, on average.
- 20% of the time both opponents call. If this happens, then the projected pot size is nine bets, not seven! Nine bets is more than enough to play a five-out hand, so you come out a little better than even.

NOTE: It's tough to bluff into a flop that has two honour cards, and it's tough to bluff into a pot with no honour cards. One honour card is just right for a semi-bluff.

Do the math! You come out ahead! By bluffing into the pot, becoming the aggressor, with *almost* enough outs to play the hand, you win more money than if you give control of the hand over to someone having position on you...because, then, you have to believe them when they bet, and fold the hand.

I cannot say enough good things about the semi-bluff, but like every other play, it must be tempered with reason. Suppose you hold 10♠-7♠ and you flop 6♠-10♦-J♣. Do you semi-bluff?

No. It's impossible to bluff into a flop containing 10-J. This flop hits too many playable hands. Anybody with two overcards will call or even raise, since they hold an inside straight draw besides the overcards. It's difficult to bluff into *any* flop containing two honour cards (two cards ten or higher). But it's sometimes also difficult to bluff into a flop that contains *no* high cards, since many people will play any two overcards. A flop like 2-8-Q may be the best for a semi-bluff attempt.

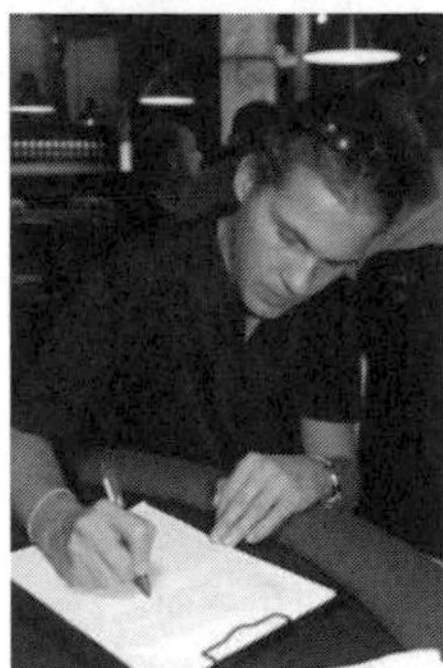

Ace Speaks...

Betting fairly weak made hands versus semi-bluffing

Actually, both of the hand examples described here (8-6 on an A-9-6 flop, and T-7 on a J-T-6 flop), are not exactly what I would call 'semi-bluffing' situations. I would describe them as situations where you can consider betting with some seemingly weak but possibly current best hands. You do this a) in order to win the hand immediately, and b) in order to defend yourself against getting outdrawn in case your very marginal hand does indeed prove to be best. Note that if people fear you and you have the image of someone who usually has the goods whenever he's betting, that these types of bets actually have a fairly good chance of success – most of all because you may be able to make your opponents fold hands that are better than the one you are betting with!

One important thing about semi-bluffing. A lot of times, this would be betting or raising with a decent hand from late position, often with the intention of taking a free card when the turn does not improve your hand and again all people check to you. While in low-limit games you will often get away with this ploy, in higher-limit games it does not work nearly as often. In these games, your opponents will take into consideration the possibility that you may have been raising for a free card with a good draw, meaning that if a blank comes on the turn, they will often bet into you again in order to make you pay for the privilege of drawing out.

It is important to take these changed game circumstances into account once you are moving up in limits, and adjust your own play accordingly. For instance, against knowledgeable opponents who recognise your possible free-card attempt and then bet into you again on the turn, you may choose to throw in another semi-bluff raise on the expensive street, because this may actually be the perfect counter-move to get him off his hand! Since he may very well be betting into you with a fairly weak made hand that can beat not much more than a draw, a hand that on top of that has very few outs to improve against the good made hand that you may well hold, then this raise of yours on the expensive street may actually be enough to make him fold the current best hand! Anytime you can make your opponents think: 'After so many signs of strength by me, I still get raised – so I may well be drawing dead against the good hand that my opponent probably holds,' any time you are able to do this, it may be worth going for this risky play on the expensive street. Keep in mind that this is an advanced play though, only to be used in slightly bigger games, and only against people who play fairly tight and who are good but not great when it comes to reading their opponents.

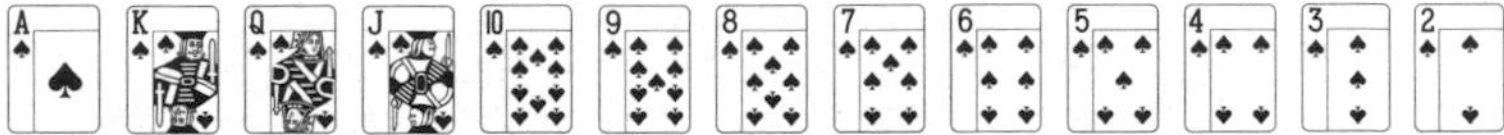

When The Board Pairs

A full house is the nemesis of any drawing hand. It beats 'em all. Of course, a full house isn't possible unless the board pairs. The best possible hand, until a pair appears on the board, is a flush.

So the question is, when the board pairs, how likely is it that somebody has a full house? Or a more reasonable question: How likely is that somebody will fill up by the river to take the pot away from you?

Clearly, a full house is more likely when the board is coordinated or full of big cards. A board like 2♠-2♦-4♣-5♠-J♣ is much less likely to bring about a full house than something like K♦-K♣-Q♥-J♠-7♥. Why? Because a hand like K-Q or K-J is much more commonly played than a hand like 4-2 or J-2. Now, it's certainly true that a person can make a full house by holding a pair in their hand. But even considering this possibility, hands like Q-Q, J-J or 7-7 are more likely to be played than 4-4 and 5-5. The second example is simply more likely to hit someone's hand, because the cards are bigger, and because the board is more coordinated.

Clearly, it also makes a difference what the pair is that's on the board. It's more likely that a person will hold a king in their hand than a two. This is significant for two reasons:

1) It is easier to turn trips into a full house than it is to turn two pair into a full house. If you have trips, then you have ten outs to make a full house; two pair has only four outs. You'll get one of those ten outs 38% of the time by the river.

2) If you *do* flop trips, then you are much more likely to stick around until the river than if you flop two pair...especially since one of those two pair is on the board!

Let's look, then, at a worst-case scenario. Suppose the cards on the table come A♥-K♠-K♥-Q♥-J♦, filling your heart flush on the turn. Could the board possibly be any more coordinated? Now let's assume your opponent will play any of about 240 starting hands (there are roughly 240 acceptable starting hands in a reasonably tight player's repertoire, from middle position).

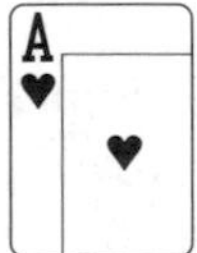

Even with a board this coordinated, your opponent will have a full house only 11% of the time... unless, of course, the betting provides ample evidence of strength

How often will he have a full house or better? The answer is, there are 26 out of the 240 hands that make a full house, or 11%. With the most incredibly coordinated board imaginable, and a pair showing, your opponent won't make a full house more often than 11% of the time!

How about the other end of the spectrum? Suppose the cards come 2♥-2♠-3♥-4♥-5♦. Now how likely is a full house? The answer is, there are *no* acceptable starting hands! Not in a 'reasonably tight player's repertoire, from middle position'. Unless, of course, enough limpers in early position make it logical for this 'reasonably tight player' to call with a pair of fives or lower.

How about something less extreme? Let's consider a typical board (if there is such a thing) like 6♥-8♠-8♥-A♥-Q♦. Now, the following hands (among those typically considered acceptable starting hands) make a full house: A-A, Q-Q, and A-8s. That amounts to eight hands, or a 3% chance of a full house. But really, wouldn't you have a reasonable guess by the pre-flop betting whether someone holds A-A or Q-Q?

Please don't misinterpret what I'm saying, and please don't make the mistake of reading players' hands on the basis of how they *should* play, rather than on the basis of how they *do* play. For some people, Q-8s, 8-6s, and A-8 offsuit are 'reasonable hands', and they'll play them religiously from any position. You've got to love these players, they're why you you're sitting at this table, but they *are* hard to read.

My point is simply this: A paired board is indeed something to be concerned about, but it's nothing that should strike fear in your heart every time it happens. Don't be overly concerned unless the board simply looks *horrible,* and the betting strength backs up your feeling of unease.

I stick by the advice I gave earlier in the book:

- ♠ If the board pairs on the flop, it's going to be awful hard for you to tell when somebody makes trips or a full house. They'll play as deceptively as possible until the bets double in size. Therefore, if there are three or more opponents, generally you should take away one of your outs on the flop. This assumes you have plenty of outs in the first place...like an open-ended straight or flush draw.
- ♠ On the turn, it's your job to determine by the betting whether or not somebody *does* have a full house. You must decide upon a reasonable percentage, and then take away that many outs. For example, if the betting seems to indicate that there is a 25% chance of someone having a full house,

you should subtract *at least* 25% of your outs. Why do I say 'at least?' Because if you *do* hit one of your outs on the river, and a full house is out there, it could get expensive for you!

- ♠ On the turn, you must also look closely at your outs to see if any of them pair the board *again*. This is because, with two pair on the board, it becomes too easy for anyone to have a full house. For example, if the board shows K♠K♥J♠7♣ and you are on a spade draw, then the 7♠ cannot be considered a reasonable out. You must drop one more out from your calculation.

If the board shows these cards, and you are drawing to a spade flush, you cannot count the 7♠ as an out

- ♠ Remember that a paired board is less likely to fit someone's hand, and it looks just as scary to them as it does to you. A paired board is often the ideal semi-bluffing opportunity.

Raising With Middle Pair

Sometimes it may seem appropriate to raise with the second-best hand. The idea is to drive out the players following you with the third- and fourth-best hands, so that you have a better chance of winning.

Let's look at an example that David Sklansky provided in his book, *The Theory Of Poker*. This book, by the way, belongs in every poker player's library, and deserves to be read more than once.

'If, for instance, the bettor has a 50 percent chance of winning the pot, you have a 30 percent chance, and two other hands each have a 10 percent chance, you improve your chance by driving those two worst hands out with a raise. Now the best hand may have a 60 percent chance of winning, but you've improved your own chances to 40 percent.'

This is an important concept in poker. But the problem with this, for our purposes, is that in games that use community cards (like hold'em in contrast to stud), the odds of each player improving are not uncorrelated. If you know that the community cards you need are *not* going to helps hands three and four, why chase those players away? Let 'em keep putting money in the pot.

Let's make no mistake about it: You have to improve to win, if you really have only the second-best hand. The only other way to win is to bluff the better hand away from the pot. So, when you raise with the second-best hand, hoping to get the remaining players to fold, there can be only one reason: You want to buy more outs. If it doesn't buy you any outs to raise, it makes little sense to chase worse hands away.

Let's look at an example. Suppose you hold A♥-9♣ and the flop comes 2♥-9♠-J♥. The player on your right bets out, and there are two more players to act after you. This is a pretty good example of holding the second-best hand, if you feel confident that you can put the lead-out bettor on a jack or an overpair. What do you do?

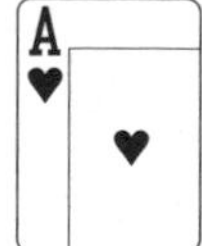

Will a raise buy you any more outs?

Well, you have about five modified outs. Four outs for middle pair, and one more out for your ace-high three-card flush. You belong in this pot, especially if there was a pre-flop raise.

Call or raise?

Let's think about it. What sort of hands are you hoping to drive out?

- The flush draws? Pairing your ace won't help them any, since you have the ace of hearts. But maybe you can buy the 9♥ as an out? Not likely. Anybody with a marginal understanding of poker odds will be in there swinging with his flush draw regardless of your raise.
- The straight draws? There aren't any. At least, not any that an ace or nine helps.
- Someone with another nine? Not on your life! The last thing you want to do is drive away another player holding a nine. If you improve... and you have to improve to win... this poor sucker is probably drawing dead.
- Someone with another jack? What's the point, if you're already beaten by a pair of jacks? Nobody with A-J is going to fold, count on that, so you won't buy your ace any more outs by raising.

It's hard to find a single hand that you might want to drive away. But let's change the example a little. Suppose, now, that you hold Q♥-9♣ instead of A♥-9♣. Again the flop comes 2♥-9♠-J♥, and you're bet into. Assuming you've decided to play (you probably shouldn't, now, without the extra out from the ace-high three-card flush), do you call or raise?

Will a raise buy *enough* outs?

Your goal, of course, is to buy outs for your queen. You want to make sure that any queen you hit on the turn is a safe card.

By raising, you may be able to move several obstacles:

1) Your raise makes it inappropriate for inside straight draws to continue. There goes K-10, Q-8 and 10-7. K-Q may not fold even if you raise. 8-7 should fold whether you raise or not.

2) Even solid open-ended straight draws have to think twice, now. 10-8 has to consider the chance that he's up against a better straight draw or a flush draw, and may fold. That's what you want; it opens up the queen.

3) It would be good to get rid of anybody with a heart higher than your queen. Maybe a hand like A♥-9♣.

4) Best of all would be if you could chase away a hand as strong as Q-J. But even if you have an extremely strong image and/or your opponents are capable of making good lay-downs, then this would be a bit too much to ask for, probably. Still, you *could* possibly make someone fold a jack with a weak kicker, or the same type of holding that you are raising with—say, a Q-9 or K-9—now, these would of course be wonderful results!

Are these reasonable hands for anyone to hold? Maybe. You'll have to decide that before you raise.

So now the question is, if you can buy some outs, is it a good investment? Let's look at some numbers.

First, are you worried about chasing people out of the pot that might pay you off if you make your hand? Don't be. They're not about to put more than one more bet into the pot anyway, unless they improve. How do I know this? Because if they would be willing to call a double-sized turn bet without improving, they'll probably call your raise on the flop just as easily. Don't lose any sleep about anybody that you chase out of the pot.

NOTE: You need big pots for drawing hands. But don't lose any sleep about anybody that you chase out of the pot with a raise on the flop. They weren't going to call a double-sized bet on the turn, anyway, if they won't call your raise.

Let's assume that both of the players following you fold to your raise, and the original bettor calls. That's a likely result. Maybe your raise made one of the two remaining people fold that wouldn't have folded otherwise. This means the pot size remains the same whether you raise or not—two bets from other players—except that this way you have put in an extra bet yourself.

The question becomes, how many outs do you need to buy, for that extra bet you paid, to make it a worthwhile investment? Well, if there was one pre-flop bet apiece, you can estimate a final pot size of nine small bets. Therefore, you'd need 4.7 outs to continue for a single bet on the flop, and roughly twice that number of outs to continue for a double bet. Thus, one bet is worth 4.7 outs. Think you can buy 4.7 outs with that raise? Of course not.

How about if there is more money in the pot? If there were two pre-flop bets apiece, that works out to an estimated final pot size of 14 bets, so you need 3.1 outs. One bet is worth 3.1 outs. Can you buy 3.1 outs? Nope.

The bottom line is, you shouldn't raise. *In hold'em, you'll find very few examples where you should raise, purely from a mathematical standpoint, with the second-best hand.* Aggressive play carries its benefits...like perhaps buying a free card on the turn...but if your raise doesn't buy you anything except an out or two, it's generally a terrible investment.

To review this idea of raising with the second-best hand, flopping middle pair is the most likely example of when this option comes into play. But it's far from a clear-cut raise, even if you have a great kicker, and even for the most aggressive games. Here is why I recommend you seldom raise holding middle pair in hold'em, if you really think you are only second best (if you're not convinced of this, then a raise may help determine exactly where you stand, and may even serve to chase better hands away):

- You can hardly ever chase a flush draw out of the pot on the flop, unless he's a bad player. This is bad news, since a flush beats anything you're drawing to! So you can't buy any outs trying to chase away flush draws.
- Straights beat what you're drawing to as well; it would be nice to drive them out. But if the board pairs, it never helps a straight draw anyway. So, two of your outs (those that make three-of-a-kind for you) are safe from straight draws already, and all you're buying is possibly the outs for you to make two pair. You might want to look and see if your other card (the unpaired one) is anywhere near any straight draws.
- What else (besides a flush or straight draw) could the remaining players have that you might want to raise them off? It's often hard to find any legitimate hands—hands that get in your way, that is—that you can scare away.
- If you have nothing more than middle pair (no flush or straight draws) it's most likely a long-shot draw. It's at best a complex draw (five or six outs), and at worst you're already drawing dead against somebody with a set. You need a reasonable pot size to continue, so driving out opponents is a catch-22.

Over-aggression with the second-best hand may be unwarranted.

NOTE: When you raise with middle pair, you're really just hoping the original bettor is on a draw.

Let's be brutally honest, then. What you're really hoping, when you raise with middle pair, is that you're not the second-best hand after all! You're hoping that you can isolate the bettor by raising the other players off their hands, and that you'll wind up with the best remaining hand. In other words, you're hoping that the first bettor is on a draw.

If you can isolate a player who is on a draw, the odds almost always favour you to win the hand.

Here is the scenario you are hoping for, to make this little ploy beneficial:

1) The first bettor is semi-bluffing with a draw, a hand currently worse than your own. Of course, it will be a good enough draw that he's willing to open the betting. This stipulation pretty much requires that the flop is two-suited, or perhaps all the same suit, because a flush draw is the most likely. Perhaps there are some straight draw possibilities as well. Anything to make it more likely that he's on a draw.

2) The remaining players cannot have any hands good enough to call your raise, so that they all fold.

3) However, presumably one or more of the other players have a hand that would have been good enough to call a single bet. Otherwise, your raise isn't necessary to chase them away, and you may have wasted an extra bet.

4) Finally, the first bettor's draw must not materialise over the turn and river...a draw that we already know is a very good one...so that you do indeed hang on to win the hand.

Let's sum it all up. Middle pair is a hand that is typically worth only four or five outs. In other words, it's right on the bubble between a complex draw and a long shot. Against only three other players, calling with a long shot is not advisable, especially since two of the three have not yet acted. Therefore, when you flop middle pair in this situation it's usually a raise or fold proposition. Not a calling hand. However, if the above four requirements must all be satisfied for you to succeed, raising with just a middle pair can be pretty much a long shot, too! But hey, it's a very satisfying gambit when it works, isn't it?

May I say it one more time? *Controlled aggression finds its reward.* Definitely add this little stratagem to your toolbox, but for gosh sakes, please don't do it all the time! Pick your moments, and raise with middle pair, trying to isolate a possible drawing hand. If there were multiple pre-flop bets, so that the pot is large enough to warrant the risk, it can be a great play. If you're raising an aggressive player who often bets a low pair...perhaps the same pair you made, but with a lower kicker...then it can be a fantastic play! Use it to mix up your play, and to add some aggression to your game. But don't do it thinking it has a positive expected return. It's still a long shot, and possibly a very expensive one.

Timing Your Raise When You Do Make Your Hand

Let's finish the chapter on a positive note.

One very important aspect of playing drawing hands is knowing how and when to extract the most money possible when you do make your hand.

Let's suppose that you called meekly on the flop with a draw, and then you hit your draw on the turn. You think you have the best hand, and so you want to raise. Do you do it now, on the turn, or do you wait for the river?

You're probably only going to get one chance to raise. You hope to extract two bets on the turn and one on the river, or else one bet on the turn and two on the river.

Which is best? Let's discuss some of the issues.

Why you should raise on the turn:

1) The most important issue, of course, is your position relative to the probable bettor. If the opportunity arises

to trap the entire table for a raise on the turn, then of course you take that opportunity. Don't trust that the same opportunity will present itself on the river!

2) On the turn, the other drawing hands are still filled with hope. By the river, those hopes are usually dashed. Therefore they may be more likely to call a raise on the turn than on the river. Make them pay to play.

3) It makes sense to take opportunity when it knocks. If an opponent bets on the turn, perhaps you should raise immediately; there is certainly no guarantee that he will bet again on the river, so the turn might be your only opportunity for raising.

4) Is there any chance you can extract a double bet on both the turn *and* the river? If the answer is yes, and your hand is good enough to do so, then of course you raise on the turn.

Why you should wait to raise on the river:

1) Are there several cards which, if they came on the river, would cause you to slow down? Maybe you've just made a straight and the board shows two clubs. Do you dare raise if a third club comes on the river? Or if the board pairs? If the answer is no...then it may make more sense to save your raise for the river. You'll raise only if a scare card doesn't appear.

2) If an opponent has a good hand but not a great hand, he is more likely to make a crying call to your raise on the river than he is to call a raise on the turn. This is because he knows calling the raise on the turn will cost him at least *two more* large bets to see the showdown.

3) If you're heads-up, is there any chance that your opponent is on a stone-cold bluff? Maybe playing just a couple of overcards? If so, there's no point in scaring him away on the turn; let him try to bluff again on the river, or maybe improve enough to call your bet.

4) If you're not heads-up, is your position such that a raise on the turn will merely chase away other callers? Then by all means, let them call, and put off the raise until the river.

The fact is, *I don't know which is best!* There are pros and cons for both sides of the argument. Perhaps by better understanding the issues, you can develop an intuitive feel for when you should raise on the turn, and when you should wait for the river.

TIP: Don't miss the chance to raise on the turn if the board is still coordinated. But you may make more money by waiting until the river to raise if it isn't!

Until you develop this feel, I suggest you follow a simple rule: Raise on the turn unless your opponent thinks you both have legitimate hands, but that he has the better one. Wow, I wish it were as simple as it sounds! But here's the secret: Be inclined to raise on the turn if there are still draws out there. Not only do you make the drawing hands pay, but your opponent may be betting on the turn only because he is afraid to give *you* a free card, and that means he has no incentive to bet again on the river. But be inclined to wait and raise on the river if there are no other possible draws; this means that when your opponent bets the turn, he either likes his hand a lot, or he's on a stone-cold bluff. Let him lead into you again on the river.

Of course, if you just hit a draw on the turn (a straight or a flush), this usually means the board is such that you want to raise immediately. It will usually mean other drawing opportunities still exist. The bottom line is this: *Don't miss out on the chance to bet your hand.*

Chapter Ten

Seven Steps to Mastery

So, do you really want to take your game to the next level? Are you committed? If you try to do it all at once, implementing everything you've learned here, you probably *will* be committed. Straight jacket and all.

We've covered a lot of material in this book. Maybe you've already begun to incorporate some of what you've learned into your play. Or maybe you're just too overwhelmed to begin. It sure won't help your game any, if all you do is spend all your time figuring outs and counting bets.

Let me give you a plan for stepping into it slowly. I'd like you to concentrate on adding one new feature to your game, each time you play. Each session should last several hours, so that you have enough time for what you are learning to really sink in, and each session will build upon the last session.

This works. I know. I went through the process myself. But you do need to take it slow, or you *will* be overwhelmed.

Before you begin, I'd like to offer a word of caution. It's natural, when learning something new, to want to give it a try as soon and as often as possible. This doesn't mean you should begin playing lots more drawing hands! *Please don't* change your starting hands standards just because you've read this book! Drawing hands like 6♥-6♠, A♥-4♥ and 8♣-7♣ are still only good hands when played against multiple players (at least four opponents, preferably more), and usually aren't worth more than a single bet before the flop.

Especially don't play hands like A♥-4♥ if you have trouble giving up the hand when an ace flops. Someone once said that more money is lost after the flop by inexperienced players who get trapped with A-x suited than any other situation, and I tend to agree...I was once one of those 'inexperienced players'.

With that in mind, you're ready to begin.

Session 1: Begin To Count Outs

You will want to begin by spending an entire session practicing counting outs, the way you learned in this book. I'm not asking you to modify your play in any way. Not yet. I just want you to practice counting outs.

Re-read chapter two, preferably just before you play, and memorise the basic rules for counting modified outs.

As you count, pay careful attention to details, *in particular two-suited flops*. Do you have any cards of the majority suit? It's important. Not only can you possibly add an out to your count if you have a high third flush card (probably an ace or king), but your drawing opportunities will be more compromised if you *don't* have the right suits. Also, if someone is on a flush draw, then a card of that suit in your hand decreases the chance of your opponent making his flush by 11%; that's not insignificant at all.

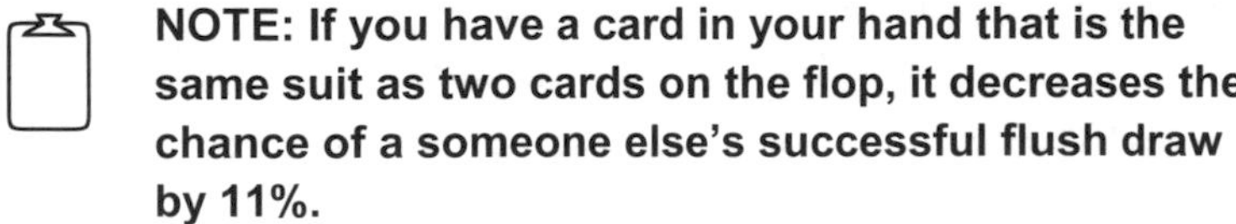

NOTE: If you have a card in your hand that is the same suit as two cards on the flop, it decreases the chance of a someone else's successful flush draw by 11%.

Watch carefully for three-card flush and three-card straight possibilities in your hand, and remember to drop these extra long-shot outs on the turn if they don't materialise. When you're dealt a low pair, carefully consider how likely it is that pairing your other card will help another player even more.

Watch for double belly-busters and inside straights; hands that you might have ignored or overlooked in the past.

In short, begin thinking of drawing hands in terms of *modified outs*.

If, after your first session, you don't think you've had enough practice, then practice at home. Deal yourself a two-card hand and a flop. Count the outs. Deal a turn card. Count any additions or subtractions.

Session 2: Begin To Classify Draws

Re-read chapter six, and begin to classify all drawing hands that you receive into the four categories. I'm not asking you yet to modify your game at all, except to use some basic guidelines for which drawing hands can be played beyond the flop.

Excellent (10+ outs)

You're there calling to the river, regardless.

Good (7-9 outs)

You're *probably* going to the river. If you are up against only a couple of opponents and the betting gets strong on the turn, you might re-evaluate and drop out. But you'd better have a darn good reason for giving up.

Complex (5-6 outs)

Call on the flop if you can get in cheaply, but think hard about whether you should call on the turn. If there's enough money in the pot, go for it.

Long shot (3-4 outs)

Call on the flop if there's plenty of money and you can get in cheaply. Fold on the turn without remorse.

Session 3: Begin Counting Pot Size On The Flop

If you're not used to keeping track of the size of the pot in your head, plan *at least* one session to practice this. Really. Until it becomes second nature, don't go past this step.

Even if you've been keeping a count in your head for years, plan a session to practice this new method of estimating the final pot size. Keep track of *every pot*, whether you're in the game or not. You're there at the table to practice.

This first pot-counting session, just keep a count through the flop. Remember, you're counting to estimate final pot size, meaning you're adding in three more bets for each player in the pot after the flop. Always add *three* extra bets for each person who calls on the flop; don't get fancy and try switching sometimes to two extra bets to account for position. But once you get through the flop, forget about the count and concentrate on your game.

Session 4: Continue Counting Pot Size Through The Turn

In your next session, keep track of the pot through the flop as you did in session three, but now begin tweaking your estimated final pot size:

1) If you haven't been, begin to add your own flop bet(s) to the count.

2) Adjust the pot size based upon the number of bettors and callers on the turn. Add one bet each time somebody puts their money in the centre.

3) Subtract three bets anytime somebody folds on the turn.

4) If the pot is raised, remember to add *two more bets* for each calling player, since a turn bet is a double-sized bet.

I'm still not asking you to modify your game very much, if at all! The only thing you may be doing differently from your 'old game' is classifying your draws and playing them with a little more smarts, as you began to do in session two.

By the time you finish this session, it should be second nature to keep track of the pot size...*the projected, final pot size*...in your head.

Session 5: Memorise The Important Charts

There are two charts in this book that you really need to memorise: The outs chart in chapter eight, and the bet odds chart in concept eight. Here is that data, again, in simplified form. The 'value bet' numbers given are for the flop: The number of opponents needed to value bet on the turn is roughly double that needed on the flop.

Number of Outs	2	3	4	5	6	7	8	9	10
Final Pot Size Needed to call One Flop Bet	23	15	11	9	7	6	5	4	4
Number of Opponents Needed to Value Bet			6	4	4	3	3	3	2

Now we're getting serious. As you attack your game this session, you want to play with the total confidence of knowing *exactly* which hands you should be in, and *exactly* which hands you should be raising on the basis of bet odds.

If it helps you get in practice, then each time you come up with a pot count (on the flop and on the turn) review in your head exactly how many outs you need to be able to continue. And vice-versa: Each time you calculate your outs, review in your head how big the pot needs to get for you to be able to call.

Learn how to extrapolate quickly. A six-out hand needs 6.8 bets in your final, projected pot size to continue for a single get on the flop, and a five-out hand needs 8.4 bets. But what if your hand is worth about five and a half outs? Then, of course, the number of bets you need would be halfway between 6.8 and 8.4. That's 7.6 bets.

Session 6: Practice Reading Opponents' Late-Street Tendencies

Review chapter seven now before continuing. This session, you want to begin paying closer attention to how your opponents play on the turn and on the river. Use this knowledge to adjust your out-count.

If you feel so inclined, begin keeping track, with a pencil and paper, of the betting action at your game. Remember how it was suggested at the end of chapter five. Somehow, writing things down reinforces what you are learning.

On the flop:

1) Add up to one out if your opponents play the late street aggressively.

2) Add or subtract about 10% to your out-count, depending upon how loose or tight your opponents are. Loose games: Add to the count. Tight games: Subtract from the count.

3) Factor in the value of position. Either add or subtract about half an out for very good or very bad position, or else drop down to two extra bets per player on the flop (instead of three) when projecting the final

pot size. Of course, then you must add two bets and subtract two bets (rather than one bet and three bets respectively) for calls and folds on the turn.

On the turn:

1) On the turn, you're paying closer attention to the actual opponents. Get to know your opponents' playing styles. Know whether they are going to keep chasing on the turn and even pay you off on the river. Know whether they will bet average hands on the river. Know whether you can raise them and receive crying calls.

2) Look ahead to the players who have yet to act. If you're pretty sure about one of them, use your knowledge. If you think he's going to fold, drop between one and three smalls bet from your projected pot size. If he's going to call, add one small bet to your pot size.

3) Plan carefully, now, what will happen on the river. What is your position? Can you extract extra bets? You are counting on one more bet from each player. Can you get more? If you think a raise will bring in extra bets, add them in, remembering that each large bet equals two small bets.

Session 7: Bring Your 'A' Game

You can now slow down, and only bother to count outs and bets when it's necessary. Instead, concentrate on your opponents and on playing poker. I mean, *Poker*.

TIP: In hold'em, you want to be feared. Before you call, think about raising instead.

Re-read chapter nine, now. Everything should fall into place, and you should begin playing 'controlled, aggressive poker' on your drawing hands as well as your leading hands. Don't be afraid to play your opponents, and don't be afraid to mix up your game, adding a little deception. Know how your game appears to others. In hold'em, you want to be feared. If your outcount is anywhere close to what you need to bet for value, it is probably correct to play aggressively. Before you call, think about raising instead. I've said it before, and I'll say it one last time: *Controlled aggression finds its reward.* Even with drawing hands. Just, please, be aware of when a raise is mathematically sound and when it's not, so that you know when aggression is costing too much.

I wish you luck, my friend!